D1738458

Government and Politics in Hungary

Government and Politics in Hungary

András Körösényi

Central European University Press
OSIRIS

Earlier version published in Hungarian as "A magyar politikai rendszer" by Osiris, Budapest, 1998

English edition published in 1999 by
Central European University Press

Október 6. utca 12
H-1051 Budapest
Hungary

400 West 59th Street
New York, NY 10019
USA

Published as part of a programme supported by the Hungarian Ministry for Education *and coordinated by the* Office for Higher Education Programmes, Hungary

Translated by Alan Renwick

Distributed in the United Kingdom and Western Europe by
Plymbridge Distributors Ltd., Estover Road, Plymouth, PL6 7PZ, United Kingdom

ISBN 963-9116-61-0 *Cloth*

Library of Congress Cataloging in Publication Data
A CIP catalog record for this book is available upon request

Printed in Hungary by AKAPRINT

To Erzsi

Contents

Chapter Six

Chapter Seven

Chapter Eight

Chapter Nine

Chapter Ten

Chapter Eleven

Chapter Twelve

Chapter Thirteen

Chapter Fourteen

Conclusion

List of Tables

Chapter One

Chapter Two

Chapter Three

Chapter Four

Chapter Five

Chapter Six

Chapter Seven

Chapter Eight

Chapter Nine

Chapter Ten

Chapter Eleven

Chapter Twelve

Chapter Thirteen

Chapter Fourteen

Conclusion

Appendices

List of Figures

Chapter Three

Chapter Four

Chapter Six

Chapter Ten

Chapter Twelve

Abbreviations

Political Parties

EKGP	United Smallholders' Party (*Egyesült Kisgazdapárt*)
Fidesz(-MPP)	Federation of Young Democrats (–Hungarian Civic Party) (*Fiatal Demokraták Szövetsége [–Magyar Polgári Párt]*)
FKGP	Independent Smallholders' Party (*Független Kisgazdapárt*)
KDNP	Christian Democratic People's Party (*Kereszténydemokrata Néppárt*)
MDF	Hungarian Democratic Forum (*Magyar Demokrata Fórum*)
MDNP	Hungarian Democratic People's Party (*Magyar Demokrata Néppárt*)
MIÉP	Hungarian Party of Justice and Life (*Magyar Igazság és Élet Pártja*)
MKDSZ	Hungarian Christian Democratic Alliance (*Magyar Kereszténydemokrata Szövetség*)
MKP	Hungarian Communist Party (*Magyar Kommunista Párt*)
MNP	Hungarian People's Party (*Magyar Néppárt*)
MP	Workers' Party (*Munkáspárt*)
MSZP	Hungarian Socialist Party (*Magyar Szocialista Párt*)
MSZMP	Hungarian Socialist Workers' Party (*Magyar Szocialista Munkáspárt*)
NPP	National Peasant Party (*Nemzeti Parasztpárt*)
SZDSZ	Alliance of Free Democrats (*Szabad Demokraták Szövetsége*)

Other

EKA	Opposition Roundtable (*Ellenzéki Kerekasztal*)
ÉT	Interest Reconciliation Council (*Érdekegyezteto Tanács*)
MEH	Office of the Prime Minister (*Miniszterelnöki Hivatal*)
MGK	Hungarian Economic Chamber (*Magyar Gazdasági Kamera*)
MMSZ	Hungarian Employers' Association (*Magyar Munkaadói Szövetség*)
MNB	National Bank of Hungary (*Magyar Nemzeti Bank*)
MSZOSZ	National Association of Hungarian Trades Unions (*Magyar Szakszervezetek Országos Szövetsége*)
MTI	Hungarian News Agency (*Magyar Távirati Iroda*)
ORTT	National Radio and Television Commission (*Országos Rádió és Televízió Testület*)
SZOT	National Council of Trade Unions (*Szakszervezetek Országos Tanácsa*)

Note: The Hungarian alphabet contains digraphs (letters written using two characters). In particular, 'sz' in the above abbreviations is a single letter, pronounced like the English 's'.

Preface and Acknowledgements

Innumerable studies have appeared in Hungarian and international political science concerning particular aspects of the political system that emerged in Hungary out of the transition to democracy in 1989–90. Researchers have been interested primarily in the political actors (particularly the parties) in the constitution and in the democratic transition. By contrast, other areas—such as the operation of the government, the public administration and the parliament—have remained largely untouched. While many books have been published on Hungarian politics,[1] none has sought to present a general survey of the Hungarian political system. Though some more broad-ranging studies have been published in Hungarian,[2] these have been concerned with state institutions and have taken a legal-constitutional perspective. In writing this book I have sought to fill these gaps and to present a comprehensive account of the Hungarian political system that includes all major aspects of the system that have not previously been dealt with.

The English- and German-language literature on Hungarian politics is for the most part composed—with some exceptions in specific aspects of the field[3]—of works analysing the transition or covering the entire region of Central and Eastern Europe.[4] In contrast, the present work analyses the character and operation of the Hungarian political system alone, surveying almost a decade of experience since the régime change. It takes not the approach of 'transitology' or area studies, but rather that of international political science, and it takes as its model other works that discuss the political and governmental systems of a single country, such as *Das politische System der Bundesrepublik Deutschland nach der Vereinigung* by Klaus von Beyme, *Governing Italy* by David Hine, *Das politische System der Bundesrepublik Deutschland* by Wolfgang Rudzio, and *The Government and Politics of France* by Vincent Wright.

Government and Politics in Hungary is an introductory, general account of politics and government in post-communist Hungary, covering basics but also offering detailed descriptions of political actors, institutions, government and political behaviour. I had two main aims in writing this book. The first was to survey the most important institutions of the political and governmental system and the cultural and behavioural characteristics of Hungarian politics. The book therefore gives a detailed description of each major political institution (from the government to the Constitutional Court) and social actor (politicians, intellectuals, parties and interest groups). It compiles the results of Hungarian and international political science on the topic, and the analysis is based upon detailed statistical data. The sixteen chapters cover, first, the non-institutional conditions and the social actors of Hungarian politics and government (political traditions, political culture, political thinking, élite groups and the political class), second, the voluntary institutions of politics (parties, interest groups and movements), and, third, the constitutional framework and the system of government (the constitution, the government, the public administration, parliament, the president of the republic and the Constitutional Court).

My second aim has been to develop a more analytical understanding of Hungarian politics. My primary concern is to analyse the two-way relationship between the cultural-behavioural and constitutional-institutional levels of politics in Hungary. The book highlights also the role played by the dominant political culture, the political thinking and role perception of the political class and the nature of the democratic transition in constitutional reform and in institution building at the time of the political transition and since. Discussion of these themes is placed within the framework of several models of comparative politics, such as those of pragmatic versus ideological political culture, cabinet versus prime ministerial government, a 'debating' versus a 'working' parliament, or consociational versus majoritarian democracy.

The first, Hungarian-language, edition of this book was written—after a lengthy period of preparatory work—between September 1996 and October 1997. I carried out the preparatory work in 1995 and 1996 in Heidelberg, with a scholarship from the Alexander von Humboldt Stiftung. The book was written at my workplace, the Political Science Department of Eötvös Loránd University in Budapest, with the support of a Széchenyi Professorial Scholarship. For the English translation, I shortened, updated and in places rewrote the original text (published in Hungary by Osiris Press) during the summer and autumn of 1998. For the benefit of readers who do not know Hungarian, I have where possible supplemented the bibliography with English- or German-language versions of directly cited sources.

I would like finally to thank the institutions mentioned above, which supported and made possible this work, and my many colleagues whose comments upon the work while it was still in manuscript form greatly helped in improving the text. I extend my thanks in particular to János Gyurgyák, who initiated both the Hungarian- and the English-language editions of the book, to Alan Renwick, who translated the text into English, and to the Felsőoktatási Tankönyvtámogatási Alap (Textbook Publishing Project) of the Hungarian Ministry of Culture and Education, whose support made the English translation possible.

Budapest, January 1999

Notes

1. For example, András Bozóki, András Körösényi and George Schöpflin (eds.), *Post-Communist Transition: Emerging Pluralism in Hungary*; Peter Katzenstein, *Mitteleuropa: Between Europe and Germany*; Gábor Tóka (ed.), *The 1990 Election to the Hungarian National Assembly*.

2. Such as István Kukorelli, *Alkotmánytan* (Constitutional Studies) and Béla Pokol, *A magyar parlamentarizmus* (Hungarian Parliamentarism).

3. For example, Attila Ágh and Sándor Kurtán (eds.), *The First Parliament: 1990–1994* (on the parliament); Csaba Gombár, *et al.* (eds.), *Balance: The Hungarian Government, 1990–1994* (on government policy); and various works by Gábor Tóka (on the party system and on electoral behaviour).

4. For example, Attila Ágh, *The Politics of Central Europe*; Klaus von Beyme, *Systemwechsel in Osteuropa*; Jon Elster, *Institutional Design in Post-Communist Societies*; Geoffrey Pridham and Paul Lewis (eds.), *Stabilising Fragile Democracies: Comparing New Party Systems in Southern and Eastern Europe*; D. Segert, R. Stöss and O. Niedermayer, *Parteiensysteme in Postkommunistischen Gesellschaften Osteuropas*; Rudolf L. Tőkés, *Hungary's Negotiated Revolution*.

Introduction

Political Traditions

In the years following the democratic transition of 1989–1990, Eastern and Western European political scientists alike pondered the same point: to what extent would the emerging democracies in Hungary and the other East-Central European countries be viable? The factors making the stabilization of these democracies more difficult included not only the social costs of the simultaneous transition to a market economy, but also the weakness of the democratic political culture and traditions. In this introduction we seek to identify which elements of the historical legacy have influenced political development since the régime transition. In doing so, we progress from the past towards the present, considering first the long-term and then the medium-term traditions, and finally assessing the influence of the most recent decades.

1

In many ways, the two most important determining factors behind Hungarian political traditions have been the country's *uneasy geopolitical location*, wedged between East and West, and its long struggle for *national and state sovereignty*. The country's dominant political culture has always had a Western orientation. But Hungary has felt itself to be on the periphery of the West, producing the feeling of national defencelessness, of having been left to struggle alone, that has often emerged during the twentieth century. This fragile position has been linked also to peculiarities in societal development, as is described perhaps most famously by Jenõ Szűcs, following István Bibó, in his essay 'The Three Historical Regions of Europe: An Outline' (Szűcs, 1983).

Hungarian statehood, meanwhile, has a long history, spanning some 1100 years. For much of that time, however, this statehood has been vulnerable. The problem of national and state sovereignty has been present almost continuously since the country's defeat by the Turks at the 1526 Battle of Mohács. For centuries the most important dividing line of domestic politics was the relationship with the Habsburgs, the occupants of the Hungarian throne, and the conflict between pro- and anti-Austrian traditions divided Hungarian politics again following the revolution and the 1848–49 War of Independence against the Austrians. As the question of the contradiction between '*homeland and progress*', this conflict continues to form a part of Hungarian political culture today: without it, it is impossible to understand the political developments and discussions of the 1990s.

From the time of the Reformation, the independence question was also coloured by the *confessional divide*, since by the seventeenth and eighteenth centuries a significant part of the Hungarian nobility that opposed the Catholic Habsburgs and the Catholic aristocracy that were loyal to them had converted to the Protestant faith. The independence tradition thus gained a Protestant, Calvinist hue.

2

Hungarian political development between the Austro-Hungarian Compromise of 1867 and the communist take-over of 1948–49 was characterized above all by a *weak democratic but strong parliamentary tradition*. With three short interruptions,[1] there existed throughout this time in Hungary a legitimate parliamentary opposition and a government commanding a majority in parliament. Yet it remains a matter of debate today whether the governmental system was truly parliamentary.

The period may be divided into three sections, the first spanning the years from the 1867 Compromise until the end of the First World War, the second covering the Horthy era between the two world wars, and the third concerning the short and limited democratic interlude between the end of the Second World War and the consolidation of communist control in 1948–49. Each of these periods will be considered in turn.

The era of the modern civic nation-state began in Hungary, as in many other European states and nations, in the mid-nineteenth century, with the events of 1848–49. It was at this time that the questions of *na-*

tional sovereignty and *modernization of the political and economic system* became intertwined, and from this time on *parliamentary government* became the central focus of constitutional and political endeavour.

The period of almost a century from the age of reform until the First World War was in Hungary the era of *national liberalism*. The *constitutional monarchy* instituted by the Compromise created the possibility of parliamentary development based on the principle of the representation of the people. The political system of 1867–1918 was a constitutional monarchy characterized by a form of *liberal parliamentarism* that was at the time far from universal on the European continent.

But there were problems. Though, throughout this period, the *parliamentary opposition* operated as an integral, legitimate part of political life, a *dominant party system* existed in which a dominant governing party was always able to secure the continuation of its position in power. In addition, the franchise remained limited: while until the mid-nineteenth century Hungary had been in harmony with most European countries in respect of the franchise question,[2] from the final third of the century Hungary was left behind in the extension of the suffrage,[3] and a breakthrough was to occur only following the First World War. Thus, while the economic and social processes of the last third of the nineteenth century opened the way to the era of political mobilization and *mass* politics, the extent of that mass mobilization in fact remained limited.

During the Horthy era between 1920 and 1944, the right to vote was already universal. But despite this, and despite the continued existence of a legitimate parliamentary opposition, the governmental system at this time was not democratic. This was so for a number of reasons.

In the first place, the secret ballot was, with the exception of the 1920 and 1939 elections, guaranteed only in the larger towns; elsewhere, open voting—and the use of the administrative apparatus—made possible abuses that benefited the governing party. This helped to ensure that the political mobilization and integration of the millions of enfranchised citizens remained weak. Political competition was limited also through the neutralization of opposition. The Smallholders' Party was absorbed into the governing party during the 1920s, while the far left (the Communist Party) and the far right (the Arrow Cross Party) were—unlike, for example, in the Weimar Republic—excluded from political competition. A range of legal restrictions on competition also existed.

These limitations had a number of consequences. First, they permitted the continuation of the dominant party system: between 1920 and 1944, no election resulted in a change of government. Changes in the balance of power within the parliament were brought about for the most part not by elections, but by the movement of representatives between parliamentary factions or by the creation of new parliamentary parties. Parliamentary elections had no direct impact upon government formation; they exercised only an indirect effect through change in the balance of forces within the dominant governing party. This *integrative* character of the governing party secured wide room for manoeuvre for the dominant political élite: even in the event of a poor electoral result, it could defend its influence over the formation of government policy.

Second, party development remained limited. Because the governing party was able to secure power through other means, between the two world wars there was no need for it to build a modern *mass party* with a mass membership and a unified national organization. Among the opponents of the conglomerate-style governing party, the Social Democrats and the Smallholders began to move towards developing nationally organized mass party structures. But neither reached that end: the development of the Smallholders' Party was halted by its incorporation into the governing party; that of the Social Democrats, meanwhile, was, as a result of the Bethlen–Peyer pact of 1921, confined to the urban, industrial regions.

Third, political mobilization remained limited. As a result of the dominant party's integrative character and of the institutionalized limitations on competition, the role of class and religious affiliation in politics, unlike in much of Europe at the time, remained weak. While the absorption of the Smallholders' Party into the governing party led by the 1930s in some sense to the political integration of the land-owning peasantry (though also to the neutralization of its potential for protest), the poorer members of the peasantry, numbering some one million, remained *excluded from the political domain*.

Fourth, however, the restrictions promoted the stability of the governmental system. In those countries that exhibited levels of social development similar to Hungary's, but where opportunities for political mass mobilization and inter-party competition were wide—in Italy, Spain, Portugal, Austria and Germany—the drift of centrifugal and polarized competition towards civil war and later authoritarian or totalitarian dictatorship could not be stopped. But in Hungary this process was halted between 1920 and 1944. In part, this was achieved as a result of the *nationally* based legitimacy that the régime gained through its efforts to secure revisions to the Treaty of Trianon of 1920, in which Hungary lost two-thirds of its territory. But in part it was achieved also through the protection of the authoritarian elements of nineteenth-century constitutionalism and parliamentarism. The limitation of political mobilization and competition meant not only the limitation of democracy, but also the limitation of those forces that might otherwise have led to the destruction of the weak parliamentarism that did exist.

It can thus be said that the limited framework within which the parliamentary system operated helped to ensure its stability. But it did so at a high cost in terms of the restriction of political mobilization. That led in turn to the low political integration of wide societal groups, and to a political culture that was characterized by widespread 'subject' attitudes (Almond and Verba, 1963). Such tendencies have recurred during the development of the democratic system in the 1990s.

3

The third subdivision of the 1867–1948 period covers the few short years from the end of the Second World War until the communist take-over in 1948–49. Three particular influences over developments during these years may be identified: the influences of the war, of the period of German occupation, and of the subsequent Soviet occupation.

The Second World War, like the First, brought the mobilization of the population by the state. The mass psychological impact of this, and later the defeat in the war and the collapse of public administration—along with the flight to the West of much of the social-political establishment following the fall of the eastern front—had huge consequences. These included not only the fundamental realignment of party-political power relations—the collapse of the old party system and the emergence of a new one—but also a change in the conditions of *political mobilization* and the rise of the era of the *mass party*. The war again brought a major push toward the extension of *political participation*.

Under the German occupation during the last phase of the war, these pressures for participation were firmly suppressed: total political-military dictatorship was introduced. By contrast, the arrival of the Soviets brought some political *pluralism*. Universal suffrage and the secret ballot were introduced in 1945. Though the short time-scale meant it was necessarily limited, between 1945 and 1947 widespread *political mobilization* occurred: in the elections of 1945 and 1947, more than 90 per cent of those eligible to vote took part. Parties competed for votes on the basis of class interests (the Smallholders [FKGP], the Social Democrats [MSZDP], the Hungarian Communist Party [MKP] and the National Peasant Party [NPP]) and on the basis of religious and confessional divisions (in 1947, the Democratic People's Party).

But the parliamentarism and democracy that operated for three years were always limited. The Smallholders' Party, which brought together the various elements of the middle class, won an overwhelming victory in the 1945 elections. Despite this, a grand coalition was formed, in which the Communist Party, with the political, financial and secret-service support of the occupying Soviet authorities, gained ever-widening formal power positions and informal influence. Thus, during the coalition period, the possibilities for democratic political participation were temporarily broadened, but the division of governmental power and responsibility was determined in large part independently of the electoral results and the parliamentary balance of forces. The composition and policies of government were, as in the previous three-quarters of a century, the product not so much of parliamentary election results as of political forces independent of these—above all, of the international and geopolitical balance of power. The Communist Party, which dominated the extra-parliamentary political domain, liquidated the multi-party democracy following the second multi-party elections of 1947. Beginning in 1948–49 it began to construct a totalitarian dictatorship.

4

Just like the period of parliamentarism that existed between 1867 and 1948, the communist era should be analysed not as a single block, but rather in three differing phases. Beginning in 1948, as a direct continuation of the emerging mass-party era, a classical *totalitarian dictatorship* came into being. During the 1960s and 1970s an *authoritarian dictatorship* existed. Finally, in the 1980s, Hungary was governed by a dictatorship increasingly unsure of its own path and increasingly unable to justify its continued existence to those who lived beneath it.

The totalitarian dictatorship that was established in Hungary in the late 1940s lasted—not counting the interruption of the 1956 revolution—for around one and a half decades, until 1963. The Communist Party that had come to power through extra-parliamentary and anti-constitutional means liquidated not only parliamentarism and the multi-party system, but also the framework of the almost century-old constitutional system and *Rechtsstaat* (the separation of powers and the freedom of association), and of civil society (such as private property). The Party became the holder of all sources of power, and it proclaimed itself the exclusive repository of all societal interests. The justification for individual and group interests ceased, and the possessors of power examined all matters according to their definition of the 'general social interest'.

The political system built an *ideological legitimacy* in which its existence was justified by the promise of the future. Political power took on a totalitarian character: every particularistic interest and every political wish and ideology, along with every social group that supported them, was excluded from political life; their organizations were liquidated, and later, attempts were made to eliminate their social bases. The legality and—through the organs of repression, the pervasive control of the political police and the instruments of terror—the possibility of effective political action by the opposition were also terminated.

The totalitarian character of the régime can be seen in the spread of the control of the party-state well beyond the political sphere to every aspect of life—from the economy, through culture, all the way to school and youth socialization. The independence of these was terminated, and they were transformed in order to fit the ideology of the Communist Party. The Communist Party and its satellite organizations (the People's Front, the trade unions, the youth organizations) became one part of the control apparatus that spread over the entire population: through their mass membership, they sought to integrate politically a large part of the society.

The other instrument of control took the form of a series of campaigns mobilizing the whole population or specific groups within it. These campaigns sought to brand as 'class enemies' those social groups that were difficult or impossible to integrate into the communist system. They also sought to achieve the production aims of the system. Political mobilization was often tied to high levels of social mobility. For this reason in particular, it proved successful: social rootlessness and atomization both eased the task of control and later that of depoliticization. Political integration based upon forced mobilization by the state, however, was to succeed only partially and temporarily. In the revolution that broke out spontaneously in 1956, the most starkly differing social groups expressed their rejection of the communist Rákosi system and turned to oppose the totalitarian régime. Though it failed, the revolution was a catalyst for long-term change. After the initial period of terror and the establishment of military and later political stability (1957–63), the Kádár régime, formed with the support of Soviet troops, became an authoritarian dictatorship with paternalistic qualities.

The *authoritarian dictatorship* of the 1960s and 1970s—the so-called golden age of the Kádár régime—abstained from mass mobilization as a general instrument of political control and integration. The mobilizing strength and function of the mass organizations was reduced. Their role in control continued, but their sphere of influence was narrowed to the groups lying at the basis of the system: the functionary strata and the organized working class. The régime preferred to depoliticize other social groups. In regard to the legitimacy of the system during the 1960s and 1970s, a twofold process occurred. First, the system's demands for ideological legitimation and its ambitions regarding political mobilization weakened. Political control pulled back from the private sphere to the political, economic and cultural domains. Second, ideological legitimation was replaced increasingly by *material legitimation*, which paralleled economic growth, or rather growth in the standard of living. The power monopoly of the Communist Party (MSZMP) and of the whole communist one-party system and leadership was justified by the economic performance of that system and by the level and growth of consumption that it secured—that is, by its performance and its success. The materialistic value system was strengthened and indeed became semi-official. The emphasis on the standard of living and the demand for material legitimacy led to the growth of expectations regarding the state's economic and social performance—expectations that had already been founded by the promise of communism and the ideology of the 1950s. As part of, and also as a result of, the policies of depoliticization and of the provision of material compensation for political repression, there emerged following 1968, within the framework of liberalizing economic reforms, the so-called *second economy*. This was the semi-legal economic sphere that was not organized by the state but that was intertwined with, and operated in symbiosis with, the state economy. Later, in the 1980s—when the growth in the standard of living could no longer be sustained, and in fact fell back, the system entered a crisis.

In the 1980s, the remaining totalitarian traits of the post-Stalinist authoritarian system disappeared for good, while the claim to material legitimacy and the paternalistic style were also pushed to the background. The existence of conflicts of interest—which had previously been denied—gained recognition. Furthermore, possibilities opened—though only within strict limits—for the articulation of interests, and in some cases for the institutionalization of such articulation. (Where such freedom was not given, the prohibition was not based upon ideological principles, as in the totalitarian era, or upon the principle that the state could do it better, as in the paternalist era. Instead, it was justified simply with reference to the existing system of power.) The ordering and reconciliation of the interests that were articulated, and the 'resolution' of any differences in those interests, remained the privilege of the party state, just as was the case with the monopoly over the identification of the 'general social interest'. From the point of view of the technicalities of power, allowing the articulation of interests within certain circles made the system, and the so-called interest-inclusion mechanism, more efficient. The decision-making organs were now able to calculate with greater precision the likely reactions of the various interest groups to the alternative paths among which they had to choose. The régime continued, however, to refuse to tolerate the articulation of *political* wishes, since this would have questioned the basis of the political system: it could have resulted in the organization of political alternatives and of alternative political groups supporting them. The authoritarian system of the 1980s became an almost entirely *de-ideologized*, 'secular' régime: the role of ideology in legitimation all but disappeared. A more moderate, 'neutral' political dictatorship came into existence.

In consequence of the economic crisis and decline in consumption that stretched over more than a decade from the late 1970s, it was necessary to give up the claim to material legitimacy. This was replaced by a legitimacy based upon *historical-pragmatic arguments*, referring to the predestined and now unchangeable historical circumstances of the establishment of one-party rule and of the geopolitical situation in which Hungary found itself ('historically, this is how it happened'). It appealed to the perception that in the given circumstances the society had no choice but to accept the system and its leaders. While the totalitarian dictatorship could legitimize itself with the promise of the *future*, and the paternalist dictatorship could do likewise with the accomplishments of the *present*, the dictatorship during the era of crisis could refer only to the circumstances given by the *past*—formed of necessity and now unchangeable—and to the existing power relations as sources of support. The combative *programme* ideology of the totalitarian era was superseded by an ever more defensive *state-of-affairs* ideology. In addition, a role continued to be played in the (self-)legitimation of the régime by the almost permanent series of reforms, by the ability of the leadership to manage the crisis, by the promise of a way out of the difficulties, and later, in the last years of the system, by the distancing of the régime from the political leaders of the 1970s (Körösényi, 1988: 120–121; Szabó, 1989: 100).

Notes

1. The 1905 constitutional crisis, the revolutionary wave of 1918–19 that followed defeat in the First World War, and the German occupation of 1944–45.

2. Indeed, in the era of the Diet, because of the large size of the nobility, the franchise had been wider than in most European countries.

3. According to domestic historiography, the main reason for this was Hungary's multinational ethnic structure and the fear of centrifugal power that this led to.

Chapter One

Political Culture

Political culture can be approached from several angles. According to one approach political culture signifies the *collective* cultural and behavioural models of the political community, combined with the modes of collective problem-solving and conflict resolution that the community employs and shares (Bibó, 1986–90; Dahl, 1971; Kende, 1994). Our political way of thinking 'is never a direct function of direct experience or acquired knowledge. It is rather a product of shared interpretations that accumulate and develop into traditions across generations. The ways of thinking and the attitudes to be found during this process are highly resistant to change, and it is customary to call the combination of knowledge, values, feelings and symbols connected with this "political culture"' (Gombár, 1989: 62).

According to a second approach—and one characteristic of those using modern survey methodology—political culture involves the attitudes, dispositions, value systems, preferences, information and abilities of the *individual* concerning politics, the political system and the political community. Here, a political community is always characterized by how the various political values, norms and attitudes are distributed among its members.

1. The Historical Legacy

If political culture is formed by the long-term factors of the collective historical experience of the political community and the everyday operational mode of the institutions, we must ask what kind of historical legacy exists in Hungary in the 1990s. We consider first the legacy of the almost half-century of communism that preceded the democratic régime change—the decades that determined the lives of the population of the 1990s. We then survey the legacy of the century to century and a half that preceded communism.

The Legacy of Communism

The communist régime came into existence in Hungary as a totalitarian dictatorship: not only did it monopolize political power, it also crushed almost every institution of societal autonomy—associations, interest groups and religious and youth organizations. Furthermore, it nationalized the church schools, the institutions of the private economy and of civic association, and the economic organizations built upon private ownership. Every remaining organization, and all aspects of public life, were placed under the strict political and ideological supervision of the Communist Party and the state. Those who did not believe in the ideas of communism, or who did not wish to join the party or its satellite organizations in order to further their careers, retreated behind the ramparts of private life. The family was almost the only community that remained more or less autonomous. Communities fell apart and society became individualized and atomized. The semi-legal but tolerated 'second economy' that began to emerge from the end of the 1960s was also based primarily upon the family. In the eyes of many, public life became suspicious, and a career in public life was associated with opportunism. Private life and the family remained a sphere free from politics. In the decades following the crushing of the institutions of political identity, consciousness of identity itself lost its strength or was extinguished completely. Around the late 1970s and early 1980s, Hungary's society became one of the most individualized in Europe (Table 1).

The opportunities for the pursuit of an individual life strategy—for a politics-free career, for professional prestige—began gradually to widen from the 1960s. Given political loyalty—or at least the ritual demonstration and affirmation of acceptance of the régime on particular occasions—professional advancement became possible. Further, as control over the economy and society was relaxed, the sphere of the second economy developed. The second economy was tied to the state institutional system only informally, and within it a space opened up in which individual or family ambitions of consumption and accumulation could be better satisfied.

Table 1. Individualization and the retreat into the private sphere (percentages of those giving the given answer to two questions)

	1 With family	2 No, there are none
Hungary	83	78
Spain	53	38
Denmark	53	49
West Germany	52	53
Belgium	51	61
The Netherlands	49	54
United Kingdom	48	60
France	47	64
Italy	36	45

Questions:
1. With whom do you most like to spend your free time—your family, friends, alone, or others?
2. Are there any values for you outside your family for which you would be prepared to sacrifice your life?

Source: Bruszt and Simon, 1994: 780–781.

This cautious economic liberalization occurred not through the open revision of the official tenets of Marxism, official party resolutions, five-year plans or the prevailing legal rules, but rather often through tacit evasion. Because of this, and because of the strengthening of the economic sphere not controlled by the state and the growth in the number of groups participating within it, a dual morality and *dual society* came into being (Hankiss, 1989: 134). The normative system, behavioural rules and modes of interaction of the second (and partly black) economy and second society, along with their language and conceptual apparatus, were different from those of the official sphere that they existed alongside and in symbiosis with.

Besides atomization, political passivity and state paternalism, the most important product of the communist decades was the *dual value system*, which gives an incentive not for adherence to the official rules of the law and the state, but rather for their violation and evasion. The dual value system involves not only the breach of norms (including legal norms) and corruption that leaks into public office, but also *political cynicism* and alienation from the political community. The legacy of this has remained a part of political culture in the democratic system of the 1990s.

Subjective Competence, Political Cynicism

Under the Kádár régime in Hungary, only a few felt that they could protect their own interests (Hankiss, 1989: 84), and their number grew only temporarily following the democratic transition. The level of this *subjective political competence* rose from 9–10 per cent to 17 per cent in 1991–92. But by 1993 it again barely exceeded 10 per cent (Bruszt and Simon, 1994: 779).[1] By contrast, in most West European countries this figure lies between 20 and 40 per cent (Gabriel, 1994: 546).

In the case of Hungarian political culture, the issue is not simply that this culture is, following the conceptual system of Almond and Verba, a *subject* rather than *participant political culture* (Almond and Verba, 1963)—though this is, of course, essential to it, since the majority of the people see the state as a power institution and authority rather than as an instrument of 'popular sovereignty' that represents and realizes their interests and the public interest. A characteristic of Hungarian political culture is perhaps the very high level of alienation from the whole of the state—not just from the 'input' institutions that shape political will, but also from the 'output' institutions. The role of, and respect for, the state resemble more those in the Italian state than those in France, Germany or the United Kingdom.

Hungarian society, despite the rapid regeneration of the so-called civil sphere, could barely be said to form a *political community*, and the level of *political integration* of the individual is low. The weak binding power of the political community is shown—as we will see later—by the low level of *national pride*. It is shown also by widespread political cynicism (Table 2): the people are sceptical not only of their own ability to satisfy their interests, but also of the ability of the elected political leaders. Trust is lowest in the representative institutions that shape political will (parliament, parties, trade unions). While parties have obtained a major role in political integration,[2] their prestige, along with that of party politicians, is low.

Table 2. Political cynicism (percentage of those agreeing with the given statement)

	1989	1990	1991	1992	1993
One can never trust politicians completely	64	71	79	83	83
Ordinary people are always excluded from politics	77	72	75	83	81
Politicians are glad if the people do not interfere in the management of the affairs of the country	60	61	72	78	72
The opinions of the people interest politicians only when there are serious problems	66	68	70	72	67
So long as things go well, it does not interest me who is in power	60	59	62	64	59
Only those who want to make a career enter politics	38	42	60	59	56
It is better for people not to enter politics, because sooner or later they will get their fingers burnt	45	45	50	53	45
In Hungary everyone can have a say in the management of the affairs of the country	34	35	28	24	23
Politicians do all they can to get to know the opinions of the people	34	21	26	22	25

Source: Bruszt and Simon, 1994: 781.

Table 2 shows the high level of political alienation and apathy. In the countries of the European Union, the level of cynicism or dissatisfaction found in answers to these or similar questions are on average 10 to 20 per cent lower. Thus, while the figures for Hungary are high, political cynicism is a general phenomenon of political culture in modern democracies. What is more important is that the level of political cynicism and alienation was very high in Hungary during the years of the democratic transition, and that it grew further during the 1990s.

The Legacy of the Nineteenth and Early Twentieth Centuries

Pessimism and the absence of political self-consciousness or political will are, however, not the product simply of the communist régime. Studies of national character between the wars, and even essays written in the nineteenth century, described the Hungarian national character in the same way as it is often described today by sociology and social psychology. During the nineteenth century, Széchenyi, and later Szekfű, cited an impulsive nature, illusionism, indolence and partisan strife as 'ancient bad traits' of the Hungarians. Prohászka, in his 'The Wanderer and the Refugee' (*A vándor és a bújdosó*, 1941) writes of the ancient '*finitizmus*' of the Hungarians, by which he means the propensity towards hiding away, reclusiveness, the mere preservation of a straitened but secure and lasting life, and the striving for protection and confinement. The 'lazy and tired' hiding of the people is interrupted only by a series of hopeless outbreaks and battles. Babits, meanwhile, turns Prohászka's pessimistic picture of the Hungarians on its head: he sees in their passive, contemplative behaviour (which he takes as having Asian origins) sobriety, the rejection of irrationality and nationalism, cautious wisdom and a realistic world-view (Lackó, 1988).[3]

The pessimistic picture of the Hungarians has been widespread since the nineteenth century. It has also been sketched by analysts of the Hungarian mentality in the period since 1945. Shifting away from the roots of the study of national character in *Geistesgeschichte* (the history of ideas), they have discussed more consciously the historical mouldedness of the Hungarian temperament (Bibó, 1986–90; Gombár, 1989). Further, from the 1980s they have used also the modern, empirical research methods of the social sciences (Hankiss *et al.*, 1982). And they have repeatedly reached similar or identical results in the description and characterization of the Hungarian (political) mentality. The high levels of individualism and atomization, the weakness of solidarity, the alienation from the political community and the political cynicism that are revealed by the sociologists have a familiar ring—the *pessimistic mentality* is, for example, a feature of the Hungarian character that has been observed and described for more than a century. Examining more specifically the nature of political will in Hungary, Csaba Gombár writes of 'velleity'—that is, of 'strengthless wishes and listless will' (Gombár, 1989: 166). He himself links this to the operational mode of the political system and the narrowed opportunities for political action under Kádár. But it clearly chimes in with the notions of Hungarian impulsiveness, illusionism, indolence and *finitizmus* that were formulated half a century or a century before. It is thus apparent that these character traits are of lasting importance. Further, as we will shortly see, they continue to be part of Hungarian political culture during the 1990s.

Another theme in Hungarian political culture that has likewise been long reflected upon in political thought is the question of (national) unity and fragmentation. In the writings of Széchenyi, Szekfű and Prohászka—

and, in the 1990s, of newspaper columnists and in mass opinion—*partisan struggle*, ceaseless and futile party activity have a *negative* meaning: they waste our powers in fruitless squabbling. The strikingly low prestige of the parties during the 1990s can, of course, be linked to the portrayal of the 'national character' painted in the writings of the past only at the level of political thought, not at that of mass attitudes. Nevertheless, it does accord with the fact, characteristic of twentieth-century Hungarian political development, that the parties have never come to act as the lasting framework for political (mass) integration.

A further dimension of Hungarian political culture is connected to the significant role the state has played in economic and social modernization. Because of the low level of political integration, attitudes regarding the state have traditionally been ambivalent in Hungarian political culture: they have been at once characterized by high expectations and low trust.

2. *The Dimensions of Political Culture*

An important feature of political culture is the extent to which the citizens identify with the political system and the political community. General, diffuse support for the political system and identification with the political community do not depend directly upon the performance of the government and of other institutions. Such support can thus serve as an important source of strength for the legitimacy of the democratic system and the smooth operation of that system. This is particularly so when a country must confront serious economic difficulties and—connected with these—political tensions. For several decades following the publication of Almond and Verba's *Civic Culture*, one of the founding tenets of political science became the connection between, on the one hand, political culture and régime legitimacy and, on the other hand, the stability of the political system and its ability to survive periods of crisis (cf. Gabriel, 1994: 103). After the collapse of the communist dictatorships of Central and Eastern Europe, political scientists both in Hungary and elsewhere raised the question: will the absence or weakness of democratic political traditions and political culture weaken the stability of the new democracies, including Hungary?

Régime Support

Support for the *institutions, abstract values and concepts of democracy* (popular sovereignty, the *Rechtsstaat*, free elections, the multi-party system and so on) was very high in Hungary, as in the other East European countries, following the régime change. In their answers to public opinion researchers, a decisive majority of Hungarians (85–90 per cent) accepted the institutions and ground rules of democracy.

Satisfaction with the *operation* of the new democratic system has, however, fallen continuously in Hungary since the régime change of 1989–90: while in the year following the régime change every third citizen was satisfied with the development of democracy, in 1993 and 1994 only one citizen in every five was satisfied (Table 3). This is one of the lowest levels of satisfaction in Eastern Europe (Vecernik, 1996: 27–28), and it is also significantly below the average among the countries of Western Europe. Only in Italy were such high levels of dissatisfaction seen during the 1970s and 1980s (Gabriel, 1994: 549), and there the political system and political élite underwent a severe crisis in the early 1990s.

The interpretation of the satisfaction index is, however, not easy: it does not distinguish the concept of satisfaction with governmental performance from that of general satisfaction with the régime. It is probably correct to consider the index of diffuse support as a *combined* indicator of satisfaction with the government and with the régime. This is all the more appropriate given that, over the long term, the two types of satisfaction become linked not only conceptually, but also in terms of their content. In West European countries, where governmental performance, real data on economic performance and satisfaction with democracy have been measured and compared for decades, it has been shown that economic decline has a negative impact on the indicator of diffuse support over the medium term. There is thus a link between the effectiveness of the government and the legitimacy of the régime (Gabriel, 1994: 103).[4] For example, the legitimacy of the political system in West Germany—starting from a very low point—was created by the effect of the 'economic miracle' upon living standards. By contrast, the United Kingdom, which in the 1950s could boast a high level of legitimacy and was, in the view of Almond and Verba, the model country of 'civic culture', had to confront a rise in dissatisfaction and protests in consequence of the economic crises that plagued it during the 1960s and 1970s.

Table 3. Satisfaction with the operation of democracy (percentages)

West Germany (1976–92)*	73.2
Luxembourg (1976–92)	69.3
Denmark (1976–92)	68.3
The Netherlands (1976–92)	61.9
Portugal (1985–92)	59.9
United States (1985)	59.0
United Kingdom (1976–92)	55.1
Ireland (1976–92)	55.0
Spain (1985–92)	54.1
Greece (1980–92)	50.8
Belgium (1976–92)	50.0
France (1976–92)	45.5
Italy (1976–92)	22.6
Czech Republic (1992/94)	38/44
Slovakia (1992/94)	28/17
Poland (1992/94)	19/23
Hungary (1991)	30.5
Hungary (1992)	22.0
Hungary (1993)	20.3
Hungary (1994)	23.0
Hungary (1995)	20.0

* After 1990, the western Länder.
Sources: Eurobarometer averages for EU countries for the years 1976–92: Gabriel and Brettschneider, 1994: 549; USA: Tóka, 1994: 248; Hungary, 1991–93: Lengyel, Molnár and Tóth, 1994: 770; Hungary, 1994–95, Czech Republic, Slovakia and Poland, 1994: Lengyel, Molnár and Tóth, 1996, 631; Czech Republic, Slovakia and Poland, 1992: Tóka, 1994: 248.

It can be seen from the cross-country data that the level of satisfaction with the operation of democracy in Hungary is very low. Further, the time-series data show that that level is continuously falling. In 1995, only a quarter of Hungarians considered the new, democratic régime to be better than its predecessor, while half of those questioned considered the Kádár system to have been better (Vecernik, 1996: 247; SOCO Survey, 1995). One explanation for this is the phenomenon, evident from the surveys (Simon, 1995: 48, 50), that many people identify democracy with well-being. Thus, the deterioration of their own economic situation leads by definition to disillusionment with the democratic system. International comparison shows that there is nothing unusual in the identification of democracy with economic well-being: it is found in many long-established democracies as well (Simon, 1995: 57).

Trust in Individual Institutions and Judgements on the Performance of Government

Diffuse support for, and identification with, the abstract concepts of the political system and with the political community are not linked directly to people's everyday experiences. Judgements concerning individual institutions are, however, formed by everyday experiences, and thus different levels of trust develop in connection with different institutions. The performance of the political system is shown in part by the extent to which the citizens trust in those institutions, such as the administration, the judiciary and the police, that serve the whole political community, manage the affairs of that community, and execute the laws—the extent to which they consider them to be free of favouritism (or corrupt) and responsive, and the extent to which they trust in the even-handedness of the office holders within these institutions.

Trust in individual political institutions has fallen in Hungary continuously since the régime change (Table 4). The picture regarding the level of, and changes in, trust is very different for different institutions. Most strikingly, the more directly an institution is involved in everyday politics, the less the people trust it and the greater has been the decline in trust since 1990.

Political Participation

If we approach Hungarian political culture from the viewpoint of empirical research—that is, from the political attitudes of individuals—it is not the level of abstract acceptance of democracy or the level of trust in particular institutions within the governmental system that differ markedly in Hungary from what is found in Western or in East-Central Europe. As Table 4 shows, the level of satisfaction and trust has fallen above all in regard to evaluations of the *performance* of democracy, belief in the value of *political participation* and attitudes to the operation of *institutions of representation that shape political will*. The lack of trust in such will-forming 'input' institutions—parties, trade unions, parliament—fits into the tradition within Hungarian political culture according to which the *participation* of the citizens plays a minimal role. The majority of those questioned consider the input institutions of democracy to be less important than the executive institutions (Lázár, 1992: 597). Further, the identification of democracy with participation, or the connection of the two, is falling (Simon, 1995: 48).

Table 4. Trust towards political institutions (evaluations on a 100-point scale)

	1991	1995	1996	Change, 1991–96
President of the Republic	79	70	66	–13
Constitutional Court	68	65*	60	–8
Local councils	61	56	45	–16
Army	66	56*	52	–14
Police	64	55*	48	–16
Courts	73	50*	51	–22
Parliament	57	39	30	–27
Government	57	37	32	–25
Trade unions	39	34	29	–10
Parties	37	32	24	–13
Press, radio, television	67	n.a.	52	–15
Average	*60*	*49*	*44*	*–16*

* The figures marked with an asterisk are from December 1995. The other figures for 1995 are averages over the year. The 1996 figures are the averages of quarterly data.
Sources: Lázár, 1992: 597; Hann, 1996: 606–607; Marián, 1997: 551.

Electoral turnout in Hungary has remained below the levels found in most West European countries. Nor has it reached the levels seen in the majority of the new democracies of East-Central Europe. The low-to-medium level of political participation is, however, not restricted to electoral turnout—it has been still more apparent in respect of certain other forms of participation (Table 5; Angelusz and Tardos, 1996). It certainly does not follow from this that 'participation' and the various forms of this are not regarded as legitimate forms of democratic behaviour. The survey evidence shows that Hungarians are highly tolerant of (or indifferent towards) even non-conventional forms of political participation and protest. Acceptance of the various forms of political protest and participation—and *potential* readiness to participate are, by international standards, very high (Gerentsér and Tóth, 1996: 640–641). In contrast to this, however, the *actual* level of political participation has remained low in comparison with that seen elsewhere (Table 5). This picture is not significantly different if we take into account the frequent referendum initiatives that took place between 1989 and 1997.

Table 5. Political participation

	Boycott	Demon-stration	Public gathering	Unofficial strike	1st parl. election	2nd parl. election	3rd parl. election
Czech Republic	10.6	34.1	52.8	17.1	96	86	76.4
Hungary	1.8	6.6	6.9	1.1	65.8	68.9	56.3
Poland	5.9	8.8	11.6	8.3	68.8	43.9	67
Slovakia	11.8	22.6	48.2	13.8	96	86	75.7
Germany, eastern Länder	4.8	43.4	66.7	2.3	–	–	–
Germany, western Länder	11.5	27.2	48.4	4.0	89.1*	84.3*	77.8*
The Netherlands	15.5	30.5	37.1	4.2	87.0*	81.0*	85.8*
United Kingdom	9.2	13.8	37.1	9.8	72.7*	75.3*	–

* Electoral turnout figures marked with an asterisk refer to elections during the decade 1981–90.
Notes: The first four columns show the percentage of survey respondents saying they had participated in the forms of political participation indicated. The remaining three columns are percentage turnout figures for national parliamentary elections. For the first two elections in the Czech Republic and Slovakia, the Czechoslovak data are used. In all cases, first-round data are used.
Sources: Vecernik, 1996: 36; Angelusz and Tardos, 1996: 13; Gabriel and Brettschneider, 1994: 587; *Magyar Közlöny*, 1998 no. 47: 3889.

Many explanations exist for the low level of political participation.

1. The lack of *interest in politics* does not in itself explain the low level of participation. The level of such interest in Hungary is low to intermediate—the proportion of those interested being around 40 to 50 per cent of those questioned—but this is no different from the situation in the long-established democracies (Hann, 1996: 604; Gabriel, 1994: 544). The level of *political knowledge*, political 'news consumption'[5] and so on is, reflecting levels of interest, limited—as it is elsewhere.

2. The low level of *(subjective) civic competence* and the high level of political cynicism that were discussed above (Table 2) may constitute one explanatory factor behind the low electoral turnout. Namely, expectations regarding the state are high, but they are combined with cynicism, such that the people do not actually believe that their own expectations

will be fulfilled. In addition, loyalty towards the state as an executive power is also low, as shown by the low willingness to pay taxes (Varga, 1994).

3. Among more general, wider explanations, the first sees the source of the low participation in the *'élite' character of the régime change*—in the fact that ordinary Hungarians were not active participants in the régime change, but passive (if consenting) observers. In Poland, East Germany, Czechoslovakia, Bulgaria and Romania communist autocracy collapsed under the pressure of mass movements or uprisings involving hundreds of thousands or millions of people. Yet in Hungary, though there were some mass demonstrations, the events were not decided on the streets. The Hungarian régime change was rather the product of internal decay, the activities of the reformers within the Communist Party, the pressure exerted by the emerging political opposition and the favourable changes in the external political environment.

4. Another explanation is the general *anti-party sentiment*, shown by the low levels of party membership and organization. We cannot explain the reticence and distrust of voters towards the new parties simply by the sharpening and apparently fruitless disputes between the parties, since these attitudes predate such disputes.

5. A further factor is the legacy of social *individualization and atomization*. The political passivity of the Hungarians seen during the régime change followed from the peculiarities of the preceding period. The 'liberal' character of the Kádár régime—which contrasted with the régimes in the neighbouring countries—made possible the organization of politics-free private spheres and living space. Society became individualized and atomized (Hankiss, 1989: 55; Bruszt and Simon, 1994: 781), and the people did not behave as 'homo politicus'. The millions observed the struggle of the intellectual élite with sympathy from behind the protected bastions of the private sphere but did not feel sufficiently pressed to participate. The 'negotiated revolution'—the *peaceful transition*—executed by élite groups and the *low level of participation* are two sides of the same coin.

6. Finally, the *legacy of demobilization* may be an explanatory factor. The reasons for this have already been discussed in the introductory chapter. Here we simply refer back to the fact that the whole history of Hungarian parliamentarism from 1867 until 1939 was marked by strong limitations on democratic rights (universal suffrage and the secret ballot)

and on competition (participation by the citizens). Except for the spontaneous mass mobilizations of 1918–19 and autumn 1956, organized mass mobilization has been limited in twentieth-century Hungarian political history to the decade following the Second World War. Even then, after the first three years, this was mobilization mandated by the state. The decade of mobilization between 1945 and 1956 was followed by more than three decades of demobilization and depoliticization under Kádár.

3. Political Culture and Democratic Stability

The claim of communism to legitimacy based upon modernization, and within this the legitimacy claim of the Kádár régime based upon materialism, has boosted the role played in the post-communist system by *material legitimacy*—governmental performance and 'output'. Negative judgements upon governmental performance have reduced not only the level of satisfaction with, and trust in, the government of the day, but also satisfaction with the democratic system as a whole.

The fall in satisfaction and trust has not been accompanied by a rise in political protest or political participation. Precisely for this reason, an important role is played in the maintenance of the stability of the system by *citizen passivity* and '*stabilizing apathy*'—even if we cannot speak, as the data on political participation show, of general political apathy.[6]

It was premature to conclude, as some did, that, because of the contradictions of the transition and the 'undeveloped' nature of political culture, the democratic system in Hungary would be unstable. This view overestimated the policy-forming role of the masses (Bruszt and Simon, 1992: 77) and the potential for protest and mobilization arising from such tensions and difficulties as unemployment and reductions in the real wage. It also underestimated the role and autonomy of the political élite(s) in the formation and operation of the democratic governmental system. The rationalist-activist model of political culture undervalued the positive role of subject political culture from the point of view of political integration and the maintenance of régime stability. The view that overemphasizes the role of civic activism—which is popular in Hungary, but also generally in Eastern and Western Europe—is characteristic more of 'civic education' textbooks[7] than of the 'civic culture' conception of Almond and Verba. The civic education textbooks prescribe the way in which citizens in a democracy should behave, and they take it as a precondition of the operation of the democratic system that there should be a participatory political culture. In this *rationalist-activist* model of political culture, the democratic citizen is politically active and conscious. His or her view of politics is rational, guided by the mind not by emotions. His or her political preferences (such as voting decisions) are well informed, based upon a careful weighing of interests and principles. These features are taken as forming 'developed', democratic political culture, while their weakness or absence is taken as signalling 'undeveloped' political culture.

But what Almond and Verba refer to as 'civic culture' in their classic work involves not only citizen participation, but also a culture in which citizens are loyal towards, respect the authority of, and show allegiance to, the political community, the state and institutions of the state. That is, there is a mixture of *participant*, *subject* and *parochial* orientations. In this *mixed* political culture, the more traditional, non-participatory orientation limits and weakens the commitment of the individual towards politics and has a moderating effect on demands and claims towards other groups or the state. Within the mixed political culture, the subject orientation of the citizens secures the autonomy for the political élite that is necessary for decision-making, while the participatory orientation makes it possible that the élite will remain sensitive to the political preferences of the voters and of society (Kavanagh, 1972: 14). Political culture in Hungary takes this mixed form, though within this, because of the low level of political participation, we must emphasize the weakness of 'participatory culture' and citizen activity. This can be regarded as an explanation for the political stability that has been seen in Hungary.

Notes

1. The figures refer to the proportion believing that they would be able to do something against a decision that was damaging to them.

2. The index of trust is lower among those not choosing a party than among those choosing a party, and lower still among non-voters (though it is also lower among voters for the Smallholders' Party).

3. Széchenyi, Szekfű, Prohászka and Babits were prominent writers of the nineteenth century (in the case of Széchenyi) and the early twentieth century (in the case of the remaining three). Their work had considerable influence on the Hungarian intelligentsia élite.

4. This link assumes that the concept of *system legitimacy* can be approached empirically.

5. For example, frequency of newspaper readership.

6. Besides the participant culture, Almond and Verba emphasize the role of subject culture as the second component of civic political culture. Others speak of 'stabilizing apathy' (Lipset, 1995).

7. The first attempt at such a book in Hungary was the 'democracy teaching' textbook *A jó polgár* [The Good Citizen] (Drahos *et al.*, 1994).

Chapter Two

The Parties

The role of political parties was decisive in Hungary during the transition, and the parties continue to be central to Hungarian politics today. Because of their importance, it is necessary that we give an overview of these parties before we proceed further in our discussion of the various elements of the Hungarian political system of the 1990s. This is the task of the present chapter. In the first two sections we consider the extent of party penetration into Hungarian political life and the roles that the parties play. We then describe briefly the principal ideological groupings into which the parties fall, and the origins of the parties. Finally, we summarize the history and character of each of the parties that have thus far played a significant role in post-communist Hungarian politics. (The electoral results and government role of the parties are given in Appendices A and B.) This account will provide the foundations to which further detail can be added in subsequent chapters.

1. The Extent of Party Penetration in Hungary

Political parties are central actors in Hungarian politics. Nevertheless, the *penetration* of the parties into state, semi-state and other public institutions is not unlimited—it is not as extensive as in Austria, or perhaps even in Germany. Strong limits have developed upon party penetration into state and social life. One such limit is created by the fact that, after half a century of one-party dictatorship, a strongly *anti-party* atmosphere and political culture emerged in the political thinking of the opinion-leading élite and intelligentsia and in mass culture.

The consequence of this anti-party political culture and the 'consensual' character of the democratic transition was that the new democratic system inherited almost the whole of the old state institutional system. The fact that the public administration remained almost entirely intact distinguished the Hungarian transition of 1989–90 not only from the previous communist and fascist or national-socialist takeovers, but also from the democratic transitions in Germany, Austria and Hungary after 1945. That is, while in these earlier cases a sweeping political clear-out of the administrative apparatus of the previous régime was conducted under the direction of the party or parties of the new system, this did not occur in Hungary after 1989. In consequence of this and of the legal exclusion of parties from the workplace, the administration's personnel—except the very highest—remained free from party influence. As a result of the personal ties created by the old party-state and *nomenklatura* system, the depoliticization of the public administration secured for the Hungarian Socialist Party (*Magyar Szocialista Párt*, MSZP)—the successor to the old Communist Party—an advantage over the other parties.

A further limitation upon party penetration is created by the fact that, in comparison with both the first half of the century and the period immediately following 1945, the structural conditions for *political mobilization* have changed. Because the parties are now able to reach almost every citizen through the modern press and electronic media, it is not necessary for them to employ the organizational instruments of political mass mobilization that would create a link between the parties and the various groups of society either directly—through party organizations—or indirectly—through satellite organizations.

The consequence of these factors and of the anti-party political culture is that the extent of party penetration into the various spheres of life is not particularly great. This is suggested by the relatively low level of party membership and the limited role played by parties on community councils. In the village local-government elections of 1990, 71 per cent of the posts available were won by independents, while the parties secured only 29 per cent. In 1994 these proportions were 81 per cent and just 19 per cent. This signifies a very low level of party penetration by international standards (Horváth, 1993: 24, 30; Bőhm and Szoboszlai, 1996).

The constitutional amendments of 1989–90, in a reaction to the four-decade-long party-state, limited the potential role of parties. The constitution states that a political party cannot exercise power directly and cannot direct an organ of the state. In order to implement this, a range of positions are made incompatible with party membership or leading party office. For the same reason, judges and public prosecutors are not permitted to be party members and cannot engage in political activities, while civil servants may not accept party office. The influence of the parties was limited also by the consensus surrounding the creation of an administration free from political influence.

2. *The Functions of the Parties*

Parties played a decisive role in the democratic transition, and they continue to play such a role in the operation of the new institutional system and in the development of models of political behaviour. They provide the personnel and leaders of the new political institutions, they participate in the formation of public opinion, and they structure the votes. Their representatives sit in parliament: as a result, the parties form the government, direct the work of the legislature and supervise the administration. In what follows, by considering in turn the various functions performed by political parties in modern representative democracies, we examine the question of what peculiarities exist in the role of parties in Hungarian democracy.

Great scope is provided for the parties in Hungary by the weakness of institutionalized interest articulation: their role in *interest integration and aggregation* is circumscribed by institutional factors (interest organizations) to a lesser degree than it is in some West European democracies possessing strong neo-corporatist structures or 'pillarized' institutions. Interest organizations are not generally connected directly (institutionally) to the parties. Where the parties do have ties to mass-membership organizations—as in the case of the MSZP and the successors to the communist trade unions—the link is based more upon personal factors, 'network capital' and cultural bonds than upon any form of institutionalized arrangement. As a result, the party leaderships remain independent and possess considerable autonomy—as shown by the socialist-led government after 1994—even in respect of policies affecting their supporters.

In Hungary, as in other democracies, parties engage in mobilization prior to elections. But the role of parties in *mass mobilization* is more limited than in the case of the mass parties of the early twentieth century.

There are two reasons for this. First, Hungarian society at the end of the twentieth century is a modern, mobilized society composed of individualized persons removed from traditional communities. Second, the former role of the parties in direct electoral mobilization has in many respects been taken over by the media. The role of the media in opinion leadership and the role of political campaigning and advertising is particularly strong because, in consequence of the very great speed of the régime change and the emergence of parties, only in part of the electorate have stable party affiliations developed, leaving a high proportion of wavering voters who can be influenced by inter-party competition.

The parties have a large role—as the dominant actors of the political sphere—in the *formation of public opinion* and the *structuration of votes*. But they are not alone in influencing public opinion: they are somewhat at the mercy of other opinion leaders and the political press. Since the spread of the modern electronic media in the 1950s and 1960s, the institutional role of the press has been greater than it was during the first half of the century, when the parties, through their mass memberships and satellite organizations, had a direct role in the formation of public opinion. Furthermore, in Hungary's case, a major role has been gained alongside the new political élite by the highly influential opinion-leading intelligentsia élite.

The role of parties in *integration* into the democratic system is also to be found in Hungary, although, because of the anti-party political culture, it is limited. Voters who support a particular party express greater trust in the institutions of democracy than do those whom no party has been able to attract.

Alongside their representative functions, the parties in Hungary—as in other parliamentary systems, but unlike those in countries with presidential systems—have a *governmental function*. 'Non-partisan' civil servants, technocratic experts and intellectuals have greater prestige in Hungarian political culture than do party politicians, and support has emerged for governments of experts or officials. Nevertheless, governments have been composed for the most part not by officials or experts but, as we will see in the chapter on the government (Chapter Ten), and as fits the logic of parliamentary government, by party politicians.

The *selection of political leaders*—from the choice of candidates for parliament to the election of government members and the president of the republic—is performed by parties. The *recruitment* of politicians, too, increasingly occurs within the parties. During the régime change and in the years immediately following it, because of the short history of most of the parties and those parties' limited leadership cadres, it was very common for non-political 'civic' figures suddenly to be appointed to leading positions. The presidents of the National Bank of Hungary, public-service television and public-service radio, who were appointed in 1990 and 1991, all rose in this way, as did some ministers. Most of those filling direct political positions (such as ministerial portfolios), however, did subsequently strive to build a personal party base, and the majority of those filling more 'neutral' posts were unable to preserve that neutrality in the midst of party-political conflicts. During the second parliamentary and governmental cycle, between 1994 and 1998, it became very rare for 'civic' figures to be appointed to governmental positions, or even to the wider circle of patronage positions at the disposal of the government. The role not only of party affiliation, but also of a party career, increased. On the other hand, non-political experts again came to the fore at the time of the formation of the Orbán government in 1998.

The function of the parties in the selection of the personnel of government and the political leadership means also that the parties—alongside the administration—have a decisive role to play in the *formation of government policy*.

3. The Three Political Camps

No 'civic forum' type of united opposition to the communist régime appeared, even temporarily, in Hungary in the late 1980s—from the very beginning, the opposition to the system was divided culturally, ideologically and personally. In consequence of this, strong competition and polarization characterized the *multi-party system* from the time of its inception. By the early 1990s, three political camps had formed—the liberal, the national-conservative/Christian and the socialist. The parliamentary parties all belonged to one of these camps. The socialist camp was formed by the Hungarian Socialist Party (MSZP), the liberal camp by the Alliance of Free Democrats (*Szabad Demokraták Szövetsége*, SZDSZ) and the Federation of Young Democrats (*Fiatal Demokraták Szövetsége*, Fidesz), and the national-conservative/Christian camp by the Hungarian Democratic Forum (*Magyar Demokrata Fórum*, MDF), the Independent

Smallholders' Party (*Független Kisgazdapárt*, FKGP) and the Christian Democratic People's Party (*Kereszténydemokrata Néppárt*, KDNP). During the second half of the 1990s, some change occurred in this structure, with Fidesz moving from the liberal camp to the national-conservative camp. The extra-parliamentary parties and the parties formed by defections from the larger parties were also, for the most part, associated with one of these camps. Each camp was tied together not only by common political and ideological orientations, but also by the very similar socio-cultural composition of their core political élites and electoral bases, and by shared political attitudes and world-views. The political cleavages that cut through society also played a role in the conflicts that divided the three camps, as will be discussed in Chapter Four, concerning cleavages. Here, by way of introduction, we summarize the main characteristics of the three camps (Table 1).

Table 1. Characteristics of the three political camps during the first half of the 1990s

	Socialist	Liberal	Conservative
Parties	MSZP	SZDSZ, Fidesz	MDF, KDNP, FKGP
Ideology	left-wing/modernizing, social democratic	based on human rights, liberal economics	national, Christian, conservative
Party élite	*nomenklatura* élite	liberal/radical intelligentsia	intelligentsia of Christian middle class
Social élite	leaders (functionaries of the Kádár era)	intelligentsia	Christian middle class
Social basis (electoral base)	former MSZMP members	those not integrated into church or communist system	church-going Christians
Cleavage	*nomenklatura*	secularized, not integrated into communist system	religion

4. The Origins and Establishment of the New Parties

The democratic transition in Hungary had led, by the beginning of 1989, to the transformation of political life into party-political life. The disintegration of the one-party system that had lasted for four decades began in the mid–1980s, and by 1987–88 had reached the stage where the various critical and oppositional groups sought to organize politically. By the time of the 1990 elections, a party system had emerged that, in comparison with the diffuse anti-communist movements of other transition countries, was relatively developed and, as was later seen, stable. The opposition to the communist system did not begin life as an *ad hoc* grouping or a united 'front'. Rather it was divided from the start by political orientations, interests and traditions. The opposition parties were established on the basis of these divisions, and they thus proved to be lasting organizations. By the time of the 1990 elections, the parties already possessed characteristic political profiles, party programmes, national organizations and relatively sizeable memberships, thus becoming similar to the majority of parties in the Western democracies. All the same, the parties in Hungary did not pass through the *mass-party* stage of development: they are rather electoral parties. Their structure and membership are comparable more to those of the middle-class parties that developed in the parliaments of the nineteenth century than to those of the social-democratic or communist parties that emerged outside parliament around the end of the nineteenth and beginning of the twentieth century. They are less centralized than the latter. They have no institutional membership, only individual members. By the end of 1991, the combined membership of all the parties was only quarter of a million—that is, only around 5 per cent of the electorate.

The parties formed in the late 1980s can be divided into three groups based upon their origins. The first group is composed of the *historical parties*—the Independent Smallholders' Party (FKGP), the Christian Democratic People's Party (KDNP), the Hungarian Social Democratic Party (*Magyar Szociáldemokrata Párt*, MSZDP) and the Hungarian People's Party (*Magyar Néppárt*, MNP). Among them, only the first two entered parliament in 1990 and 1994, and only the Smallholders gained parliamentary representation in 1998. The common feature of all of these parties was that they had a historical past. They operated for a longer or shorter time and gained political significance before the communist take-over of 1948–49—between the wars or during the short period of limited but still competitive democracy following the Second World War. The historical parties combined won around one-fifth of the votes in 1990 and around one-sixth of the votes in both 1994 and 1998.

The second group comprises the *new parties*, formed from the dissident intelligentsia groups during the last years of the Kádár era. The Hungarian Democratic Forum (MDF), the Alliance of Free Democrats (SZDSZ) and the Federation of Young Democrats (Fidesz) belong to this group. The 1990 elections brought success for these parties—they won in total more than half of all the party-list votes cast. In both 1994 and 1998 they won close to 40 per cent of the votes, but their relative strengths had changed totally by 1998: while Fidesz had by then become a large party, the SZDSZ had gradually fallen back, and the MDF—the electoral victor in 1990—had become very small indeed.

To the third group belong the successor parties to the old Communist Party. The Communist Party (officially, the Hungarian Socialist Workers' Party, or *Magyar Szocialista Munkáspárt*, MSZMP) split into two at its October 1989 congress. The reformers, who gained the upper hand at the congress, formed the Hungarian Socialist Party (MSZP), while the conservatives continued to operate under the old MSZMP banner, later shortening it to the Workers' Party (*Munkáspárt*, MP). The MSZP was able successfully to enter competition with the opposition. It entered parliament as the fourth largest party in 1990, with 11 per cent of the votes, and in 1994 it was the electoral victor. The MSZMP/Workers' Party has, by contrast, been unable to enter parliament and has fallen back to the political periphery.

A further group comprises the parties formed as a result of splits from the six major parties that entered parliament in the 1990 and 1994 elections. Among these are the United Smallholders' Party (*Egyesült Kisgazdapárt*, EKGP), the Hungarian Party of Justice and Life (*Magyar Igazság és Élet Pártja*, MIÉP) and the Hungarian Democratic People's Party (*Magyar Demokrata Néppárt*, MDNP). By 1998, the first of these had already disappeared. MIÉP entered parliament in the 1998 elections, while the MDNP—despite failing to win parliamentary representation—gained a place in the Orbán government formed after those elections.

Having surveyed the political palette briefly, we now consider the features of each of the major parties in terms of policy character, leadership and social base.

5. The Character of the Parties

The traditional divisions of the Hungarian intelligentsia had a considerable impact upon the pluralization of Hungarian politics and the development of the political structure between 1987 and 1990. These divisions, inherited from the first half of the century, ran in latent form through the communist era and were revived during the 1970s and 1980s. The politically most active critical intelligentsia was divided into *urbánus* and *népi-nemzeti* groups, and the line between them was drawn by major differences in ideology, mentality and political tactics.[1] In 1987 and 1988, the two intelligentsia subcultures established their own political organizations and later political parties: the *népi-nemzeti* intelligentsia created the MDF, while the *urbánus* intelligentsia formed the SZDSZ (Bozóki, 1990; Körösényi, 1989).

The Hungarian Democratic Forum (MDF)

The Hungarian Democratic Forum was formed in the autumn of 1987. The first period of its history, lasting until autumn 1989, was defined by a *népi-nemzeti* orientation, and its character was that of a movement rather than a party. The conceptual universe of the *népi-nemzeti* orientation was characterized by national and democratic values, national traditions, grassroots radicalism and a view of the future based upon the so-called third way between capitalism and communism. The *népi-nemzeti* group, and at this time the entire MDF, saw the national reform wing of the MSZMP led by Imre Pozsgay as a political ally. In its political tactics, the MDF sought to keep its distance from both the radical opposition (Fidesz and the SZDSZ) and the ruling MSZMP.

The second half of 1989 brought major changes in both the leadership and the policies of the MDF. The transformation of the political character of the MDF is shown well by the change of personnel in its leadership. In the autumn of 1989, Zoltán Bíró, who had once worked as the colleague of reform communist Imre Pozsgay and who cultivated a personal and political alliance with him, was replaced as president of the party by József Antall. While Bíró was unambiguously the representative of the *népi-nemzeti* movement and a believer in grassroots democracy and the third way, József Antall came from the traditions of national liberalism and liberal conservatism. He represented a wider social and political spectrum: the national and Christian middle class. In the democratic interlude after 1945, his father had been a politician in what was then the largest *bürgerliche* party, the Smallholders' Party, and a government minister. In József Antall there appeared on the Hungarian political landscape for the first time in decades the figure of the *bürgerliche* politician. It was characteristic of his prestige that during 1988 and 1989 all three large parties emerging on the centre-right—the MDF, the Smallholders' Party and the Christian Democratic People's Party—offered him the post of party leader. By the time of the elections in spring 1990, the MDF had become the party of gradual transition.

The MDF became a rightist-centrist *people's party* or 'omnibus' party. From the spring of 1990 it could, given its electoral base, be regarded as a *catch-all party*. That position as a people's party entailed a somewhat blurred political character—the party was characterized more by symbols and values than by a policy programme worked out in great detail. Following its electoral victory in 1990, the MDF formed a centre-right coalition and became the leading party in government for four years (see Appendices A and B).

During the two years following those first elections, the *political character* of the MDF was defined by two major policy orientations. The first and decisive orientation was the *liberal-conservative*, pragmatic orientation led by Prime Minister Antall, the political thinking of which was strongly influenced by Hungarian constitutional and legal traditions. In comparison with the approach of the conservative and Christian democratic parties of Western Europe, Christian and traditional values and the concept of nation received greater emphasis in the political rhetoric of the MDF. This was in part a consequence of the search for political continuity and the effort to establish a clear identity. While the party was more ideological, the governmental circle was characterized by more pragmatic attitudes, as is often the case in European politics. The major laws delineating the final stages of the régime change—such as those on local government, civil servants and compensation—were connected with the MDF-led government.

Alongside the leading pragmatic-conservative orientation, considerable influence was exercised within the party by the *right-wing, popular-radical* wing. This group was very popular among party members, and its role grew after the departure of the left-wing *népi-nemzeti* politicians and supporters of the third way. It was characterized by anti-communist as well as anti-liberal rhetoric. Its members believed in the 'cleansing' of former communist functionaries and party members from the state administration and state industry and advocated the removal of the leaders of television and radio, who were said to pursue 'un-national' programme policies. They saw as their principal opponent the 'cosmopolitan', 'liberal-bolshevik', 'Jewish' SZDSZ, which, because of the Jewish origins of its leaders, its viewpoint on the national question and its radical liberalism, they viewed as having a mentality alien to that of the Hungarians. The shift of the national radicals to the right, and, from 1992, their open opposition to the pragmatic-conservative governmental centre within the MDF led eventually, in 1993, to their departure from the party. A number of far-right parties were then formed. The most important of these is the Hungarian Party of Justice and Life (MIÉP), led by István Csurka, which will be discussed separately below. The presence of the national radicals within the MDF and their shift to the right significantly reduced the authority of the party and increased the influence of its opponents upon public opinion.

Following the death of József Antall in late 1993 and the serious electoral defeat of the party in 1994, the erosion of the MDF that had begun with the departure of the national radicals and of a number of centrists and 'national liberals' continued. A sharpening internal struggle for the party leadership between the more conservative wing headed by Sándor Lezsák and Péter Boross and the centrists led by Iván Szabó culminated in 1996 with the victory of the former. Lezsák was elected party leader, leading to the departure from the party of the group led by Szabó, which embraced almost every leading governmental and parliamentary figure from the Antall period. This group then established a new party, the Hungarian Democratic People's Party (MDNP). With this, the disintegration of the MDF into the various groups that had once formed its broad base to all intents and purposes came to a close.

Three successor parties to the original MDF took part in the elections of 1998: the rump MDF, the MDNP and MIÉP. The performance of MIÉP will be discussed below. The MDNP was able to secure only 1.3 per cent of the list vote and did not enter parliament. The MDF itself also scored badly, winning just 2.8 per cent of the list vote. Nevertheless, as a result of an electoral agreement with Fidesz—according to which Fidesz and the MDF ran joint candidates in seventy-five of the single-member electoral districts—seventeen seats were won by MDF candidates. Following the elections, the MDF entered the governmental coalition with Fidesz and the Smallholders, and the MDNP has also gained a limited role in the government. At the time of writing, the future of both the MDF and the MDNP is rather uncertain. Co-operation between Fidesz, the MDF and the MDNP is increasing (for example, in the local elections of October 1998), and the possibility has been floated by senior figures in each of the parties that in the future they will form a party alliance or even merge into one.

The Hungarian Party of Justice and Life (MIÉP)

MIÉP is the party of the national radicals who left, or were expelled from, the MDF in 1993. Its predecessor was the Movement of Hungarian Way Circles, which was founded by István Csurka when he was still an MDF parliamentary deputy as a counterforce to the centrist policies of the MDF and the government led by József Antall. The group around Csurka left the MDF in 1993 after Csurka failed to win the party presidency from Antall and failed to effect a radical right turn in the party's orientation. MIÉP was formed by a group of around a dozen parliamentary deputies.

The direct catalyst for the split was the fact that Csurka's supporters did not vote in parliament for the Hungarian-Ukrainian treaty signed by the Antall government, which, among other matters, recognized the existing borders between the two countries. This points to the fact that, unlike all the other parties in Hungary, MIÉP considers possible the revision of the borders established by the Trianon Treaty of 1920. The party's radical national profile is built not only upon its attitudes to the border question and the issue of ethnic Hungarians living in neighbouring countries, but also upon anti-capitalism—particularly opposition to international and banking capital—and anti-Semitism. MIÉP seeks to represent Hungary's 'real' interests against the 'liberal-bolshevik' forces that serve alien interests. Its political goal is to cleanse the media and the state administration of former communists and 'alien', 'non-Hungarian' elements. It calls for real régime change, the re-examination of privatization, and protectionist economic and social policies. On the international stage, it fosters particularly close ties with Jean-Marie Le Pen and his French National Front.

MIÉP represents the radical anti-communist strand within the third-way *népi-nemzeti* movement that played a key role in the formation of the MDF. It draws heavily upon the *kurucos* anti-Habsburg independence tradition, and the Calvinist (Reformed) character of that tradition is a feature of MIÉP too. The majority of the fourteen MIÉP deputies who entered parliament in 1998 are members of the Reformed Church. MIÉP constitutes the far right of Hungarian politics, and the other parties refuse to deal with it directly. Its relationship with the parties of the moderate right is thus ambivalent—it was not a member of the MDF-led government in 1993–94, and it gained no place in the Fidesz-led centre-right government coalition formed following the 1998 elections, but it does consider itself to be an external supporter of that Fidesz-led government. In 1994, MIÉP was unable to pass the 5 per cent threshold on entry to parliament. In 1998, however, it succeeded in doing so, and it has thus been able to form its own independent parliamentary group in the new parliament (see Appendix B, Table 3).

The Alliance of Free Democrats (SZDSZ)

The Alliance of Free Democrats was formed in 1988 as the political organization of the so-called Democratic Opposition. The Democratic Opposition came into existence in the late 1970s in solidarity with the Czechoslovak human-rights movement Charter '77. The *intelligentsia élite* that founded the SZDSZ was composed of left-wing intellectuals, philosophers, sociologists and economists who had broken with Marxism during the 1970s. A significant number of them were of Jewish origin and came from communist functionary backgrounds. The critical intelligentsia that gathered under the banner of human rights stood in radical opposition to the Kádár system. One product of this was support for the group from many veterans of the 1956 revolution, a number of whom—such as Imre Mécs and Árpád Göncz—later became SZDSZ politicians. Partly out of necessity and partly through choice, the *dissidents* remained outside the official institutions. They published *samizdat* (illegal) newspapers and built ties with the human-rights movements in Czechoslovakia and Poland. The broader circle of the dissident intelligentsia, numbering several thousand people, consisted of social scientists and researchers in Budapest. The connections of this circle within the intelligentsia and its capacity for dissemination—exercised in particular through its press—had a significant effect in the more liberal atmosphere of the 1980s upon the political thinking of the politicized intelligentsia and the alternative élite.

The notion of liberal human rights and, in the 1980s, of democratic institutions, stood at the heart of the *political thinking* of the Democratic Opposition, and this left its stamp upon the conceptual universe of the SZDSZ too. While the *nation* was central to the thinking of the *népi-nemzeti* intelligentsia circle that formed the MDF, the thinking of the Democratic Opposition was 'cosmopolitan'. Its aim was not the independence of the nation, but rather the 'liberation' of (civil) society from the rule of the state. It proclaimed the primacy of universal rights. For example, while the situation of the Hungarians living in the neighbouring countries was treated by the MDF as a national question, in the politics of the SZDSZ it was seen as a problem of human rights. In consequence of the SZDSZ's human rights principles, a part came to be played in its policies by the representation of the interests of the various (religious, ethnic and cultural) minorities. The representatives of a range of minorities—the Jews, the Gypsies, non-conformist churches such as the Methodists and the *Hit Gyülekezete* (Congregation of Faith)—appeared among the party's members and leaders, and later among its parliamentary deputies.

The liberalism of the SZDSZ during the late 1980s and the 1990s has been radically individualist. It takes as its model not the social and political community of nineteenth-century continental European (national) liberalism, but rather contemporary American society based upon human rights and multiculturalism.

During 1988 and 1989, the SZDSZ became, along with Fidesz, the party of *radical régime change*. At the time of the roundtable talks in the summer of 1989, the MDF was ready to compromise with the reform wing of the MSZMP led by Imre Pozsgay over the nature of the transition to democracy and the basic pillars of the governmental system being created. The SZDSZ, however, was not. Together with Fidesz it initiated a—successful—referendum in the autumn of 1989 to realize its goals. The programme of the 'coherent régime change' and radical anti-communist propaganda significantly broadened the base of the SZDSZ. The party developed to such an extent during the referendum campaign that, in terms of membership numbers, organization and popularity, it had become the principal rival to the MDF by the time of the parliamentary elections of spring 1990.

Following the 1990 elections, the SZDSZ became the largest party in opposition to the centre-right government of the MDF, FKGP and KDNP (see Appendices A and B). During the first year following the elections, it engaged in highly combative politics. Enjoying the support of much of the press, it exerted constant pressure on the Antall government, which did not cohere well, appeared very weak and uncertain during its first year and was gradually unravelling. The years 1991 and 1992, however, brought gradual change in the politics of the SZDSZ. The change of direction involved the exclusion of any opening to the right—towards the government coalition—in the coalition policy of the party and a move instead in the direction of the MSZP, which the party had seen in 1990 as its chief opponent. This culminated in the socialist-liberal coalition that followed the 1994 elections. While the radicalism of the SZDSZ had, until the 1990 elections, manifested itself in the party's anti-communist campaign against the MSZP, from not long after those elections—that is, from around the autumn of 1990—it was directed primarily against the MDF-led government coalition. The strategy of the 'anti-fascist' coalition around the *Democratic Charter*[2] was to brand the centre-right government and the parties within it as extremist, to identify the whole government and government coalition with the national radicals led by István Csurka, and to paint them as reactionary, far-right or simply fascist. The most important resource in this campaign was the intelligentsia circle around the party, which gained a major role in the press and other, electronic opinion-leading instruments. The background of the SZDSZ in the intelligentsia and the activities of the left-wing and liberal intelligentsia in support of the SZDSZ was symbolized by the party's national list in the 1994 elections, at the bottom of which the names of around two dozen nationally recognized members of the intelligentsia appeared.

The conclusion of a coalition agreement with the MSZP in 1994 signified the abandonment of the party's previous official policy, the policy of the 'liberal block'. But, taking into account the nature of broader political relationships, the signing of this coalition was not entirely unexpected. Believers in the coalition within the intelligentsia (such as the writer György Konrád) had been preparing the way for it since 1991–92 within the framework of the Democratic Charter. Its opponents too (such as the national-radical István Csurka) had for years seen a coalition between the two as natural.

Following the formation of the coalition, the SZDSZ lost much of its early character as the protector of minorities and of liberal human rights. It placed its liberal and monetarist economic policies in the foreground and fell into line with the modernizing ideology of the Socialists who led the coalition (Bozóki, 1996). On the other hand, the SZDSZ became a more pragmatic party after 1994. Besides the party's participation in government, this was tied also to the fact that many of the 'founding fathers' who had previously been dominant within the party leadership relinquished their positions and handed them over to more pragmatic career politicians.

The SZDSZ suffered a serious setback in the parliamentary elections of 1998. Its support fell by almost two-thirds to just 7.57 per cent of the list vote, and its representation in parliament fell from sixty-nine seats to twenty-four (see Appendix B). Much harm was done to the popularity of the SZDSZ by the years of coalition government with the Socialists—a series of corruption scandals surrounded the government, and the party lost its distinctive profile within the coalition.

The Federation of Young Democrats–Hungarian Civic Party (Fidesz-MPP)

The Federation of Young Democrats was formed as a youth political organization in the spring of 1988. Besides political liberalism, it was characterized initially by radical anti-communism and the alternative, activist features of youth subculture. Following its electoral success in 1990, it consciously pushed its youthful, movement-like character to the background. This character later disappeared completely, and in 1993 the age limit on party membership (of thirty-five years) was dropped. Fidesz donned the image of a 'serious' parliamentary party.

The founders of Fidesz were young—at the time of the régime change, in their twenties—and came from the prestigious colleges of the universities in Budapest. They grew up on the *samizdat* literature published by the Democratic Opposition and, like the members of the SZDSZ, they were characterized by liberal political values and the radical rejection of the one-party system. The decisive figures in the Fidesz leadership graduated from university in the early and mid–1980s. In contrast to the leaders of the SZDSZ, whose background was mainly in the humanities, literature and sociology, the Fidesz politicians were mostly lawyers and thus possessed more practical knowledge. The leaders of Fidesz were different from those of the SZDSZ also in terms of their origins and family background. Many came from provincial middle-class families, and they were often 'first-generation' members of the intelligentsia (Tőkés, 1990: 37).

As regards *ideological and policy orientation*, Fidesz has gradually moved further and further from the SZDSZ. It has a more authoritarian conception of government—indeed, even in the early 1990s it believed in strong government and a strong executive. Its anti-statism is weaker than—or different in character from—that of the SZDSZ. In addition, it has kept its distance from organized interest groups, particularly trade unions. It believes in governmental responsibility and opposed, for example, the creation of autonomous 'functional self-governments' in social security. These were established by the Antall government; the Fidesz-led Orbán government abolished them in one of its first acts after gaining office in 1998. In terms of economic philosophy, Fidesz was more libertarian than the SZDSZ during the early 1990s. But in response to the restrictive monetarist policies of the socialist-liberal government between 1994 and 1998, and also in part as a reflection of its conservative shift, in the mid–1990s the party placed greater emphasis upon the social responsibility of the state and the need for social policy to support the middle strata.

Following its electoral failure in 1994 and the establishment of the MSZP-SZDSZ government, Fidesz took a decisive turn to the right. It became the principal organizer of one of two rival attempts to ally the fragmented parties of the opposition to the government—that of the centre-right 'Civic Alliance' (*bürgerliche Koalition*). Following the failure of this, and in consequence of the splits within, and weakening of, the MDF and the KDNP, its position among the right-wing parties further strengthened—not just in terms of parliamentary politics (where its numbers grew through defections from the other parties), but also at the ballot box. Its strategy of gathering under its wings all of the forces of the moderate opposition was signified also by a change in its official name—to the Fidesz–Hungarian Civic Party (Fidesz-MPP). The party became the integrative force of the centre and right, and subsequently the victor in the 1998 elections (see Appendices A and B). Through co-operation with the Fidesz-MPP, both the MDF, and the Christian democrats who left the increasingly radicalized KDNP, were able to enter parliament. Whether this pressure for integration will lead to a new, unified party of the centre-right remains to be seen.

The Independent Smallholders' Party (FKGP)

A leading role was played in the reorganization of the Independent Smallholders' Party in 1988 by veterans of the period before 1948. During the inter-war years, the Smallholders' Party was the party of the land-owning peasantry, and it was one of the leading parties of the opposition alongside the Social Democrats. It achieved a remarkable victory in the elections of 1945 as the party of the whole right wing, winning a total of 57 per cent of the votes cast. When the communist system fell, however, it was unable to regain that position. The more agile political groups gathered around the MDF or the SZDSZ, and the Smallholders started with a disadvantage from which they have never fully recovered. The FKGP was again seen as the party of rural areas and of the peasantry and former small and medium-sized landowners. It is a radically anti-communist party, which campaigned for the abolition of the collective farms and the *re*-privatization of the land (the return of the land to the original owners) in order to re-establish private farming. Its political élite has been recruited primarily from members of the provincial middle class with agricultural backgrounds. The FKGP has entered both centre-right government coalitions formed since the régime change—in 1990 and in 1998.

The Smallholders' Party has, since its refoundation, consistently supported economic and social policies giving favourable treatment to small, independent economic actors—the land-owning peasantry, small traders and industrialists, and independent members of the liberal professions. As regards privatization, it favoured not sale to foreign buyers and compensation for former owners, but rather the return of assets to the pre-communist-era owners. It was the lack of such reprivatization that led to the departure of the Smallholders from the Antall government in 1992.

After the FKGP, led by József Torgyán, left the government, it formed a *right-wing opposition* to the centre-right government, and between 1994 and 1998 it continued to occupy a position on the right of the parliamentary opposition. Because of the party's populist understanding of democracy (seen, for example, in its support for allowing the recall of parliamentary deputies, for disbanding the Constitutional Court and for introducing direct presidential elections), its resulting conception of the constitution, and its leader's populist political style and anti-élite approach, much of the political and media élite viewed it as unfit for membership of a government coalition. The other right-wing parties that formed the opposition between 1994 and 1998 were greatly divided by their relationship with the Smallholders' Party. This weakness was connected to the fact that the FKGP was the only one of the parliamentary parties lacking any intelligentsia or media support. A further weak point for the party was that it lacked any significant international ties—it was excluded in the first half of the 1990s from the European Democratic Union, the grouping of European conservative Christian-democratic parties.

In the 1998 elections, the Smallholders' Party was unable to achieve the levels of support that it had reached in the opinion polls a year earlier, though it was able almost to double its representation in parliament in comparison with 1994 (see Appendix B). Despite having been shunned as populist by the parties of the more moderate right, the Smallholders did, as a result of parliamentary arithmetic, enter the Fidesz-led centre-right governmental coalition following the elections (see Appendix A). There is, however, little chance that the party would join any union of right-wing parties in the near future.

The Christian Democratic People's Party (KDNP)

The Christian Democratic People's Party was officially refounded in early 1989. Its immediate predecessors were the Áron Márton Society (a grouping of Catholic intellectuals) and the National Association of Large Families. The refounders of the party had been politicians in the Democratic People's Party that operated between 1945 and 1948. The KDNP emerged more as a Christian-social than a Christian-democratic party. It is the only one of the parliamentary parties that regards itself as attached to a *Weltanschauung*: it defined itself as an ideological party based upon Christian morality and existing above any particular denomination. On the basis of its history, the circumstances of its foundation and the denominational affiliation of its leading élite, however, it is better seen as a Catholic party, and this is borne out by the nature of its electoral base (Enyedi, 1997: 91, 126). The former Democratic People's Party and earlier Hungarian Christian parties were also Catholic: political activity based upon Christian foundations has taken place in Hungary within the framework of political Catholicism. The party became more or less tied to the Catholic Church, and has been strongly embedded in Catholic subculture (Enyedi, 1995, 1997: 131). Its leaders emerged from among Catholic political veterans and the Catholic intelligentsia, while the Calvinist intelligentsia élite was present in large numbers among the founders of the MDF.

In the 1990 elections, the party won just 7 per cent of the votes. With 21 seats, it became the smallest party in parliament (see Appendix B). The party congress that followed these elections resulted in the ousting of the 'historical' party leadership. A 'double' generation change took place: the party leadership was taken over by politicians in their forties, as exemplified by the election of László Surján to the party presidency. A determined process of party organization began, resulting in a sevenfold increase in the party membership and the development of party organizations nationwide. Even the party's own politicians acknowledged, however, that the party's policies were 'grey' and were adapted to fit the line taken by the Antall government. Clear, independent party policies were formed concerning support for the churches and religious education, as well as in regard to social questions.

Following the 1994 elections, which were again a failure for the KDNP, a leadership crisis developed within the party. The power struggle that emerged between the 'moderates' led by Surján and the 'radicals' led by György Giczy, who was elected party president in 1995, proved intractable. In party political terms, what was at stake was whether the party would become oriented more towards the populist, national-radical Smallholders (and the far-right MIÉP) or more towards the centre-right axis of Fidesz, the MDF and the MDNP. In mid–1997 this dispute caused the party to split in two, with the moderates leaving the party to form the Hungarian Christian Democratic Alliance (*Magyar Keresztény-demokrata Szövetség*, MKDSZ).

A number of these moderates ran in the parliamentary elections of 1998 under the Fidesz banner and were thereby able to enter both parliament and the government. The KDNP itself, however, fell far short of the 5 per cent of list votes necessary to gain parliamentary representation. The bulk of its previous supporters apparently moved towards other parties on the right.

The Hungarian Socialist Party (MSZP)

The Hungarian Socialist Party came into being at the time of the split in the Communist Party in October 1989. It was the party of the reformers and moderates within the old MSZMP. Though they took an entirely different view from the opposition as to how the democratic transition should proceed, these reformers played a major role in the success of that transition. A number of the party's leading politicians were highly popular, but this popularity could not be translated into votes for the party in the 1990 elections: it won 11 per cent of the votes and thirty-three seats in parliament. Between 1989 and 1992, the MSZP, as the successor party to the old régime, was pushed onto the defensive and confined to the margins of politics.

The shift from the MSZMP to the MSZP was not an immediate one. The membership of the old party was not transferred automatically to the new—rather, members had actively to re-enter the new party. While the MSZMP still had 700,000 members in 1989, one month after the formation of the MSZP, the party's membership numbered only 30,000. Despite the political renewal, the *political élite* of the MSZP—as seen in Chapter Five ('Political Elites')—was recruited from the functionaries of the old party, its youth organization and the trade unions, as well as from the local-council, administration and enterprise leaders of the communist era. Furthermore, that élite retained the character of its origins. Meanwhile, the party's electorate displayed the same pattern. Even in 1994, at the height of its success, the party gained a higher proportion of votes from top- and middle-ranking leaders than from any other occupational category.

The political and *ideological* orientation of the MSZP has, since the party congress of 1990, officially been left-wing and social-democratic. Alongside the acceptance of political democracy, it counted as one of its aims the creation of social democracy. The party requested admission to the Socialist International, the international organization of social-democratic parties, as early as 1989. In 1993 it gained observer status, and since 1996 it has been a fully fledged member, showing it to have become a party with international respectability. The ideological character of the MSZP, and later the basis for its popularity, have, however, been given primarily not by the 'social-democratic' orientation defined by the party congresses and party programmes, but by the legacy of *deideologization* that began during the 1980s. The slogans of pragmatism, expertise and modernization that the party employed from the end of the 1980s onwards proved more attractive in 1994 to those disappointed with the new political élite and the régime change than did the rhetoric of the new parties based upon the grand ideologies of liberalism, conservatism and Christian democracy. Ideology-free pragmatism led to the development of the *ideology of modernization* and technocratic expertise, which later served also as the ideology of the MSZP-SZDSZ coalition.

The party's return from the political margins began with the change that took place in 1991 in the politics of the SZDSZ. The MDF and the right wing as a whole replaced the MSZP as the principal opponent in the eyes of the SZDSZ leadership and in the political thinking of the opinion leaders of the intelligentsia. At the same time the MSZP, previously regarded as an outcast, came gradually to be seen as more acceptable. At this time the formerly left-wing intelligentsia leaders of the SZDSZ formed social-liberal and social-democratic platforms within their party. The party moved not only towards the Liberal International, but also, like the MSZP, in the direction of the Socialist International. The rapprochement between the two parties was also encouraged by the SZDSZ leaders' realization that the conservative coalition was further removed from them culturally, ideologically and in terms of social background than were the party-state functionaries. The rapprochement was prompted primarily by party-political factors, but it was eased also by the fact that the economic experts of both parties belonged to the same 'reform economist' subculture.

The elections of 1994 resulted in a fundamental shift in the political balance of forces in favour of the Socialists (see Appendix B). In consequence of disappointment with the régime change, the voters punished in particular the government parties, but also more generally the parties that had brought the transition, and they rewarded the Socialists, who now represented the security of the Kádárism of the 1970s and 1980s. Perhaps the most important factor explaining the MSZP's electoral victory was nostalgia for the relatively high levels of well-being, security and stability of the years prior to the régime change. This, in turn, was linked to the worsening economic situation following the transition and the deterioration in the position of the middle strata. Around one-quarter of the population lives in very difficult financial circumstances, and two-thirds of the population has been affected by the decline in real incomes. Only one-fifth of the population has seen a rise in real incomes. While the MSZP is the party of the so-called *nomenklatura* élite—it has the support of around half of those identifying themselves with the 'upper class' and of those in leading positions—a large number of the 1.5–2 million voters who were behind its landslide victory in 1994 came from those dissatisfied with the economic transition.

The popularity of the MSZP—unlike that of its smaller coalition partner—did not significantly decline during the years of government between 1994 and 1998: the party finished not far behind the victorious Fidesz in the elections of 1998 (see Appendix B). The MSZP has an 'above-class' character in regard to both ideology (or pragmatism) and electoral base. It is the most popular party among both high-status leaders and workers—among those placing themselves in the upper class and those seeing themselves as belonging to the working class. Its support is higher in these two groups than in the middle strata (Gazsó and Stumpf, 1997: 516). This paradoxical class basis has not, however, led to serious tensions within the party. Prime Minister Horn and his government did face some tensions during the period between 1994 and 1998 but were still able to achieve a workable balance between the demands of the market-oriented élite, the economic interests of the former *nomenklatura* and the need for political gestures towards the ordinary people.

Notes

1. The division of the Hungarian intelligentsia into *népi-nemzeti* and *urbánus* groups originates in the literary life of the first half of the twentieth century. This split gradually extended to the whole Hungarian intelligentsia, and it is still alive today. It can be explained by ideological, political, sociological and psychological factors. The relationship between the two groups is marked by deep mutual distrust and animosity. While '*népi-nemzeti*' has sometimes been translated as 'populist-nationalist', this is misleading, and the original term is retained here. The *népi-nemzeti* movement emphasizes the importance of the Hungarian nation, of tradition, of the land, and of the peasantry, which it sees as the embodiment of the nation. It sees *urbánus* (urban) liberalism as the intellectual

expression of the Budapest Jewish middle class and bourgeoisie. For many in the *népi-nemzeti* tradition, liberalism both presents a danger to traditional Hungarian values and promotes the power monopoly of alien social groups. The *népi-nemzeti* group advocates a 'third road' between East and West, and between capitalism and socialism. It is seen by *urbánus* intellectuals as provincial, nationalist and anti-Semitic, and sometimes as a (proto-)fascist grouping.

2. The politicians and intelligentsia supporters of the SZDSZ formed this anti-government left-wing political block, aiming at the creation of a 'popular front'. It was the opposite number to István Csurka's Hungarian Way movement, which saw the SZDSZ-MSZP grouping as its liberal-bolshevik opponent. The Democratic Charter paved the way for the rapprochement between the SZDSZ and the MSZP.

Chapter Three

The Party System

By the *party system* we mean the array of parties and the structure and dynamics of inter-party competition. This involves the system of interaction between the parties—how the individual parties are placed on the political spectrum, on what dimensions and in what ways inter-party competition takes place, what the role of ideology is, the extent to which particular parties are influenced by other parties, and how rival parties react to movements within the political spectrum. We deal here first with the left/right scale—which is the main dimension of competition in Hungary as elsewhere—second with the role of the political-cultural and economic dimensions, and finally with the main issues of political competition in Hungary.

1. Left and Right in Hungarian Politics

The competitive multi-party system that reappeared in Hungary with the elections of 1990 more or less fitted into the general European tradition of the left/right dichotomy. In consequence of the logic of political competition and party politics, and perhaps because of the decisive role of the ideology-oriented *intelligentsia* in the formation of the new parties, the political actors understand the great majority of political conflicts in ideological terms. Following the pluralization of political life in Hungary, the left/right scale became the most important referential framework and coding system of politics and inter-party competition.

The ideological character of Hungarian politics can be summarized in the following three points.

1. One unusual feature of the Hungarian political spectrum of the first half of the 1990s is that, unlike in most West European countries, right and left signify, in terms of content, primarily an *ideological-cultural* dimension, and only in second place an *economic-distributive* dimension. In Western Europe during the decades following the Second World War it was the economic left/right axis that became dominant. A further unusual feature is that in Hungary these two dimensions cut across each other. While the parties quickly established their positions in respect of the ideological-cultural dimension, the picture regarding the economic-distributive dimension has remained more hazy and confused.

2. The second feature of the emerging multi-party political spectrum in Hungary is linked to the first. It is the absence of *social democracy* in the West European sense, organized on the basis of economic class conflict. One reason for this is that the political significance of economic questions was, until the mid–1990s, and particularly just before the 1990 elections, very low: these questions did not divide the parties. Consequently, the *economic* left/right divide did not develop. The political spectrum did not become divided between a left wing representing workers and trade unions and a right wing representing owners and the middle class. There were no fundamental differences among the economic policy programmes of the major parties at the time of the 1990 elections—they all gave priority to privatization, deregulation and liberalization. That is, they all adopted right-wing economic programmes. When conflicts of economic policy did emerge in the course of the first parliament, they concerned not the alternatives of increasing or reducing the level of state intervention, but rather such issues as the methods and speed of privatization. The parties became sharply divided over economic and social policy for the first time with the unveiling of the 'Bokros' package of economic austerity measures in 1995. The package, which was aimed at improving the government's finances and which cut back the system of social redistribution, was unanimously criticized by the opposition from the standpoint of (in economic terms) the left. Yet this did not produce any fundamental change in the left/right placements of the parties on the ideological-cultural dimension (either in the parties' own self-definitions, or in the perceptions of the voters, or in the evaluations of experts).

3. The third important characteristic of the Hungarian political spectrum is that, while the *economic* left/right division has emerged only

slowly, in terms of the *political-ideological* plain the distinction between left and right is very marked. The most important test for the relevance of the left/right axis is the extent to which it serves as a reference point for the leading actors of politics—politicians and political parties—in the competition for political power. In Hungarian politics, it clearly does act as such a reference point. The left/right dimension has become the basis for coalition and government formation (see Appendix A). In 1990, a centre-right coalition combining the MDF, the FKGP and the KDNP was formed, while a left-liberal (SZDSZ and Fidesz) and socialist (MSZP) opposition emerged. In 1994 a centre-left (MSZP-SZDSZ) government coalition and a right-wing opposition appeared. In 1998, a government of the centre-right was formed by Fidesz, the FKGP and the MDF, with opposition from the left (in the form of the SZDSZ and the MSZP) and the far right (MIÉP).

2. The Structure of the Party Spectrum: The Political-Cultural and Economic Axes

While the relations of the parties to each other can be simplified to a single left/right scale—and while this scale did accurately characterize Hungarian politics in the electoral contest of 1990—these relations are better analysed in twentieth-century European politics in two-dimensional political space. In this, the two meanings of left and right—the ideological-cultural and the economic—are separated from each other. The ideological-cultural axis is characterized by the dichotomy between '*progressive*' and '*traditionalist*', or, in other words, between '*liberal*' and '*authoritarian*'. The economic axis, meanwhile, is formed by the dichotomy between *egalitarian income-redistributive* and *anti-state-intervention, market-based* positions. Historically, the second dimension appeared alongside the traditional liberal/conservative opposition when the goal of greater equality and state income redistribution emerged, represented by social democracy and Christian socialism. Economic and redistributive questions gradually gained in importance and have been dominant in European party politics since the Second World War. By contrast, as we have seen, in Hungary, as generally in the new democracies of Eastern Europe, the ideological-cultural dimension became dominant in the first half-decade following the régime change. The role of the economic-social dimension on the economic agenda and in inter-party competition has grown since the mid–1990s—in Hungary, since the announcement of the Bokros package in 1995.

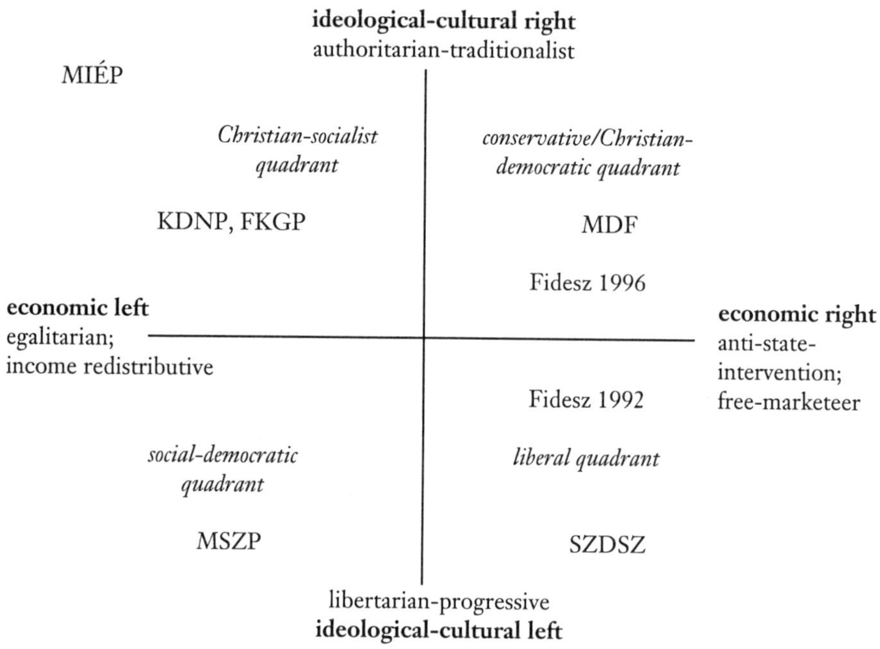

Figure 1 The Hungarian parties in two-dimensional political space

The points that have been raised are illustrated in Figure 1, showing the positions of the parties in Hungary within a political space divided by the two dimensions that have been discussed (Bozóki, 1996; Körösényi, 1993a; 1993b). The lower left quadrant, representing the progressive side of the ideological-cultural dimension and the economic left, is filled in European politics by *social democracy*, and it is here that the MSZP is to be found. In the bottom right is the *liberal* quadrant, combining the ideologically 'progressive' and economically right-wing positions. Among the Hungarian parties, the SZDSZ belongs here, as did Fidesz before 1994 (though it was always further from the progressive pole than the

SZDSZ). From 1994, Fidesz moved decisively in the direction of the traditionalist pole. The upper left quadrant combines traditionalism on the ideological-cultural dimension and the moderate left on the economic dimension. It is the quadrant of *Christian socialism*, represented in Hungary by the KDNP and the FKGP (and by MIÉP, which may be placed beyond the Smallholders and Christian Democrats, in the far top left corner). Finally, the upper right is the culturally traditionalist, economically right-wing *conservative (Christian-democratic)* quadrant. The MDF is found here, as is the MDNP (which left the MDF in 1996) and, since 1994, Fidesz.

In summary, while in Western Europe for close to a century the political-cultural left has been tied to the economic left and the political right to the economic right, in Eastern Europe—including Hungary—since the collapse of communism, these two dimensions have cut across each other. There is no consistency between the political and the economic left, or between the political and the economic right. The economic right can be connected to the cultural right or the cultural left, as the examples of Fidesz and the SZDSZ show. Similarly, the economic left may be linked to the cultural right as well as the cultural left, as shown by the examples of the 'Christian-socialist' KDNP and the agrarian- and social-protectionist FKGP and MIÉP. Despite this, the SZDSZ is not a right-wing party and the FKGP, KDNP and MIÉP are not left-wing parties. This shows the association of the concepts of right and left in Hungary with the progressive/traditionalist dichotomy. In comparison with this, the economic dimension is of only secondary importance.

3. The Ideological and Political Agenda

The ideological character of the party élites, like their socio-cultural character, has an effect independent of party strategies in orienting the voters. The ideological character of the parties assists the voters in their orientation among the parties and the establishment of their political identity. Alongside this, a part is also played by consciously employed party strategies in delivering the ideological message of the parties to the voters. A third factor in the formation of the political spectrum and, through this, of political dividing lines, is that of the political agenda—the issues that are prominent in political debate and conflict.

Hungarian analyses of the *ideological* character of the Hungarian parties unanimously conclude that those parties have from the time of their foundation possessed clear ideological images. The analyses also conclude that in comparison with contemporary West European politics the political battles of the first parliament (though to a lesser degree the second parliament) were concerned with ideological questions to an unusual degree (Ágh, 1993; Fricz, 1991; Körösényi, 1993, 1993c; Schöpflin, 1990). From our current point of view, this means also that ideology and the political agenda have played a significant role in Hungary in the creation of political camps and the articulation of political cleavages, and that they have contributed to the politicization of these lines of conflict. It has also been a matter of consensus in the literature on the Hungarian party system of the early 1990s that the Hungarian party spectrum can be depicted by the 'triangle' of the socialist (MSZP), the liberal (SZDSZ, Fidesz) and the Christian-national or conservative (MDF, KDNP, FKGP) parties (Figure 2). This ideological triangle has become the framework for the analysis not only of party programmes and the relationships between the parties, but also of political attitudes and of the ideological self-placements of the political élite and the voters (Angelusz and Tardos, 1994; Kovács and Tóth, 1992; Katalin Lázár, 1996; Tóth, 1992; Lázár and Marián, 1996).

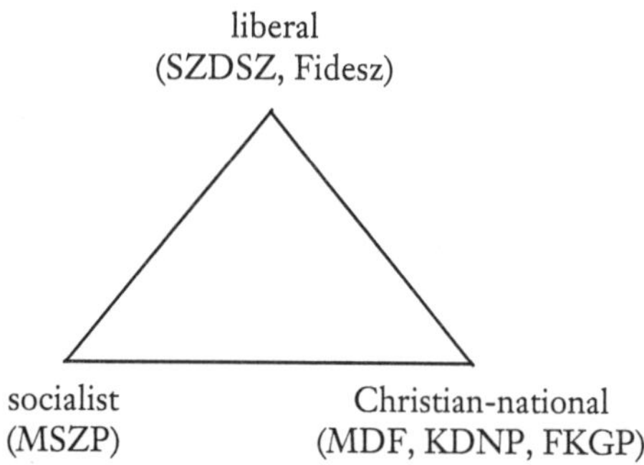

Figure 2 The ideological triangle of the Hungarian party system

In consequence of the usage of the left/right conceptual pair as a coding system, the liberals come to be placed between the left-wing socialists and the right-wing Christian-democratic, conservative and national parties, in the 'centre' of the political space.

What questions and *themes* stood at the heart of political debate during the first period of the development of parliamentary democracy in Hungary? During the period beginning with the democratic transition, the *agenda* of party-political conflict and of legislation in large part concerned the social groups defined by the three central cleavages of Hungarian politics (see the following chapter, 'Political Cleavages', for details). Issues affecting the communist *nomenklatura* based upon the *communist/anti-communist* cleavage concerned, for example, the question of the assets of the political and mass organizations of the former system, lustration,[1] the question of justice for crimes committed under the communist system, and the prohibition of the symbols of communism (such as the hammer and sickle). The *religious/secular* cleavage was strengthened by conflicts over the compensation of the churches for losses incurred during the communist era, religious education, abortion and the financing of church schools, as well as other matters in the relationship between church and state. The *rural/urban* cleavage appeared primarily in the debates over the land question—the issue of whether agricultural land should be returned to the original owners or whether those owners should be given only compensation.

These questions gave occasion for the creation of political 'camps' and the strengthening of group and political identities. Besides the ideological conflicts, a large part was played in the political agenda by the opposition of the élites and parties of the liberal (SZDSZ and Fidesz) and, in part, socialist (MSZP) camp versus the Christian-national camp (MDF, KDNP, FKGP). The parties were divided in this way by questions of symbolism and history, such as the issue of national symbols (the national coat of arms and national celebrations) and by evaluations of political and historical traditions—for example, the debates over the reburials of the figures of the 1956 revolution and of the inter-war leader Admiral Horthy. But they were divided in the same way by interpretations of constitutional principles (for example, the separation of powers) and the operation of the institutions of the governmental system (such as the role of the president of the republic and the independence of the public-service media). Table 1 gives a summary of the positions taken by the left- and right-wing parties on the various political issues.

Table 1. The relationship between left and right on key political issues

Issues	Cultural-ideological left	Cultural-ideological right
Attitudes to the communist system		
Compensation	no, or divided	yes
Trials of communist leaders	no	yes
Removal of former communist personnel	no	yes, or divided
Historical traditions		
Historical focus	revolutions (breaks with past)	1000-year statehood (continuity)
Coat-of-arms debate	favoured Kossuth arms	favoured crown arms
National celebrations	focus on 15th March (1848 revolution)	focus on 20th August (founding of kingdom)
National question	'weak'	'strong'
Hungarian minorities in neighbouring countries	question of human rights	national question (collective rights)
Church-state relations	anti-clerical	clerical
Optional religious teaching in schools	no	yes
Attitude to church schools	negative	positive
Moral questions		
Abortion	yes	no, or limited
Death penalty	no	yes/no (divided)
Human rights v. state authority		
Police powers	when in opposition: restrict when in power: extend	extend
Behaviour of state towards deviant groups	'softer', more permissive	'harder'
Defence policy	in favour of NATO membership*	in favour of NATO membership*
Economic policy		
Social policy	limit welfare state	maintain welfare state
Agricultural land and strategic sectors	can sell to foreigners	should stay Hungarian-owned

* The views of the Workers' Party and MIÉP—that is, the far left and far right—'meet' on this issue: both oppose NATO membership.

Note

1. That is, the issue of whether appointees for certain posts should be screened for past involvement in the communist secret service.

Chapter Four

Political Cleavages

At the end of the 1980s and the beginning of the 1990s, after four decades of political dictatorship and homogenizing social policies, many believed that Hungarian society was politically *diffuse* and *undifferentiated* and that the great majority of the voters who had suddenly obtained the right of electoral choice possessed no kind of political identity.[1] In fact, however, politics in Hungary since the democratic transition has been marked by deep political cleavages—cleavages that cut through both the political élite and the wider electorate.

In this chapter and the two that follow it, we examine those cleavages and the effects they have within the political system. Here we outline the cleavages that have emerged, as well as assessing how they came about—how they regenerated after four decades of social and political homogenization. In the two chapters that follow, we consider in greater detail, first, the political élite and, second, the electorate. Among other points, we analyse how the parties differ from each other in terms of the sociological and ideological profiles of their élites and their wider support bases. The three chapters as a whole will show that important cleavages exist in Hungarian politics and that those cleavages are central in the structuring of the political landscape.

1. Cleavages

In most West European countries, the two most important political cleavages are those expressed at the organizational level by church attendance and by membership of a trade union. Germany provides a good example: the great majority of church-goers belong to the Christian-democratic/Christian-social political camp, while most union members belong to the social-democratic camp. This organizational tie is associated with membership of political camps more closely than is occupation or social status.

The political divisions that are in the process of regeneration in Hungary fit into the wider European traditions only partially. The most important difference is to be found in the fundamentally different character of the class division. As a consequence of the economic and social programme of the communist system, a *political* class division emerged in place of the economic one. This has become a factor structuring the emerging multi-party system. Three cleavages can be identified in Hungarian politics—two stronger and one weaker. These appear at the levels of both élites and voters, at the organizational level and in the sphere of political culture and ideology. The two stronger cleavages centre upon religion and the *nomenklatura* (the political class of the communist system), while the third is tied to the traditional urban/rural (industrial/agricultural) dichotomy.

The rapid regeneration of political differentiation is due in part to the fact that the political homogenization of society pursued during the communist years was successful only in part and on the surface. Though the earlier cleavages lacked institutional, organizational or political articulation, they survived the long decades of communism in attitudes and value systems and among subcultures, and they changed only slowly. When the channels of political articulation opened, significant groups were mobilized along the lines of the old cleavages. An additional factor influencing the development of political differentiation was the role of political actors. There is no pre-existing political differentiation *per se* in society. The statistical or sociological stratification of society (into demographic groups and strata) does not imply the presence of any pre-existing *a priori* differentiation of political relevance; this emerges only through the activities of political actors (Sartori, 1969). Some of the main socio-cultural group divisions and group conflicts within society are 'selected' through the ideologies of political élites and the mass-mobilizational and organizational activities of parties, and they thus become organized and institutionalized into lasting cleavages that structure political life. This occurred in Europe around the turn of the century, and it has been the role also of parties in Hungary and generally in East-Central Europe since the democratic transition. The *parties and political élite* play a decisive role in cleavage-based political mobilization. It depends upon their activities which of the many group conflicts within society become politicized and deepen into political cleavages. The role of the élite in post-communist Hungary has perhaps been still greater than that in Western Europe at the turn of the century, since, through the formation of parties, the pluralization of politics and the political differentiation of the élite occurred much more quickly than could be articulated at the societal level by interest groups or institutionalized on the organizational level on a mass scale.

We will see in the following chapter ('Political Elites') that there are significant socio-cultural differences among the party élites (the parliamentary party groups). The three cleavages that have been described divide the parliamentary party élites into three groups (Table 1). The MSZP deputies were recruited from the *nomenklatura* élite of the communist system; those of the MDF, KDNP and FKGP from the Christian middle class; and those of the SZDSZ and Fidesz for the most part from less religious, 'bourgeois intelligentsia' strata.[2] The Smallholder deputies are differentiated from those of the MDF and the KDNP by their lower social status and their primarily rural, agrarian origins.

Table 1. The socio-cultural characteristics of the parliamentary party élites

	MDF	KDNP	FKGP	SZDSZ	Fidesz	MSZP
nomenklatura	–	–	–	–	–	+
religion	(+)	+	+	(–)	–	–
rural		–	+	–	–	
education	+	+	–	+	+	+
age		+	+	–	–	

Note: The table is based upon the data presented in the chapter on political élites (Chapter Five). The '+' sign indicates a positive correlation and the '–' sign a negative correlation between the character of the parliamentary party group and the given socio-cultural factor.

2. *The Three Cleavages of Hungarian Politics*

The Religious/Secular Cleavage

As in Europe's other Catholic countries and countries of mixed religion, the *religious/secular* divide has become an important cleavage in Hungarian politics. Christian morals and policies have been represented at the level of the political élite by the conservative parties, particularly the KDNP, whose élite has a strongly Catholic background. Religion appears at the societal and sociological level too, as a world-view if not a direct political ideology: it is one of the most important factors influencing voting behaviour. The religious, particularly regular church-goers, have become voters above all for the KDNP, the FKGP and the MDF. The historical churches provide an organizational and institutional background to this: their organizational continuity was not broken even during the communist period. The clerical/anti-clerical conflict became one of the most important dimensions of party and cultural battle during the 1990s. The anti-clerical side was formed during the early 1990s by the left-wing and liberal parties (the MSZP, the SZDSZ and Fidesz), which possessed non-religious ideology, party élites and voter bases. By the mid–1990s Fidesz, in line with its turn to the right, had begun to move gradually to the clerical side, though this change was felt only partially in the religiosity and church attendance of its potential voter base.

The empirically measurable indicator of the religious/secular cleavage at the level of individual preferences—religiosity and church attendance—divides the voters (as it does the party élites) into three major groups. The more religious (frequent church-goers) show significantly stronger preferences for the centre-right parties. The more the strength of religiosity (the frequency of church attendance) falls, the greater becomes support for the liberal and socialist parties. According to a late 1992 survey using a subjective self-placement scale of religiosity, liberal-party (SZDSZ or Fidesz) sympathizers were twice as common among the non-religious as among the most strongly religious, while socialist (MSZP) sympathizers were three times as common. By contrast, MDF sympathizers were four times more common in the latter than the former category, FKGP sympathizers five times more common, and KDNP sympathizers nine times more common (Gazsó and Gazsó, 1993: 123). A late 1997 survey found that the sympathy index of the KDNP was sixteen percentage points higher among regular church-goers than among non-church-goers. The index was twelve percentage points higher among church-goers in the case of the MDF, nine points higher for the FKGP, eight points higher for the MDNP and four points higher for both Fidesz and MIÉP. It was two percentage points lower in the case of the SZDSZ. Another survey, from autumn 1991, found that around three-quarters of regular church-goers voted for the KDNP-FKGP-MDF 'block' and one quarter voted for the SZDSZ or Fidesz, while virtually none voted for the MSZP (Table 2). This well illustrates the fact that the voters, like the party élites, can be split into three groups on the basis of level of religiosity. In consequence of Fidesz's gradual shift to the right during the second half of the 1990s, its voter base has slowly altered, and the proportion of church-goers within it has grown.

Table 2. The distribution of party preferences according to frequency of church attendance, October 1991 (percentages)

Frequency of church attendance	FKGP-KDNP-MDF	Fidesz-SZDSZ	MSZP
At least once a month	73	26	1
A few times a year	42	49	9
More rarely or never	28	63	10

Source: Tóka, 1992a: 152.

The Political Class Cleavage

Alongside religion, the *class divide* has become the most important cleavage in European politics. In Hungary, the roots of the cleavage based upon the classical worker/capitalist dichotomy and the division between the working class and the middle class disappeared (just as did the social role of the property-owning bourgeoisie and the middle class) when, at the end of the 1940s, the communist régime abolished private property and capitalism. Economic class division was replaced in the communist system by a social structure built upon political and administrative position. The most important institutional instrument of the rule of the *nomenklatura class* (composed of party functionaries and the members of the *nomenklatura*) was the Communist Party, which embraced between a fifth and a sixth of the society and which comprised, besides the *nomenklatura*, a wide circle of communist supporters and beneficiaries (Gazsó, 1990; Szakadát, 1992: 113). The party-state had a closed ideology and was built upon sociologically circumscribable groups (just as its perceived opposition was formed from well-defined groups). It placed its political class and its supporters into a unitary organizational system, into the party and into the party's satellite organizations (such as the trade unions, the Popular Front and the workers' guard).

It is no coincidence that the second major cleavage of Hungarian politics since the transition has been that based around integration into, or separation from and oppression by, the communist/socialist state-party system. This has remained a part of the new ideological universe, of electoral and parliamentary party politics and of political discourse. The successor to the Communist Party, the MSZP, is a 'cadre' party—it remains the party of the *political class* of the former system. Its political élite is recruited from the former *nomenklatura*, and the core of its voter base is formed in large part by former party members. Its ideology is still modernizing in character, but in place of the classical ideas of socialism, it combines left-wing redistributive populism with a technocratic system of argumentation. On the other side of the communist/anti-communist dichotomy created by the rule of the *nomenklatura* are the pre-communist élites and middle class, the politically unintegrated middle class of the communist era and some new élite groups that have appeared since the régime change.

The classical worker/capital class division does not exist in post-communist Hungary at the level of voters: the *class voting index* is very low (Bruszt and Simon, 1994a: 75; Gazsó and Gazsó, 1993: 123–125). However, the *political class division* created by the communist system strongly divides not only the political élite but also society. This cleavage is tied to political integration or non-integration into the communist system, the most important organizational indicator of which is former Communist Party (MSZMP) membership. Analyses of voters' party preferences show this indicator of integration to be closely tied to support for the MSZP—the successor party of the communists—after 1989 (Angelusz and Tardos, 1991, 1995; Bruszt and Simon, 1994a; Tóka, 1996). Support for the MSZP has been consistently and significantly higher (by 13 to 28 percentage points) among former MSZMP party members than among voters in general since 1990 (Table 3).

Approaching the same point from the other side—from the voter bases of the individual parties—it can be seen that the proportion of former party members is much higher among MSZP voters than among voters as a whole (Table 3) and several times the level found in the other parliamentary parties. In early 1997, for example, former MSZMP members comprised around 40 per cent of potential MSZP voters, while the same proportion stood at just 3 per cent in the case of the MDF, 4 per cent for Fidesz, 6 per cent for the SZDSZ and the FKGP and 13 per cent for the KDNP (*HVG*, 8th March 1997: 113).

Table 3. The link between former MSZMP party membership and support for the MSZP (percentages)

	May '90	Oct. '91	Sep. '92	Jan. '93	Dec. '93	Apr. '94
MSZP supporters: proportion among all voters	8	8	14	14	34	35
MSZP supporters: proportion among former party members	21	30	34	40	62	57
Former party members: proportion among all voters	18	15	16	13	18	17
Former party members: proportion among MSZP voters	50	55	39	36	33	28

Sources: Tóka, 1996: Table 3; for 1990 figures, TÁRKI-CENTER.

Analysis of the votes cast in the first round of the 1994 elections has shown also that the likelihood of voting for the MSZP increases as the degree of family integration into the communist system increases. In families where neither spouse had been a party member, 26 per cent of voters voted for the MSZP. By contrast, 49 per cent of those whose spouse had been a party member and 54 per cent of those who had themselves been members voted for the MSZP. Finally, in those cases where both partners had been members, 73 per cent voted for the Socialists (Angelusz and Tardos, 1995).

The Urban/Rural Cleavage

The third cleavage of Hungarian politics—and one again characteristic of many European countries, particularly during the first half of the century—is the *urban/rural* or industrial/agrarian conflict. This is represented by the FKGP, which, as in other European cases, is more a 'sectoral' party than a party with any coherent ideology: it is the party primarily of land-owning farmers and of the strata of the former rural middle class that saw their social status fall during the communist period. Besides the FKGP, these strata are represented at the interest-organization level by such groups as the Peasants' Alliance and '*Hangya*'.[3] The Smallholders' Party is characterized ideologically by agrarian populism, national radicalism and anti-communism. At the level of voters, the urban/rural, industrial/agrarian cleavage sharply distinguishes the FKGP, and to a lesser extent the KDNP, from the other parties. The old, rural-dwellers and the less educated are strongly over-represented among voters for the Smallholders' Party and the KDNP (Angelusz and Tardos, 1991; Závecz, 1995), as are agricultural workers and farmers. More than half of the FKGP's voters are rural-dwellers, and this proportion approaches 50 per cent in the case of the KDNP. For the other parties, by contrast, it lies between 24 and 40 per cent (see Table 2 in Chapter Six, on electoral behaviour). In all three parliamentary elections to date, the FKGP has obtained most of the votes in the agricultural south and east of the country, particularly in the Protestant east. In 1998, as well as in 1990, the party won 10 percentage points more votes in these regions than in Budapest, and in 1994 it won 5 percentage points more (Körösényi, 1991; Bíró, 1994; *Magyar Hírlap*, 11th May 1998: 6). The voter base of the FKGP is thus strongly defined by social position, place of residence and region.

The Absent Cleavage: The Economic Class Division

We have seen that social stratification is only a secondary factor explaining political preferences in Hungary and that the classical *economic class division* is absent from among the political cleavages.[4] Both blue- and white-collar workers are divided into blocks of integration into the former communist system (MSZP), religion (KDNP, FKGP and MDF) and 'negative' embeddedness (SZDSZ and Fidesz). Each of these blocks has an 'above class' character. Clear divisions according to social status have appeared only within the right wing:[5] whether we look at education, occupation, income or subjective self-placement of class position, MDF voters are of higher social status than those of the FKGP or KDNP. In 1990 and 1994, the KDNP and particularly the FKGP were more strongly blue-collar parties than the MSZP, while Fidesz, the SZDSZ and the MDF had equal support among blue- and white-collar workers (Gazsó and Stumpf, 1995: 9–11; and Table 4 in Chapter Six, on electoral behaviour). The FKGP and the KDNP could, however, hardly be thought of as workers' parties, and the remaining parties can be described unambiguously as 'above class' parties. Nevertheless, in terms of their voter bases, the MDF and the SZDSZ—and to a lesser extent Fidesz—have a middle-class and upper-middle-class character, while the MSZP was characterized in 1990 by the dominance of the *nomenklatura* class and in 1994 by a combination of the *nomenklatura* and the working class. The role of the working class is stronger and that of the upper and upper-middle classes weaker in the MSZP if we look at class self-placements than it is if we consider occupational and educational data. This points in part to the fact that the MSZP has been successful in retaining the ideologically 'trained' and organized worker base of the Communist Party. In part, the examination of the middle and upper strata shows also that, in terms of socio-cultural roots, there are three middle classes within Hungarian society: the Christian-bourgeois middle class, the secularized bourgeois middle class and the *nomenklatura* middle class that rose during the years of communism (Table 4).

Table 4. Cleavages and the classical class division

	Nomenklatura	Liberal	Religious	
				rural/agrarian
Middle class	MSZP	SZDSZ Fidesz	MDF	
Lower status	MSZP	SZDSZ Fidesz	MDF	FKGP KDNP

3. Cleavages and the Party System

The development of the party system is tied to the macrosocial and socio-cultural divisions within society, and in particular to those divisions that are, in the course of *political mobilization*, deepened by political actors into political cleavages. The political divisions are thus not sociologically determined. The structure of the party system depends upon what strategies of mobilization are employed by the political actors dominant at the time the competitive party system is formed and upon which existing but unarticulated socio-cultural fissures are deepened through the instruments of political mobilization into cleavages. We have seen how the Hungarian political élite, itself strongly divided by three cleavages, has deepened the existing socio-cultural divisions of society into political cleavages through the instruments of parties, policy, ideology and organizational development. It has been possible by means of these cleavages to mobilize politically the major groups of society.

The model that we present below shows how the political cleavages that have developed structure the party system. The religious/secular and political class cleavages have led to the creation of three positions (Figure 1). These positions are the following: those who were politically integrated into the communist system (those who were MSZMP members) are the voters of the MSZP (position 1); the religious are the voters of the centre-right, comprising the MDF, the KDNP and the FKGP (position 2), within which the rural/agrarian groups support primarily the FKGP; finally, the non-integrated form position 3.

To this third position belong those who are integrated into neither the church, nor the political class of the former communist system, nor the agrarian sphere. This is a huge group, comprising at least one-half of Hungarian society. The majority of the members of this group are not clearly positioned in terms of the political cleavages, and from among them come the *floating voters* who lack any lasting party preference. But it is from here that the liberal parties (the SZDSZ and Fidesz) also win their supporters. We cannot come closer to a definition of the core electorate of the liberal parties using the cleavage approach.

The ideologies and world-views of the parties correspond to the socio-cultural character of their electorates. The MSZP, which represents the political class of the communist system, has a left-wing, modernizing, technocratic ideology. The ideology of the three centre-right parties that represent the religious is Christian-national in character. Finally, the SZDSZ and Fidesz, built upon those not integrated into the large systems of collective socialization, have an ideology that is individualist and liberal.

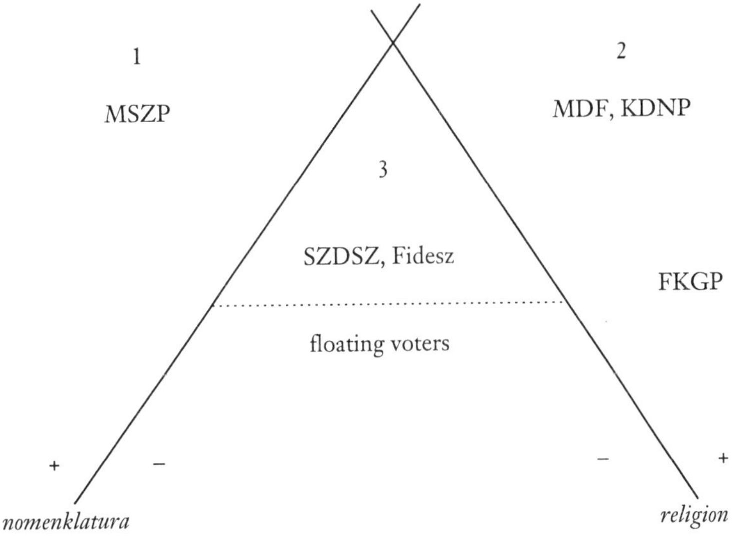

Figure 1 Cleavages and the party system

The positions within the party structure defined by the cleavage approach offer two mutually compatible means of interpreting the socio-cultural embeddedness of the SZDSZ and Fidesz electorates. 1. If we assume that the political identity of the group of voters placed in position 3 in Figure 1 can be defined only negatively, by the absence of embeddedness (those voters are non-religious, not integrated into the communist system and non-rural), the conclusion follows that the structural situation makes the SZDSZ and Fidesz the most market-oriented parties. This interpretation is strengthened by the example of Fidesz. In terms of social embeddedness, Fidesz is the least integrated of the parliamentary parties. 2. If, however, we invert this negative definition of the socio-cultural embeddedness of the liberal parties, we see that the social segment that is non-religious, not integrated into the communist system and non-rural, is at the same time the social segment into which the secularized, urban, civic-intelligentsia middle strata can be placed. In Europe, it is precisely from this group that the electorates of the liberal parties have emerged. It would appear that the same trend has operated in Hungary since 1989. This interpretation is strengthened by surveys showing the SZDSZ electorate to be highly qualified and to have considerable cultural and economic power (Angelusz and Tardos, 1991: 648–649). Surveys conducted at the time of both the 1990 and the 1994 elections showed the SZDSZ to have higher support than other parties among those with university education, those engaged in intellectual work and those with higher incomes (Angelusz and Tardos, 1990; Körösényi, 1990: 50–51; Gazsó and Stumpf, 1995). On the basis of this we can postulate that the electorate of the liberal parties—or at least the stable electorate of the SZDSZ—has come since 1990 from the secularized, urban, civic-intelligentsia middle strata.

We saw earlier that the parties have employed primarily market-based rather than organizational strategies of political mobilization. We saw also that, as a consequence of this, no *mass party* has developed in Hungary and the social embeddedness of the parties—at least at the organizational, institutional level—has been relatively weak (see Chapter Two, which deals with the parties). In this chapter, by contrast, we have seen that, on the ideological and socio-cultural level, political cleavages structuring the party system have indeed clearly emerged.

Notes

1. In parliamentary elections during the one-party era, citizens had right only to *vote*, not to make a *choice* between political parties.

2. The concept of the 'bourgeois intelligentsia' may be better expressed using the German term '*Bildungsbürgertum*'. This is a property-owning class, but it must be differentiated from both the 'Christian middle-class' and the communist cadres.

3. *Hangya* is a rural trading co-operative.

4. A differing investigation of the link between subjective class identification and party choice is given by Péter Róbert (1994).

5. On the left, the tiny, extra-parliamentary *Munkáspárt* (Workers' Party)—the party of the unreformed communists—has a blue-collar profile.

6. In contrast to what is done here, the long-term continuity of the party-political camps is examined on national and regional ('macrosocial') levels in Körösényi (1991), using the analysis of the geographical division of political preferences. On the 'microsocial' level it is considered by Wiener (1997) using the analysis of the political composition of electoral districts and wards in Budapest.

Chapter Five

Political Elites

Classical élite theories emphasize the point that the distribution of power and influence in every society is unequal. In every political community and political system, there are people and groups that possess greater political power and influence than the others. They form the *political élite*. The individuals and groups forming the political élite either possess direct political power through holding *positions* of public power, or they possess *influence* over political decisions through their influence over those who make those decisions.

Who belongs to the political élite? The political élite is composed of the members of the political leadership and of members of other spheres—such as the public administration, interest groups, large enterprises and opinion leaders—who have an influence over political decisions.

The political élite is not identical with (though it does overlap with) the circle of professional politicians. The professional politicians form the *political class* (von Beyme, 1993). One part of the political class—the party leaders, ministers, leaders of parliamentary groups and committees, and the direct advisors of these—does belong to the political élite. But a second and perhaps larger group of professional politicians—including back-bench members of parliament, party functionaries and party employees—has a genuine influence over political decisions that remains far behind not only the power of the political leaders, but also the influence of the leaders of business, the interest groups and the churches, and of opinion leaders. While the latter belong to the political élite, the back-bench professional politicians do not.[1]

A characteristic of individual political systems is who belongs to the political class and the political élite. Radical change in the political system—whether caused by revolution or defeat in war, or by institutional reforms—generally entails the failure of the political élite and therefore involves complete or partial *élite change*. Changes in the economy or in the structure of society, by contrast, affect the composition of the political élite and political class only over the longer term, and after a certain delay.

In what follows, we begin by taking a historical look at the political élite in Hungary, focusing upon the '*nomenklatura*' élite of the communist era and the ability of that élite to sustain its position after the transition. We then try to answer the question of who makes up the Hungarian political élite of the 1990s—of the character of élite recruitment, the career paths leading into the political élite, and the nature of the divisions within the élite. This we do in three sections. First we consider how the political élite is divided into groups by its political origins. Then we assess the changes that have taken place in the sociological and cultural composition of the political ruling stratum—the parliamentary deputies—during and since the régime change, and the character of the world-views, ideologies and typical career paths of those deputies. Finally, we turn to the wider political élite by considering the political role of the various institutional and social élite groups.

1. *Nomenklatura* and Transition

The history of the political élite in Hungary between the Austro-Hungarian Compromise of 1867 and the régime change of 1989–90 can be divided into two parts. The political changes between 1944 and 1948 separated these two longer periods. During the first, the political élite was recruited above all from the historical ruling classes, while during the second it was recruited from the members of the communist *nomenklatura*. Before 1944—though political crises, the extension of the franchise and other factors did influence the personnel of the political ruling class, and though personal and political realignments did occur—the recruitment base of the political class did not change fundamentally. Between 1944 and 1949, however, the defeat in war and the three political régimes that followed each other in quick succession resulted in radical élite change. Not only the personal, but also the social composition of the political ruling class changed totally, as did the mechanism of recruitment to it. The administrative élite was also replaced, while certain social élites disappeared totally. Between 1945 and 1948 a new political élite replaced the old. It was recruited from a wider social base, and it was socially more open and pluralist, but it disappeared very quickly. Under the emerging one-party communist dictatorship, élite recruitment came to be strictly controlled and supervised. Highly centralized control over the recruitment of political and other leaders became one of the most important elements of the communist power monopoly.

Ideological commitment to the party-state and political loyalty to the system and the leadership were expressed by membership of the Communist Party. This was an indispensable element, a precondition, for a political (or leadership) career. Because the Communist Party placed other spheres—administration, education, economy, culture and so on—under political supervision, the entire social and political élite came under the control of the top of the political ruling class: the Communist Party leadership. Societal élites independent from politics—that could have influenced the political ruling class 'from outside'—disappeared. A more or less united power élite (*nomenklatura*) came into being. The *nomenklatura* system became the most important institution of control over recruitment to leading positions. The most important stages in a political career were the following: service in the communist youth movement or in other mass organizations, such as the trade unions; membership of the Communist Party; and service in a series of party and state positions. These mechanisms were loosened somewhat only in the 1980s, towards the end of the communist era.

The concept of the *nomenklatura* has two principal meanings. 1. The *nomenklatura* system signifies above all the list of power positions and the system of appointments to those positions through the leading party organs. There were several thousand such positions on the Political Committee (Politburo) and Central Committee of the Communist Party, while at the local and intermediate levels during the 1960s and 1970s a total of 300,000 to 400,000 party positions existed. This is the number of positions over which political control was exercised (Szakadát, 1992). The *nomenklatura* system thus signifies the institutionalized and politically directed and/or controlled mechanism for recruitment to leading positions in politics, the economy, culture and elsewhere. 2. In a second sense, the *nomenklatura* is a *societal* formation, coming into existence through the operation for decades of the recruitment mechanism that has just been described. That is, in a sociological sense, it signifies the leading social stratum or class (Szalai, 1994; Szelényi, 1995; Szelényi, Ezal and Townsley, 1996). In what follows, we use the concept in the second sense. We thus see the *nomenklatura* as a societal formation, indicating the political and social ruling class of the communist system.[2]

The *nomenklatura* is a politically created societal formation—unlike the capitalist class division, in the communist system the source of social rule is political in character. In the communist system, the economic class division was replaced by a social structure based upon political and administrative positions. In place of the economic class division, *nomenklatura* rule thus created a *political class division*. The most important institutional instrument of the rule of the politically based *nomenklatura* was the Communist Party, which, besides the occupants of *nomenklatura* positions, included a broad circle of supporters and beneficiaries—between one-sixth and one-fifth of the society, once their families were included. Membership of the Communist Party was an expression of ideological commitment to the party-state and of political loyalty to the system and the leadership. It was thus an indispensable precondition for any kind of political or leadership career. Nevertheless, the ruling structure of the Communist Party cannot be characterized simply by the dichotomy of 'up' and 'down'. The privileged political class and broader social clientele of the communist system—from the top political leadership to the workplace party officers—also created a *vertical* division through society. The former was supported by the *nomenklatura* positions, the latter by the mass-party organization of the Communist Party and the broad circle of satellite organizations (trades unions and youth and sectoral organizations). This structured the society politically in a broader sense. That is, the members of the Communist Party—at no matter what level of the division of labour—were politically distinct from other groups within society and in a certain respect formed a privileged stratum.

In examining the political élite of the 1990s, we can consider previous Communist Party membership as an approximate indicator of membership of the *nomenklatura*. A stronger indicator of such membership is whether a party member occupied a *leading position* during communist times. It is unlikely that better indicators of political integration into the communist system or membership of the *nomenklatura* can be found.

Though during the 1970s and 1980s entrance into the various social sub-élites beyond the political sphere was gradually opened up, in some, above all professional, spheres, the *nomenklatura* system continued to operate until the end of the 1980s. This continued to be the only channel through which the recruitment of political functionaries took place (Gazsó, 1990). On the other hand, during the 1980s the role of qualifications and expert knowledge alongside political loyalty increased in the selection process (Gazsó, 1993).

At the time of the régime change, both the *nomenklatura* and the Communist Party as an institution and an organ of power disintegrated. But the *nomenklatura* as the dominant *social actor* in politics for half a century did not cease to exist, just as the nobility did not disappear as a social actor when the feudal legal system was abolished. The *nomenklatura* is tied together by the common experiences, forms of behaviour and socialization acquired in the Communist Party and the satellite organizations, as well as by the system of personal contacts and by the common interests that have arisen out of the conflicts of the political, social and economic transformation. All of this is only weakly true for the former party membership as a whole.

Regarding the relationship between state and society and the communist system's claim to legitimacy, a shift occurred first from totalitarianism to paternalism, and later in the direction of authoritarianism. But the method of selection of the political élite and the leading stratum did not significantly change. For this reason the question of the democratic régime change was closely tied in Hungary to the question of political, and broader societal, *élite change*. The collapse of the communist régime also gave rise to considerable expectations for political élite change, and the events of the régime change seemed at first to justify these.

Two postulates have been formulated within élite research concerning élite change and the democratic transition. According to the *élite circulation* approach, a new élite replaces the *nomenklatura* élite, or the earlier (pre-communist) élites return to the fore. Even on the eve of the régime change, however, some emphasized the likely ability of the *nomenklatura* élite to preserve its position. The *élite reproduction* approach generally starts from the position that the régime change that followed the collapse of the communist systems in 1989 brought little significant change in the composition of the political (and social) élite: the members of the *nomenklatura* élite were able to retain their positions or to transfer to new positions within the élite. According to the 'grand coalition' picture, a group or class alliance emerges between the strata of enterprise managers and new entrepreneurs and those within the state and the party bureaucracy (Hankiss, 1989: 310). Half a decade following the democratic transition—at the latest, after the second parliamentary elections—it became apparent that change in the social and political élites, though significant, had been partial, and that the former *nomenklatura* élite had considerable capacities of 'reproduction' and the preservation of their power. Though the *nomenklatura* élite lost its power monopoly, it remained, as the party élite of the MSZP, a political élite group with a decisive role to play alongside the new political élite groups that had entered the political stage. This political élite group was recruited from the former *nomenklatura*, and this continues to form its recruitment base after the régime change.

Within the political class, the position of the *nomenklatura* élite depends upon the electoral results of the Socialist Party. The proportion of former Communist Party members in parliament sank to just 13.5 per cent in 1990 as a result of the poor electoral performance of the Socialist Party, but following the Socialists' electoral victory in 1994 it rose to 44.2 per cent (Table 1).

Table 1. The representation of the *nomenklatura* élite (former Communist Party members) in parliament, 1990 and 1994 (percentages)

	1985*	1990	1994
MSZP deputies as a proportion of the whole parliament	-	8.5	54.1
Former MSZMP members as a proportion of the MSZP group	-	88.6	76.7
(Former) MSZMP members as a proportion of the whole parliament	75.1	13.5	44.2

* The last one-party parliament.
Sources: For 1985, Tőkés, 1990; for 1990 and 1994, Körösényi, 1996b: 90.

Institutional, organizational and personnel changes did occur in the administration, the economy and culture—as in politics and the political system—as a result of the régime change. But, in contrast to the régime changes of 1945 and 1948–49, there was no *institutionalized* élite change. Compared with the political class—the composition of which depends directly upon the voters—continuity was strong in other politically influential social élites. This indicated two parallel tendencies: high individual fluctuation in élite positions, but much smaller élite change. That is, fluctuations at the individual level do not necessarily imply élite change in a social sense. While the fluctuations have been high—one survey found that 79 per cent of economic leaders questioned had been appointed between 1991 and 1993—every second appointee was a former Communist Party member (Lengyel, 1995: 318). The representation of the former *nomenklatura* thus fell by only a quarter (Table 2). Among the spheres examined, élite change was greatest in politics, more limited in the public administration, and least extensive in the economy.

Table 2. Former Communist Party members in certain segments of the élite, 1990 and 1993 (survey data, in percentages)

	1990	1993
Ministries	81	43
Parliament	n.a.	26
Banks	64	44
Public companies	74	70
Private companies	n.a.	66
Economic élite combined	74	56

Source: Lengyel, 1995: 315.

2. Political Elite Groups

We turn now to consider more systematically the Hungarian political élite of the 1990s. We begin by assessing the divisions in that élite that are created by differences in the political origins of its members.

The political élite that organized the new parties and controlled the process of the democratic transition was highly fragmented. The new parties were formed on the basis of the traditions and political groups of three successive political régimes. The 'historical parties' (FKGP, KDNP) had their roots in the 1945–48 period, the MSZP was the successor party to the communist one-party system, while the completely new parties (MDF, SZDSZ, Fidesz) were derived from the dissident intellectual groups of the 1980s. These three groups may each be considered, beginning with that rooted in communism.

1. The *communist leadership* became polarized in part over the numerous plans for economic reform and in part over the leadership and succession crisis that developed from 1985 onwards, combined with the political liberalization—and possibly democratization—that was connected to the economic reforms. The eventual victory of the reformers and pragmatists over the hard-liners was linked to the breakthrough of the democratic régime change in 1989. The splitting of the MSZMP in autumn 1989 confined the hard-liners who formed the Workers' Party (*Munkáspárt*) to the perimeter of the political stage.[3] The pragmatic-technocratic and reformist part of the *nomenklatura* élite formed the MSZP, which became the legal successor to the MSZMP and which was able to retain the old party's property and sources of strength. The MSZP entered parliament in 1990 and was the electoral victor in 1994.

The political élite within the MSZMP and later the MSZP was not homogeneous in 1989: it was split (as are most parties) into rival groups and competing political tendencies (Bihari, 1996: 85–95; Gazsó, 1996). The MSZP, formed in late 1989 as a participant in multi-party competition and political mobilization, is, however, a united political actor. A broad range of political groups—with the exceptions of only a few politicians who left the party (such as Imre Pozsgay, a leading reform communist of the 1980s)—have remained politically loyal to the successor party. The sociological bonds that hold them together—personal ties, shared socialization, political style and world-view, and their distance from the other political actors (the new parties)—are much stronger than the personal and political conflicts within the party. The MSZP constitutes a single political camp. Of course, this is hardly surprising, given that lying behind it are the value system, symbols, forms of behaviour and interaction, and language of half a century of rule. The party élite of the MSZP has been recruited from the *nomenklatura* that gives it its membership and, as we will see in the following chapter, that also forms the core of its voting base.

2. The opposition élite that operated during the Kádár era was divided into two principal groups on the basis of the so-called *népi/urbánus* dichotomy.[4] The radical opposition to the communist system—the so-called *urbánus* (urban) intelligentsia—formed the SZDSZ, which became the party of the *liberal-radical élite*. (Fidesz, which was based upon the opposition youth organization, became the second liberal party.) The more moderately oppositional, so-called *népi-nemzeti* movement, which

consisted of writers and other members of the intelligentsia with origins mainly in the humanities, formed the MDF. During 1989 and 1990 the *liberal-conservative pragmatists* led by József Antall gradually came to the fore within the MDF, and in the autumn of 1989 they entered the party's leadership. The conflict within the party between the conservatives and the increasingly vocal, anti-communist 'national radical' group led in 1993 to the victory of the conservative moderates under Antall and the secession from the party of the national radicals under István Csurka. The latter formed a number of new parties, most prominently the Hungarian Party of Justice and Life (*Magyar Igazság és Élet Pártja*, MIÉP).

3. The third source of the regeneration of the pluralist political élite were the now-elderly founders of the historical parties—the former Catholic People's Party, now the Christian Democratic People's Party (*Kereszténydemokrata Néppárt*, KDNP), and the Independent Smallholders' Party (*Független Kisgazdapárt*, FKGP). Continuity has been characteristic of the party élite of the KDNP: though significant younger blood has been brought into the party leadership, the character of the party élite has changed little. By contrast, the rejuvenation of the FKGP's party leadership led in 1993–94 to a significant policy break within the party and the sidelining of the original party leadership. The new party leader, József Torgyán, gave the party a populist, anti-establishment style.

3. The Political Class: Deputies in the Pre- and Post-Transition Parliaments

We turn in this and the following three sections to the second element of our investigation of the élites of the 1990s—the consideration of the 'political class'. The democratic transition brought with it changes for the entire political élite. But it was in the case of the more narrowly understood political class that those changes were greatest.

We approach the political class by analysing the group that best represents it—namely, the parliamentary deputies. First we compare the composition of the last one-party parliament, elected in 1985, and the first two democratic parliaments, elected in 1990 and 1994. This will allow us to draw conclusions concerning the question of élite change. Then, on the basis of the curricula vitae of the deputies in the 1990 and

1994 parliaments, we consider the socio-cultural character of the various party groups. We examine family background, religiosity, place of residence, education, occupation, life path and political and existential integration into the communist system.[5]

A radical transformation occurred in the personnel of parliament between the last one-party parliament and the first democratically elected parliament. As a result of the first free parliamentary elections, 95 per cent of the parliamentary deputies were replaced (Loewenberg, 1993: 440; Tóth, 1992: 81). This involved not simply change at the individual level. It also brought with it élite change—that is, the arrival of a new élite with different qualifications, different occupations and different socio-cultural background—and change in the political character of the parliament. The extent of the latter is shown by the fact that the proportion of those who had been members of the MSZMP fell from 75.1 per cent of the deputies in the 1985 parliament (Tőkés, 1990: 1) to 13.5 per cent of the deputies in the 1990 parliament (Table 1). Meanwhile, the Communist Party secretaries and other party and local-council functionaries, who filled 15 per cent of the seats in the 1985 parliament, completely disappeared from the parliament following the elections of 1990 (Table 3).

The *level of education* and the professional composition of the parliamentary élite also changed. The deputies in the democratically elected parliament were more highly qualified than their predecessors: the proportion with higher education qualifications rose from 59.3 per cent in the old parliament to 88.9 per cent in the new (Tóth, 1992: 82), thereby increasing further the over-representation of the most educated part of the population in the legislature. Meanwhile, the nature of their degrees also changed considerably. Among those possessing degrees, the proportion having agricultural or technical degrees fell from 53 per cent to 18 per cent, while the proportion with degrees in law or the humanities leapt from 23 per cent to 51 per cent (Tóth, 1992: 82).

When examining the *occupational composition* of the last one-party and first multi-party parliaments, it must be remembered that during the communist period the social and occupational composition of the members of the legislature was manipulated to give every social class and stratum representation reflecting its share of the population as a whole. The workers, the peasantry and the intelligentsia—which were, according to communist ideology and 'scientific socialism', the two fundamental classes and the fundamental stratum of socialist society—were represented in parliament in proportion to their shares of the population. This artificial representation disappeared from the Hungarian parliament following the free elections of 1990.[6] In comparison with the previous parliament, the proportion of industrial and agricultural workers fell in 1990 from 21.7 per cent to just 3.7 per cent (Table 3).

Table 3. The occupational distribution of parliamentary deputies, 1985 and 1990 (percentages)

	1985	1990
Workers	21.7	3.7
Industrial and agricultural managers	32.3	11.1
Party secretaries, party and council functionaries	15.0	0.0
Trade-union and interest-group functionaries	5.9	2.6
Civil servants, soldiers, policemen	3.3	3.9
Teachers, doctors, veterinary surgeons	12.1	18.1
Intelligentsia	8.8	40.1
No occupation or no data	0.7	20.7

Source: Loewenberg, 1993: 442.

At the same time, the ending of the artificial manipulation of the composition of parliament brought with it a reduction in the representation of women—from 21 per cent of the deputies to 7.3 per cent (Tóth, 1992: 82). Alongside the complete expulsion of Communist Party functionaries from the parliament, the representation of the industrial and agricultural leaders who had formed the economic élite of the Kádár system fell by two-thirds—from 32.3 per cent to 11.1 per cent. In contrast to the exclusion of the political and economic élite of the Kádár era from the parliament, the share of seats held by the intelligentsia rose fivefold—from 8.8 per cent to 40.1 per cent. This unparalleled rise shows that the dominant social group (in professional/functional terms) of the régime change was the intelligentsia. This new intelligentsia political élite was composed primarily of lawyers, university teachers, scientific researchers, writers, newspaper columnists and other independent members of the liberal professions (Loewenberg, 1993; Sugatagi, 1994).

4. The New Political Class: The Origins, Socio-Cultural Composition, Political Socialization and Career Paths of the Parliamentary Deputies

The socio-cultural character of the parties changed little between the first (1990–94) and the second (1994–98) parliaments following the régime change. The party élites can, on the basis of their socio-cultural character, be divided into three groups. The first is the MSZP, which represents the former *nomenklatura* élite. The second is formed by the parliamentary groups of the MDF, KDNP and FKGP (and the party groups that separated from them during each of the first two parliaments), the members of which are mainly Christian, middle-class intellectuals. The third is composed of the groups of the SZDSZ and Fidesz, recruited from the more secularized, civic intelligentsia and middle classes.[7] (Detailed analysis of the parliament elected in 1998 is not yet possible. It is likely, however, that the only major change has been some alteration in the composition of the parliamentary group of Fidesz, reflecting the party's shift to the conservative camp described in Chapters Two and Three, on the parties and the party system.)

The cleavage based on membership or non-membership of the previous *political class* sharply divides the successor to the Communist Party—the MSZP—from all the other party groups. Membership of the political class of the communist régime can be best measured using the indicator of Communist Party (MSZMP) membership: this is an indicator of political integration into the communist system that separates the political class of the communist system from other groups in society. As we will see, Communist Party membership is linked to a range of other factors, such as socio-cultural embeddedness, origin, career path and work position.

The New Socialist Party Elite

The new Socialist party élite was recruited from the political class of the communist system—from the *nomenklatura*. The overwhelming majority of its members had been Communist Party members (88.6 per cent in 1990 and 76.7 per cent in 1994) *and* filled leading positions during the communist era (78.8 per cent in 1990). This sharply distinguishes the

Socialist party élite from the élites of all the other parties (Table 4). For example, among the thirty-three Socialist deputies who entered parliament in 1990, five had been members of the Communist Party leadership or had had their principal employment in the party, eight had been ministers, state secretaries or other leading office-holders, and two had been trade-union functionaries (Kiss, 1993: 601). Of the MSZP's 176 single-district candidates in the 1994 elections, 149 of whom entered parliament, ninety-one had possessed one or more political positions prior to the régime change. Among them, thirty-four had been party functionaries, twenty trades-union functionaries and thirty-seven local-council functionaries, while twenty-seven had held office in the Communist Youth Alliance and six had been members of the previous parliament (*Beszélő*, 5th May 1994: 12). The MSZP was thus the successor to the Communist Party not only politically, but also in a sociological sense, as the representative of the former *nomenklatura*.[8]

Table 4. Indicators of political integration or non-integration, by party group in the 1990 and 1994 parliaments (percentages)

		MDF	SZDSZ	FKGP	MSZP	Fidesz	KDNP
Former MSZMP member	1990	6.5	4.0	0.0	88.6	0.0	0.0
	1994	7.9	7.1	0.0	76.7	10.0	0.0
Holder of leading position during communist era	1990	31.1	24.2	38.6	78.8	0.0	0.0
Victim of persecution	1990	36.1	45.5	59.6	22.7	22.7	63.6
	1994	31.6	31.4	46.2	3.3	20.0	50.0
Oppositional past	1990	31.7	26.3	43.2	6.0	9.1	28.6

Note: These figures are based upon the deputies' own self-descriptions and thus indicate tendencies only.
Source: Körösényi, 1996b: 90.

The MSZP party élite represents for the most part the stratum of functionaries and *nomenklatura* that rose from below within society during the communist period. Those with a background in the working class or peasantry form the largest group among Socialist deputies, while smallholders and those with a middle-class family background are the least represented (Table 6). A further indicator of the social rise of this élite is given by the fact that, despite their origins in the lower social strata, they have high levels of education (72.7 per cent of the 1990 party group held a university degree). Meanwhile, a very low proportion of Socialist deputies are religious (4.5 per cent in 1990 and 2.4 per cent in 1994). This differentiates the Socialists not only from the Christian-conservative party groups but also from those of the liberal parties (Table 5). While in the cases of some of the Socialist deputies they themselves had moved up through the hierarchy of society, in the cases of other, younger deputies it was often their parents who had risen from the lower strata. The latter come from families of functionaries, and they form the second—now ex-communist—cadre generation (Table 6).

While the principal characteristic of the Socialist deputies' *career paths* is strong *political integration* into the communist system—Communist Party membership, occupation of a leading position during the communist period—the career paths of the members of the other party élites are characterized by non-integration into the communist system—the absence of party membership, persecution, the disruption of careers and an 'oppositional past' (Table 4).

Table 5. The religiosity of parliamentary deputies (according to their own self-descriptions), by party group, 1990 and 1994 (percentages)

		MDF	SZDSZ	FKGP	MSZP	Fidesz	KDNP
Religious family background	1990	84.7	56.8	97.7	51.5	45.5	100.0
Deputy him/herself religious	1990	35.5	28.3	63.8	4.5	22.7	95.5
	1994	39.5	20.0	42.3	2.4	15.0	68.2

Note: These proportions of the deputies consider it important to mention their family background or their own religiosity. The figures thus show primarily tendencies only.
Source: Körösényi, 1996b: 89.

The Elite of the Christian-Civic Parties

Alongside the overwhelmingly non-religious Socialist deputies, the proportion of religious deputies is low also in the parliamentary groups of the liberal parties, standing between 15 and 30 per cent. It is higher in the MDF and very high in both the KDNP and the FKGP (Table 5). The level of religiosity thus separates the parliamentary groups of the KDNP and the FKGP (and to a lesser extent also the MDF) from those of the MSZP, Fidesz and the SZDSZ. The KDNP is not only religious, but, at least in the first half of the 1990s, also had close ties to the church (Enyedi, 1995).

The majority of KDNP and MDF deputies have a family background in the Christian middle class, while FKGP deputies generally have a background in the peasantry or lower middle class (Table 6). Such backgrounds were associated during the communist years with low levels of political integration (the absence of party membership) and high levels of persecution (Table 4). Among the historical parties, which have mainly older deputies, high religiosity is most characteristic of the KDNP (Table 5). The social roots of the KDNP party élite have been characterized in part by a middle-class, petit-bourgeois or peasant background, and in part by strong embeddedness in the Catholic subculture (Enyedi, 1995; Körösényi, 1993a, 1993b).

Table 6. The social origins of parliamentary deputies, by party group, 1990 and 1994 (percentages)

		MDF	SZDSZ	FKGP	MSZP	Fidesz	KDNP
Middle class	1990	40.2	47.5	25.5	25.0	59.1	50.0
	1994	47.4	47.1	19.2	19.0	35.0	45.5
Lower middle class	1990	21.9	18.2	14.9	18.2	18.2	27.3
	1994	15.8	12.9	19.2	17.1	15.0	18.2
Farming	1990	11.2	6.1	34.0	9.1	4.5	9.1
	1994	5.3	4.3	38.5	7.1	0.0	9.1
Working class	1990	24.3	20.2	21.3	34.1	13.6	13.6
	1994	18.4	20.2	19.2	40.5	25.0	9.1
Cadre	1990	1.2	4.0	0.0	13.6	0.0	0.0
	1994	2.6	5.7	0.0	2.9	0.0	0.0
Other/n.a.	1990	1.2	4.0	4.3	0.0	4.5	0.0
	1994	10.5	10.0	3.8	13.3	25.0	18.2

Note: The figures are based on the self-descriptions of the deputies and show mainly tendencies only.
Source: Körösényi, 1996b: 88.

The FKGP has certain features that differentiate it from all the other parties: it has a *rural-agricultural* character. One-third of the Smallholder deputies (in 1990 the proportion was 34.0 per cent; in 1994 it was 38.5 per cent) originate in farming, *land-owning* families. During the decade of collectivization following 1948, they were often classed as '*kulaks*' and were subject to vilification and discrimination. In contrast to this, in comparison with the party élites of the other non-socialist parties, the proportion of FKGP deputies having middle-class backgrounds is significantly lower (at 25.5 per cent in 1990 and 19.2 per cent in 1994; Table 6). The Smallholders' parliamentary group is differentiated from the other party groups by other factors too. Almost half of the members of the 1990 parliamentary group and one-third of the 1994 group were born in villages, while in both parliaments close to a third were also resident in villages (Table 7). The Smallholders have also had less formal education: only 56.8 per cent of the 1990 group and 50.0 per cent of the 1994 group possessed a university degree. Many of them are themselves farmers or are self-employed, and many were among those who suffered a decline in their social status during the communist period: they did not integrate, and they were confined to the bottom of the social hierarchy. This is shown in Table 4 by their lack of Communist Party membership and their frequent references to persecution and an 'oppositional past'. Under the communist régime, the Smallholder party élite was forced to remain outside not only the political élite, but also the social, cultural and economic élites. As a result of the régime change, they moved from the periphery of society to the heart of the political élite.

While the parliamentary groups of the KDNP and the FKGP show very particular characteristics, the third 'religious' party élite—the parliamentary group of the MDF—is much more heterogeneous. The MDF party élite is characterized in large part by religious, middle-class family background (Tables 5 and 6) and lack of integration into the communist system (Table 4). Low levels of persecution compared to the Smallholders, Christian Democrats and Free Democrats point to the fact that, though the members of the MDF élite were recruited mostly from the non-*nomenklatura* middle strata of the 1970s and 1980s that were not integrated into the communist system, they did not belong to any of the groups—such as the '*kulaks*' (FKGP), those attending church schools (KDNP), or the dissidents (SZDSZ)—that were subjected to the most persecution. Around half of the MDF deputies in 1990 were school, college or university teachers, or doctors—the local social élite, who entered parliament through the single-member electoral districts.

Table 7. (a) The birthplace of parliamentary deputies, by party group, 1990 and 1994 (percentages)

Birthplace, 1990	MDF	SZDSZ	FKGP	MSZP	Fidesz	KDNP
Budapest	25.6	31.6	4.5	36.4	36.4	28.6
other town	41.4	45.3	43.2	27.3	54.5	38.1
smaller community	29.9	17.9	47.7	36.4	9.1	23.8
other (n.a./abroad)	3.0	5.3	4.5	–	–	9.5

Birthplace, 1994	MDF	SZDSZ	FKGP	MSZP	Fidesz	KDNP
Budapest	44.7	32.9	15.4	23.0	25.0	27.3
other town	28.9	50.0	46.1	48.8	55.0	40.9
smaller community	21.1	14.3	30.8	26.3	20.0	27.3
other (n.a./abroad)	5.3	2.8	7.7	1.9	–	4.5

Sources: Based on Tóth, 1992: 86 and Kiss, 1996: 742.

(b) The place of residence of parliamentary deputies, by party group, 1990 and 1994 (percentages)

Place of residence, 1990	MDF	SZDSZ	FKGP	MSZP	Fidesz	KDNP
Budapest	31.7	37.9	22.7	69.7	77.3	61.9
other town	47.6	49.5	47.7	24.2	22.7	28.6
smaller community	20.7	11.6	29.5	6.1	0.0	9.5
other (n.a./abroad)	–	1.1	–	–	–	–

Place of residence, 1994	MDF	SZDSZ	FKGP	MSZP	Fidesz	KDNP
Budapest	65.8	45.7	30.8	26.8	40.0	54.5
other town	26.3	47.2	38.4	62.2	60.0	41.0
smaller community	7.9	7.1	30.8	11.0	–	4.5
other (n.a./abroad)	–	–	–	–	–	–

Sources: Based on Tóth, 1992: 86 and Kiss, 1996: 742.

Table 8. (a) The education of deputies' fathers: proportions of the least and most educated groups, by party group, 1990 (percentages)

Father's highest education level	MDF	SZDSZ	FKGP	MSZP	Fidesz	KDNP
primary school (eight years)	26.6	11.6	59.1	36.4	13.6	23.8
university	38.4	44.2	20.4	36.4	63.6	42.2

Source: Based on Tóth, 1992: 87.

(b) The deputies' own education: proportions of the least and most educated groups, by party group, 1990 and 1994 (percentages)

Deputy's own highest education level, 1990	MDF	SZDSZ	FKGP	MSZP	Fidesz	KDNP
primary school (eight years)	0.0	0.0	0.0	0.0	0.0	0.0
university	72.6	80.8	56.8	72.7	63.3*	85.7

Deputy's own highest education level, 1994	MDF	SZDSZ	FKGP	MSZP	Fidesz	KDNP
primary school (eight years)	0.0	0.0	7.7	0.0	0.0	0.0
university	86.8	80.0	50.0	60.8	75.0	77.3

* This figure does not include university students.
Sources: Based on Tóth, 1992: 84 and Kiss, 1996: 743.

The Elite of the Liberal Parties

The deputies of the two liberal parties—the SZDSZ and Fidesz—are differentiated from those of the MSZP by their low level of political integration into the communist system, by their oppositional past and by their frequent persecution (Table 4). They are distinguished from the MDF, FKGP and KDNP deputies above all by their low level of religiosity (Table 5). That low religiosity applies to both the deputies themselves and their family backgrounds. These are the parties having the lowest proportion of deputies with village origins, and their élites have been recruited above all from the educated urban middle classes and intelligentsia (Tables 7 and 8).[9] The proportion with university degrees is very high, and the deputies also come from the most educated family backgrounds (Table 8).[10] As regards place of residence, the liberal parties have the least village-based and most urban party élites except that of the MSZP (Table 7). This is shown also by the fact that they have the lowest proportions of deputies with farming or '*kulak*' origins (Table 6). The liberal party élites originate above all in the secularized intelligentsia and the middle classes.

5. The Ideological Characteristics and World-Views of the Party Elites

Marked differences exist between the various party élites in terms of the ideological orientations and world-views of their members. The deputies of the MDF, KDNP and FKGP describe themselves predominantly as *Hungarian/national* and *Christian/religious*, while those of the SZDSZ and Fidesz characterize themselves as *liberal* (Table 9). The MSZP deputies, meanwhile, choose the labels *left-wing* and *social-democratic* much more often than do those of any of the other parties. But, in the closed-ended questionnaire on which the data here are based, they choose the 'other' category still more often, and more often than do the deputies of any other group.

Table 9. The parliamentary deputies' characterizations of their own world-views, by party, 1990 (percentages)

	MDF	SZDSZ	FKGP	MSZP	Fidesz	KDNP
Hungarian/national	92.1	2.1	65.9	3.0	4.5	36.4
Christian/religious	56.7	16.8	68.2	0.0	40.9	100.0
Liberal	24.4	72.6	2.3	6.1	100.0	0.0
Left-wing	1.8	4.2	2.3	60.6	4.5	0.0
Social-democratic	0.0	4.2	0.0	51.5	18.2	0.0
Radical	3.7	9.5	2.3	3.0	27.3	0.0

Note: The label 'democratic' was chosen by 100 per cent of every party group and is therefore not shown in the table. Nor is the 'other' category shown. It was mentioned by 24.4 per cent of MDF deputies and by 78.8 per cent of MSZP deputies.
Source: Based on Tóth, 1992: 89.

6. *Recruitment and Career Paths*

The democratic transition transformed both the mode and the base of the recruitment of politicians. We have seen in the foregoing that the recruitment base of the political class widened and became more pluralistic in both political and socio-cultural senses: the doors into the political class opened for those who were of middle-class origin, who were religious or who were not politically integrated during the communist era. At the same time, however, the role of education increased greatly in comparison with the artificially 'representative' parliament, and also somewhat in comparison with the *nomenklatura* élite of the late 1980s: 59.3 per cent of the deputies in the 1985 parliament, and 88.9 per cent of those in the 1990 parliament possessed a higher-education qualification (Tóth, 1992: 82). The proportion of the MSZMP leadership who had completed higher education was 66.4 per cent in 1985 and 84.9 per cent in 1989. In the parliaments of the 1990s, those with less education had significant chances of entering the political class only in the Smallholders' Party (Table 8).

Not only the base of political recruitment, but also its methods changed. It is perhaps more appropriate that we speak of the career paths leading to parliament than of an institutionalized recruitment mechanism. Five characteristic career paths stand out from the curricula vitae of the deputies.

1. The first and, at the time of the first elections after the régime change, the most important, career path was that built upon *political capital* obtained at the time of party foundation or earlier (Pokol, 1993a; Róna-Tas, 1991: Sugatagi, 1994). Many sources existed for such political capital. One source that played a part in every party was the politician's role in the organization or reorganization of the parties. Another, important in the historical parties—including the MSZP—was former party membership. Political 'veterans'—including those who had been involved in the events of 1956 and the activists of the dissident subculture—played a part in the new parties as well. A small number of members of the last communist parliament who broke away from the MSZMP were able to enter the multi-party parliament as independents or candidates for one of the new parties.

2. The second path to a political career is built upon *expert knowledge*. Several experts founded significant political careers upon participation in

the roundtable talks of 1989. In addition, the structure of the parliamentary committees and the government based upon expertise provides permanent career opportunities for party experts.

3. A similar but less frequent career path has been that of *representatives of interest organizations* who became candidates and secured parliamentary mandates. For example, in 1990 leaders of the Recsk Alliance, the Phralipe Gypsy Alliance and the National Association of Entrepreneurs entered parliament under the banners of, respectively, the MDF, the SZDSZ and the MDF. Through this, the interest organizations and their leaders hoped for greater publicity and political influence, while the parties sought the enrichment of their images and the broadening of their support bases.

4. The fourth career type is built upon *recognition and positions filled within the local community*. As a result of the electoral system, 176 of the 386 parliamentary seats are won in single-member districts. We stressed earlier the intelligentsia character of the Hungarian parliament—particularly during the first parliamentary cycle. While those entering parliament on the party lists were often intellectuals working in the humanities and the social sciences who had already gained political capital and entered the party élite, the deputies from the single-member districts tended to come from the local élites and possessed local prestige and authority—they were doctors, veterinary surgeons, pharmacists, teachers and priests (Sugatagi, 1994: 49). The parties avidly searched out and sought to win for themselves local figures who would have greater chances of victory in the elections. Except for the local candidates of the MSZP, they had not previously engaged in political activities that could have given them political capital. Only with the establishment of the local organizations of the parties did they enter political life. The single-member-district deputies of the MSZP were of somewhat different character: many were members of the old *nomenklatura*, including presidents of agricultural co-operatives, agronomists and local-council presidents who had become mayors.

5. A fifth career type emerged at the time of the second free parliamentary elections: one built upon party membership and activities within the party organization—that is, upon an *internal party career*. At the time of the first elections this career path was found mainly in the MSZP—since the other, newly founded or newly reorganized parties had no direct organizational predecessors. For a period after the foundation of

the parties, everyone within them still counted as new. But time spent in the party organization has come to play an increasing and, by the time of the 1994 elections, visible, role. For those who entered the parties after their foundation, a career inside the party—or in public office—is already a precondition for entry into parliament and the political élite.

7. *Institutional and Functional Groups within the Political Elite: The Political Influence of Sub-Elites*

We have been concerned in the foregoing with the composition, political breakdown and socio-cultural roots of the parliamentary deputies—that is, with the political class composed of professional politicians. We now turn to the question of how the members of the Hungarian political élite outside the political leading stratum—outside the political class—are recruited.

When we look at the political influence of the various institutional élites, it is important above all, as generally in Europe, that we consider the role of the *civil-service élite*. As in other democratic political systems, leading civil servants participate directly in political decision making in Hungary. While many civil servants became members of parliament (38 per cent of the 1994 parliament were state employees, many of whom were civil servants[11]), their role and influence are greater and more direct within the executive itself: besides the politicians in the government, it is the civil-service apparatus of the ministries that prepares and reaches decisions. This apparatus largely retained its position and political weight after the democratic transition: unlike in earlier Hungarian and other European régime changes, the transition did not involve a purge of the civil service or the reduction in the influence of the civil servants that this would have entailed. Further, at the time of the power vacuum during the transition, and then in consequence of the governmental and administrative inexperience of the political leaders who entered government in 1990, the political influence of the top civil servants became for a time perhaps greater still.

In contrast with the leading civil servants of the central administration, the influence over national politics of the *local civil servants* and *leaders of the local governments* established in 1990 is not significant. As we saw when considering the recruitment of parliamentary deputies, a role in local society can give prestige and recognition and thus act as a launching pad, via the single-member electoral districts, for a career in the political class. The repeal of incompatibility rules following the 1994 elections increased the possibility that a local political career could lay the foundations for a career in national politics.

As is generally the case in European democratic systems, the political presence and influence of *army* and *police* leaders has remained minimal. In contrast with the inter-war period, military leaders already had negligible political influence in Hungarian politics during communist times. This was the consequence of the complete replacement of the military élite following defeat in war and the communist take-over, of the occupation of the country by Soviet troops until 1991, and of the insignificance of Hungary in international military and strategic terms. The police and military élites played no role in the democratic transition, and their social prestige, decision-making competence and political influence remained insignificant after 1990. All the same, their lack of political weight did not mean party-political neutrality. The office corps of the army and police—a large proportion of whom were Communist Party members before the régime change—support mainly the Socialist Party at the ballot box (Mészáros and Szakadát, 1995: 50–53).

Of greater significance is the political influence and power of the *leaders of the justice system* and the *élite of the legal profession*. This is tied closely to the building of the constitutional state and of legal institutions and, more broadly, to the role played by the legal profession in the new political élite that determined the course of the régime change. This role in the intellectual élite originates in the constitutional reforms and the creation of the constitutional state, which extended favourable career opportunities to traditional, above all self-employed, lawyers.[12] It is in part from this latter circle and in part from the élite of the university and academic lawyers that the judges of the new and powerful Constitutional Court, which symbolizes the strengthening of the constitutional state, have been appointed.

In consequence of the transition to a market economy that has occurred simultaneously with, but over a much longer time period than, the political régime change, the political influence of the élite of *economists and financial experts* has increased greatly. The financial, monetarist approach to economics already appeared in Hungary in the 1980s in competition with the branch-based view and the approach focusing on development of the real economy, which dominated the communist planned economy. But it did so mainly as a result only of its indispensable role in crisis prevention. In consequence of the total breakdown of the planned economy, the beginning of the process of privatization, the internal and external debt crisis and pressure from the international financial agencies, a complete realignment took place at the end of the 1980s and the beginning of the 1990s within the Hungarian economic élite (the academic élite and those involved in economic policy) and among opinion leaders. Believers in neo-liberal, monetarist economic ideology became dominant not only in the scientific community, but also in the opinion-leading intellectual élite and among the *éminences grises* of economic policy. The banking and financial spheres strengthened *vis-à-vis* the production and transportation sectors. The institutional and policy independence of the central bank increased *vis-à-vis* the government, and the central bank became a power in its own right in financial affairs and economic policy. The realignment within the government and the central administration in favour of the financial sphere was shown by the strengthening of the Ministry of Finance at the expense of the sectoral ministries. Since 1990, the prime minister has been almost the only person more important than the finance minister in Hungarian government policy, and in political life more generally. The political influence of the financial and banking leaders was further increased by the fact that, except for the government budget, theirs were the greatest resources available in Hungary for distribution. Besides a number of domestic and foreign entrepreneurs, it has been mainly the banks that have financed the press, the foundations and institutes linked to the parties and, indeed, electoral campaigns in Hungary during the 1990s.

At the time of the democratic transition, only a few members of the élite of *company owners and managers*—those who were interest-group leaders or who had links to the political parties—possessed any great political influence. Later, however, as privatization proceeded, a greater role was gained by multinational companies operating in Hungary, by financial investors and by the strengthening group of domestic entrepreneurs.

Our survey of the origins of the parliamentary deputies has already shown the prominent position of the *cultural intelligentsia* in Hungarian politics. The proportion of deputies in the parliament elected in 1990 who held degrees—at close to 90 per cent—was very high (Tóth, 1992: 82).

The concept of the intelligentsia refers here, however, to a much narrower circle—to the social group that generates ideology and symbols, and that leads culture and public opinion. The proportion of the parliament filled by the cultural intelligentsia and those working within the liberal professions, at 40 per cent (Table 3), was exceptionally high by international standards. This new intelligentsia political élite was composed primarily of lawyers, university teachers, scientific researchers, writers, columnists and other intellectuals in the liberal professions (Loewenberg, 1993; Sugatagi, 1994).

The various investigations of Hungarian élites agree that the intelligentsia is not simply the recruitment base of the new political class: it also has its own political role and influence (Bozóki, 1997; Konrád and Szelényi, 1992; Pokol, 1993a; Szalai, 1994, n.d.; Szelényi, 1995; Szelényi *et al.*, 1996). During the democratic transition and the half-decade that followed, the intelligentsia became perhaps the most important group in the political élite, and was certainly of unparalleled importance by European standards.[13] Just one factor behind this is the fact that the cultural intelligentsia, along with the legal and economic intelligentsia, formed, in numbers, a significant, and the most influential, part of the new party élites and the membership of parliament. The second factor is that on occasion certain intelligentsia groups became direct political actors and pressure groups. The characteristic instrument of this was the organization of movements above the parties and of protest actions—the publication of declarations, collection of signatures, boycotting of publications, and so on—all of which was carried out in the name of the nation, society, the freedom of the press or the defence of democracy.

A third factor increasing the political influence of the intelligentsia was the role of the cultural intelligentsia as the dominant opinion-leading élite. The so-called media intelligentsia and media élite are intertwined with, and emerged from, the cultural élite. They form an important group within the cultural intelligentsia and possess key institutional positions. A particularly important role was played in setting the scene for the régime change by the press. From the mid–1980s the press gave an outlet for the reform communist intelligentsia, and from the late 1980s it provided space for the *dissident* opposition intellectuals. An important element of the political influence gained by the intelligentsia in the course of the régime change was the fact that they determined and moulded the *language* and *agenda* of the democratic transition and of political discourse

(Konrád and Szelényi, 1992; Pokol, 1993). They largely retained this function after the transition.

Several further factors increased the role of the press and thus the political influence of the media élite.

1. One stemmed from the fact that all of the parties were established around the same time, during the régime change. The weakness of party identities caused the role of the press in the formation of public opinion and party choices to increase.

2. The Hungarian press is, however, more than an instrument in the hands of political actors: it has its own independent political role. It does not simply deliver the 'message' of politicians and other political actors but, because of its conception of its role, also influences public opinion itself.

3. The understanding many among the media élite have of their role is not that of journalists, but rather that of the intelligentsia. A significant number of journalists see their role as similar to that of the media intelligentsia who are afforded many column-inches by the newspapers. They select stories not on the basis of their 'news value', but rather according to their personal world-view and political value system and orientation. The media élite is in large part a politically committed—though certainly not homogeneous—actor in Hungarian politics, and through its influence it forms a part of the political élite. The majority of the media élite is left-wing or liberal, while a smaller part is right-wing, nationally oriented and/or conservative.

4. A further factor increasing the political influence of the media élite is the fact that the parties, the intellectuals around them, and the governments themselves try to extend their influence to the media, almost dividing up among themselves the newspapers, radio stations and television channels.

The fight between certain intellectual groups in the parties and the media élite for influence over the media led, during the first half of the 1990s, to the so-called media wars. During this time, for example, the programmes—including political news programmes—on public-service television and radio were parcelled out to the various rival political groups and orientations. Through the establishment of the National Radio and Television Commission (*Országos Rádió és Televízió Testület*, ORTT), the political control of the parliamentary parties over the public-service media was institutionalized. Both this law and the establishment of two nationwide private television channels in 1997 exercised a balancing influence within the media.

Between 1989 and 1992, during the years of the régime change, the political influence of the trades unions and the *trades-union élite* fell significantly. The leaders of the new unions entered the foreground through their party and political links, while the leaders of the so-called successor unions were pushed onto the defensive. The new parties that dominated parliament and politics, as well as opinion leaders and the media, all preferred the new unions over the old.

But despite this, those new unions were able to achieve only modest—and temporary—success in the development of their organization and membership. The strengthening of the MSZP that began in 1993 and, even more, the victories of the successor unions in the so-called trade-union elections of 1993 greatly strengthened the political influence of the old trade-union élite. The former communist trade unions were characterized during the political transition and the years following it by organizational transformation but continuity of personnel. Despite some personnel changes within the leaderships of the successor unions, no élite change occurred: the union leaders belonging to the old *nomenklatura* stratum preserved their positions. The links between the old union élite and the élite of the MSZP were rebuilt at the political level: in 1994 many trade-union leaders entered parliament and governmental office wearing Socialist colours. The rise of union influence was a product also of the fact that the unions obtained institutionalized positions of power—in part through institutionalized interest reconciliation (the Interest Reconciliation Council) and in part through control over the so-called social-security self-governments.[14]

One consequence of the régime change was the rise in the political weight of the *church leaders* in comparison with their almost complete insignificance during communist times. This occurred not only because the administrative and political restrictions imposed by the communists on the churches and on religious belief were lifted, but also for a number of other reasons: the policies of the conservative government between 1990 and 1994; the compensation of the churches for losses incurred under the communists; the strengthening of the optional religious education in schools; and, in particular, the appearance on the party spectrum of the KDNP, which was built upon Christian-social political traditions. Nevertheless, the political influence of church leaders and the

Catholic and Protestant intellectual and social élite during the 1990s—though not tied exclusively to the KDNP or to the period of conservative government—remained only moderate.

8. Links between the Economic and Political Elites

A certain level of intermingling occurs in every modern mixed economy between the political and the economic élites. Such intermingling is promoted by the redistribution by the state of 40 to 60 per cent of GDP, by the economic policy of the government, by economic legislation and by the activities of economic actors such as lobbyists and interest representatives. The intermingling is further increased by the government's patronage power over the state sector of the economy and by the demands of the parties for financial resources (such as campaign finances).

In Hungary, as in most East-Central European countries, a range of other factors exist, the combination of which has spawned a particularly marked intertwining of economics and politics. These relate partly to the inherited situation (the state sector was still dominant at the time of the political régime change) and partly to the economic transformation (the transition to a capitalist market economy gave the state further responsibilities, such as that of privatization). A third factor increasing the linkage is tied to a further peculiarity of the communist system: the economic and political élites of that system were institutionally intertwined, and the communist élite, though it no longer holds a monopoly of power and though it was temporarily pushed to the periphery of the political class, has been able to retain a significant position in the new system. This is indicated by the fact that it is heavily over-represented within the rapidly developing private sector—for example, two-thirds of the leading managers in large companies are former party members (Table 2). Other studies have found that this ability to find a position within the new system has not been confined to big business—former party members are over-represented also among small and medium-sized private enterprises (Kovách, 1994; Róna-Tas, 1994). All of this strengthens the so-called capital transformation hypothesis, which posits that the *nomenklatura* élite can 'transform' the political capital it obtained during the communist period into economic capital (Szelényi and Szelényi, 1991).

One indicator of the intermingling of the political class and the economic élite is given by the number of parliamentary deputies who occupy leading positions within companies. This is, of course, only one channel of many through which such intermingling could occur, but we must content ourselves here with the channel for which data are available. Between 1994 and 1996, of the 386 deputies, 143 held a total of 251 positions in companies—as managers or as members or chairmen of boards of directors or supervisory boards. The largest number of posts, in both absolute and relative terms, was held by members of the MSZP group, recruited from the *nomenklatura* élite: 43 per cent of the Socialist deputies held leading company positions. In the parliament as a whole, more than one-third (37 per cent) of the deputies held such posts, and only in the parliamentary group of the Smallholders' Party was it unusual for deputies to perform such functions.[15]

9. Concluding Remarks

Having surveyed the socio-cultural and political composition of the political élite of the 1990s, we can draw out certain conclusions. To some extent these conclusions question the thesis frequently voiced in Hungarian political science that a wide chasm exists between the political leaders and political élite on the one hand and society on the other, and that the parties 'float' above society.

1. The recruitment and socio-cultural composition of the Hungarian political ruling stratum between 1990 and 1997 was pluralistic: the various party élites have different characters and represent different social groups. As we shall see in the chapter that follows, on electoral behaviour, the electorates of the parties also differ from each other in their composition, and these differences in part reflect the differences in the party élites.

2. Even in comparison with the long-established European democracies, the link between the socio-cultural characteristics of the groups of the political class (religiosity, former party membership, family background) and party-political affiliation is strong. Thus Hungary does not have a homogeneous 'functional élite', differing from the population as a whole only in its higher level of education (Herzog, 1975, 1982). Rather, its political élite may be better compared to the 'representative' élite that

appeared, representing various social groups, during the European democratization of the late nineteenth and early twentieth centuries (Putnam, 1976). All of this is connected with the changes that occurred in the Hungarian political class at the time of the régime change and with the early stage of the professionalization of politicians (Sugatagi, 1994).

3. The political élite is also pluralistic in its composition, and the élites of the various social spheres all, if to differing degrees, possess some level of political influence.

4. The notion of the separation of the political class and élite from society is also rebutted by the fact that, during the years of the political and economic transition in the first half of the 1990s, the range of career paths leading into the political class and élite broadened and the opportunities for entry into those groups grew. Both élite change and élite reproduction were present simultaneously.

The Hungarian political leading stratum and political élite are thus recruited from, and are the representatives of, broad social, professional and occupational groups. Contrary to the views of some élite critics, they do not constitute a 'power élite' separate from those groups. It is another question whether the traditionally ambivalent attitude in Hungarian political culture towards the state and political institutions (parties, parliament, the government) has influenced negatively judgements upon the personnel of these institutions—that is, upon the whole political class and political élite. This appears to be a judgement that the political class that entered power in the wake of the régime change has been unable to improve.

Notes

1. In what follows we thus understand the political élite as including political leaders, top civil servants, and the most authoritative members of influential groups.

2. By seeing the *nomenklatura* as a broad social group we can understand why the *nomenklatura* later became, following the fall of the communist régime, the basis of a macrosociological political *cleavage* (see Chapter Four on political cleavages).

3. The Workers' Party has been unable to enter parliament during the 1990s.

4. See footnote 1 in Chapter Two ('The Parties') for an explanation of the terms '*urbánus*' and '*népi(-nemzeti)*'.

5. Regarding the deputies in the 1990 and 1994 parliaments, we rely on two types of sources. One is István János Tóth's study of the 1990 parliament '*Képviselők és frakciók a*

parlamentben' ('Deputies and Party Groups in Parliament'), based upon data from the *Jelenkutató Alapítvány* (Current Research Foundation) (Tóth, 1992). The other is a study based on the author's own research results (Körösényi, 1996b, 1999). The original sources for information on the deputies are the volumes *A magyar országgyűlés almanachja* (Almanac of the Hungarian Parliament; Kiss, 1993) for the 1990 parliament, and *Országgyűlési választások 1994* (Parliamentary Elections 1994; Kecskés and Németh, 1994) for the 1994 parliament. Because these sources were not structured questionnaires but rather the curricula vitae offered by the deputies themselves, the tables based upon them must be treated with some caution: they show tendencies rather than precise data.

6. Before the régime change the genuine political élite in Hungary, as in the other communist countries, was composed not of the parliamentary deputies, but rather of the members and secretaries of the Political Committee and Central Committee of the Communist Party. Real political leadership and power were in the hands of the Communist Party leadership and party bodies, while the role of the legislature was only representative and symbolic. The *parliamentary group* of the Communist Party's successor, the MSZP, in the 1990 and 1994 parliaments better represented the *nomenklatura* élite than did the manipulated composition of the last communist legislature.

7. Among the demographic features of the party élites, generational differences are particularly noteworthy. The parliamentary deputies elected in 1990 and 1994 represented three generations of politicians. The generation that first entered politics in the years following the Second World War was to be found primarily in the historical parties, and to a lesser extent in the MSZP and the MDF. The generation that was socialized at the time of the 1968 movements and reforms appeared mainly among the representatives of the SZDSZ, MDF and MSZP. Finally, the so-called post-communist or protest generation, socialized at the time of the disintegration of the Kádár régime, was found above all in Fidesz (Stumpf, 1996). (For the age composition of the parties' parliamentary groups, see Tóth, 1992: 86; Kiss, 1996: 742).

8. Other investigations of élite sociology have reached similar results (cf. Machos, 1997).

9. Data are available on place of residence and education only for 1990 and 1994.

10. Following the KDNP, university education is most frequent in the case of the SZDSZ. At the time of their election, a significant number of the Fidesz deputies were still students, explaining the apparently lower level of university education suggested for this group by the table.

11. Based on statistics concerning the occupational composition of parliament (Kiss, 1996: 748–749).

12. Beyond this, the principal professional career path into the political class, besides that of the economists, belongs to the lawyers. While 6.1 per cent of the deputies in the 1985 parliament who possessed a degree completed their studies in law, in the 1990 parliament, this proportion was 21.6 per cent (Tóth, 1992: 82).

13. The historical background to the political careers of the intelligentsia in Eastern Europe is well known. In consequence of the difficulties in achieving national independence and, later, democratic transformation, that these nations faced for a century and a half, the intelligentsia, in times of national and political oppression, often represented the 'nation' and 'society' against the centre of power. Thus developed the role of writers and

poets as 'prophets', something that was maintained during the communist era. In the communist systems of Central Europe, the intelligentsia formed both the ideological opinion-leading stratum that served the system and the 'dissident' opposition that emerged from the 'internal' opposition to the régime. In consequence of their lauded role and status, the intelligentsia became one of the chief bearers of the régime change in Poland, Czechoslovakia and Hungary, and it appeared that the political élite of the new democratic system would emerge from it.

14. The 'social-security self-governments' were set up by the Antall government in 1993. They were partially independent from the government and had extensive powers in respect of the implementation of social-security policy. In terms of composition, half of their members were elected by the trade unions, and half were delegated by employers' organizations. They were disbanded in 1998 by the newly elected Orbán government.

15. Author's own calculations, based upon *HVG*, 12th December 1996: 122–123.

Chapter Six

Electoral Behaviour

This chapter considers electoral behaviour at the micro-level—the level of the individual voter. First we analyse the level of volatility in voters' party preferences. Then we assess the extent to which patterns nevertheless exist in those preferences—that is, we assess the degree to which party preferences and a range of demographic, sociological and other variables are linked. Finally, we consider the value systems and political attitudes of the voters and the connection between these and party preference. We will turn to the macro-level of electoral studies—that of election results and the overall distribution of support between the parties—in the next chapter (a short overview of the election results is given in Appendix B).

1. The Openness of the Political Market: The Instability of Party Preferences

One indicator of the state of the political market is the extent of the stability or instability of party preferences. One of the principal characteristics of the Hungarian political market is that the popularity of a party among potential voters can change over a short period to an almost unbelievable extent. The results of the parliamentary elections of the 1990s—and the findings of surveys conducted between them—show that the proportion of floating voters 'flowing' between the parties was very high.

For example, we may measure the change in votes between consecutive elections using Pedersen's index of electoral volatility.[1] Between

1990 and 1994, this stood at 28.3 percentage points—several times higher than the average for the countries of Western Europe in the 1980s, which stood at 8 percentage points (Tóka, 1994: 461; 1995: 3–4). It was higher also than the figures for the first electoral cycle in the new party systems established in southern and Western Europe after 1945, which stood at between 13 and 20 percentage points. Between 1994 and 1998 it rose further, to 33.6 percentage points (Tóka, 1998: 2)

Nevertheless, party choice had stabilized somewhat by 1994 in comparison with four years earlier. While in 1990 only 27 per cent of the electorate had decided more than two months in advance of the elections which party they would vote for, by 1994 this proportion had risen to 51 per cent. In 1998, 58 per cent of respondents said they had decided long before the elections which party they would support (Table 1).

Table 1. 'When did you decide which party you would like to vote for?' (percentages)

	1990	1994		1998
More than two months before the elections	27	51	Long before the elections	58
1–2 months before the elections	23	16	1 month before the elections	16
3–4 weeks before the elections	13	9		
1–2 weeks before the elections	18	10	1 week before the elections	7
A few days before the elections	12	8	A few days before the elections	10
On the day of the elections	4	2	On the day of the elections	5
In the voting booth	3	4	Don't know/won't say	4

Sources: For 1994, Szonda-Ipsos; for 1990, *Magyar Közvéleménykutató Intézet* (Hungarian Public Opinion Research Institute), *Népszabadság*, 1st June 1994; for 1998, *Századvég Politikai Elemzések Központja* (Századvég Political Analysis Centre), *Politikai Barométer*, June 1998, Figure 6.

Further light can be shed upon the strength of the link between parties and voters by asking to what extent the parties are successful in mobilizing the voters—by asking how high is the level of *electoral turnout*. Surveys show the proportion of those uncertain of their party preference to be higher among non-voters than among voters (Simon, 1991: 120–121; Bruszt and Simon, 1991: 609), and that non-voters are those who have become uncertain of their party choice and have 'wandered' between parties—those who would no longer vote for the party they had chosen earlier, but still do not know which party they would now choose (Fábián, 1996). Actual turnout in parliamentary elections in Hungary during the 1990s has fluctuated between 45 and 69 per cent. This is low not only in comparison with the figures for Western Europe, but also, as mentioned earlier, in comparison with those for the other former communist countries (Angelusz and Tardos, 1996). Besides the lack of development of party preferences, the second major reason for the lower level of turnout is that there was relatively little political mobilization in Hungary at the time of the régime change: the great bulk of the citizens remained passive throughout. The transition in Hungary was rather the product of the internal disintegration of the communist system, the activities of the reform communists within the MSZMP and the pressure exerted by the emerging political opposition.

2. The Electoral Bases of the Parties

It was the almost unanimous view of political analysts in Hungary during the first half of the 1990s that the link between the new parties and society—between the parties and the voters—was very weak. The parties were said to 'float' above society. Despite the evidence that has just been seen for instability in party preferences, we do not share this 'floating' hypothesis. It was evident even from early analyses (around 1990) that the notion of 'wandering' votes was inadequate for explaining the emerging relationship between the parties and their voters. The *distribution of political preferences* is not uniform across all the parties, and even the first investigations of preferences showed them to be related to *socio-cultural background*. Though one part of Hungarian society does display a lack of political differentiation, in another part the lines of political division have already been drawn. That is, if we disregard the genuinely huge masses of wavering voters, each party does have a characteristic core voting base. This link is stronger still if we consider not parties but rather the relationship of the *political camps* to each other. The political camps differ not only in socio-cultural composition, but also in their voters' value systems, political attitudes and ideological self-placements. In what follows we survey the relationship in Hungary between party preferences and certain factors pertaining to demography (age, place of residence), sociology (occupation, income, class position), organization (former MSZMP membership, church attendance) and culture (religion, value preference), and also the relationship between party preference and attitudes in regard to particular political questions.

The Smallholders, the Christian Democrats and the Socialists had the most clearly defined electorates in the early 1990s. In contrast, the electorates of the three new parties were less clearly defined in their sociological characteristics. The large changes in the popularity of the various parties have of course had an impact upon the composition of their (potential) electorates. At the height of their popularity, the MDF in 1990, the MSZP in 1994 and Fidesz in 1998 all had much broader electorates, resembling those of 'catch-all' parties, than they did at other times. Changes in the size of the party electorates have affected the composition of those electorates in the cases of the other parties too. Nevertheless, lasting features of the various parties' support bases can be observed (Tables 2 to 6).

Table 2. Party electorates by place of residence (percentages)

	MDF	SZDSZ	FKGP	MSZP	Fidesz	KDNP	MIÉP
Budapest							
1990	26	32	12	31	22	13	-
1994	20	25	9	22	19	20	n.a.
1998	n.a.	28	14	20	19	n.a.	26
other towns							
1990	40	43	31	40	44	36	-
1994	44	49	38	46	45	35	n.a.
1998	n.a.	46	39	47	49	n.a.	40
smaller communities							
1990	34	25	57	29	34	51	-
1994	36	26	53	32	36	45	n.a.
1998	n.a.	26	47	33	32	n.a.	34

Sources: Závecz, 1994: 453; *Századvég Politikai Elemzések Központja* (Századvég Political Analysis Centre), *Politikai Barométer*, May 1998.

Table 3. Party electorates by religiosity (percentages)

	MDF	SZDSZ	FKGP	MSZP	Fidesz	KDNP
Religious, follower of church teachings						
1990	15	13	33	9	10	61
1993	23	10	28	4	10	55
Religious, with own approach						
1990	56	52	52	40	44	35
1993	51	42	61	49	50	39
Not religious, or don't know						
1990	29	34	15	51	45	4
1993	26	48	11	47	60	6

Sources: For 1990, Tomka, 1991: 49; for 1993, Stumpf, 1994a: 161.

Table 4. Party electorates by occupation, 1994 (percentages)

	MDF	SZDSZ	FKGP	MSZP	Fidesz	KDNP
Manager/high-ranking	5	8	2	7	5	4
Professional/white-collar	16	24	9	19	22	12
Worker	19	30	27	28	32	14
Farm worker	3	3	8	3	3	3
Unemployed	6	7	8	6	9	4
Inactive	51	29	47	37	29	63

Source: Based on Tóka, 1994: 486.

Table 5. Party electorates by age (percentages)

1990	MDF	SZDSZ	FKGP	MSZP	Fidesz	KDNP	
18–33	21	28	15	10	56	7	
34–49	38	40	27	37	30	21	
50–65	27	12	36	30	10	33	
65-	14	10	22	23	4	39	
1998	**MDF**	**SZDSZ**	**FKGP**	**MSZP**	**Fidesz**	**KDNP**	**MIÉP**
18–24	n.a.	10	9	8	18	n.a.	15
25–34	n.a.	26	14	14	23	n.a.	21
35–44	n.a.	24	18	16	21	n.a.	18
45–60	n.a.	27	31	34	24	n.a.	28
over 60	n.a.	13	28	28	14	n.a.	18

Sources: Závecz, 1994: 453; *Századvég Politikai Elemzések Központja* (Századvég Political Analysis Centre), *Politikai Barométer*, May 1998.

Table 6. Party electorates by education (percentages)

	MDF	SZDSZ	FKGP	MSZP	Fidesz	KDNP	MIÉP
up to 8 years / primary							
1990	34	30	58	43	30	56	-
1994	38	19	51	32	30	50	n.a.
1998	n.a.	28	58	44	31	n.a.	34
vocational training							
1990	17	20	17	15	20	18	-
1994	19	23	27	29	31	20	n.a.
1998	n.a.	19	24	16	22	n.a.	20
secondary education							
1990	31	35	20	20	35	18	-
1994	23	38	17	30	29	20	n.a.
1998	n.a.	31	15	26	32	n.a.	31
higher education							
1990	18	15	5	22	15	8	-
1994	20	20	5	9	10	10	n.a.
1998	n.a.	22	3	14	15	n.a.	15

Sources: Závecz, 1994: 452; *Századvég Politikai Elemzések Központja* (Századvég Political Analysis Centre), *Politikai Barométer*, May 1998.

The secret of the *Hungarian Democratic Forum's* success in 1990 was that it was the party that, by the time of the elections, had best succeeded in becoming a 'catch-all' party. This catch-all character was both social and political in nature. First, the party was at that time successful in gaining votes in almost equal proportions from every social group. Its voters were equally divided among groups based on educational level, place of residence, occupation and age. Second, it was the electoral victor not only in the provincial towns: it was also able to defeat the Smallholders in the villages and rural areas, and the SZDSZ in Budapest. It was supported by both the religious and the non-religious. In 1994, the MDF was able to retain only a small part of its 1990 electorate, while in 1998 that electorate shrank to almost nothing. The composition of the core voter base that remained loyal to the MDF in 1994 was much less broad-based than that of four years earlier: the proportions of the elderly, the religious, the educated and the upper middle class were all higher than previously. By 1998 the MDF electorate had contracted to such a small size that measuring its composition became very difficult.

The *Alliance of Free Democrats* emerged from both the 1990 and the 1994 elections as the country's second largest party. It was particularly strong in Budapest and in the country's north-western counties. Its voters came above all from the educated, young and middle-aged, urban population. The proportion of SZDSZ voters was particularly high among residents of Budapest, among those with secondary and higher education, and among high income groups. From the party founded by the Budapest intelligentsia, the SZDSZ became the party of society's various élite groups, and it was less successful in winning support from the (lower) middle class. The unusual feature of the SZDSZ's electoral base in 1990 was, however, that, while its support in the middle class was lower than that among the élite groups, like the Smallholders' Party and Fidesz, it was successful in winning votes among the least well-off. This can be seen if we look at the party's results in 1990 in the single-member districts of Budapest: it led in the élite districts in the hills of Buda, and in the materially and socially most deprived districts (for example, in Csepel, Angyalföld and Ferencváros), while it was defeated by the MDF in the city's middle-class districts and in the outer suburbs. The élite strata (those with high incomes, those occupying leading positions and the intelligentsia) were attracted to the SZDSZ by its promise of a rapid transition and its pronounced Western orientation. What attracted the marginalized groups within society with low incomes and low social status, meanwhile, was the party's radical anti-communism. Later the SZDSZ lost much of its support among workers and low-status groups. The secularized middle strata that were not integrated into the communist system came to dominate its electoral base. By 1998 that electorate had shrunk to between a third and a half of its earlier size. Within it, the proportions of urban dwellers and the more educated rose further. It also grew older, as the proportion of the middle-aged increased. In regional terms, the SZDSZ gained most votes in both 1990 and 1994 in Budapest and the country's more developed, urbanized western regions. In 1998 the latter were won over by Fidesz, and Budapest became the SZDSZ's main base.

The *Independent Smallholders' Party* has, in terms of the social composition of its electorate, become a rural, agrarian party. Its electoral base is composed above all of less educated, elderly, religious rural-dwellers of low social status. Support for the Smallholders is lowest among managers, the intelligentsia and white-collar workers, while the proportions of blue-collar workers (Gazsó and Stumpf, 1995: 11), those on low incomes and the poor are highest. The party's support in the agricultural counties of southern and eastern Hungary has exceeded by a significant margin that in other parts of the country. These are the counties where a strong political tradition existed behind the Smallholders in the period prior to 1948 and where the proportion of the population tied to agriculture remains significant. The support for the Smallholders in the 1990s can thus be explained mainly by political tradition and the party's position on agricultural issues. The concentration of the Smallholders' Party's votes in these groups, places of residence and regions points to the fact that the party's electoral base is formed by a numerically significant social group that possesses strong party identity and that was directly affected by the collectivization of the communist era. This basis was, however, rather *closed*, and the party has been able to attract support outside this sharply defined interest group for only brief periods.

The *Socialists* gained greater support than average in 1990 among residents of Budapest, those possessing university degrees and those in leading economic or administrative positions. At this time, the MSZP was, despite its social-democratic rhetoric, unable to count upon the votes of the workers, and it performed less well in small communities than it did in the larger towns. In the 1990 elections, the MSZP was above all the party of the *nomenklatura*—the ruling élite of the communist system—and the greater part of its voters were members of the *nomenklatura* (former members of the MSZMP and those who occupied leading positions during the communist years were strongly overrepresented in the MSZP electorate).

Because the MSZP won around three times as many votes in 1994 as it did in 1990, the demographically and socio-culturally very particular electoral base that the party possessed in the first elections had become diluted by the time of the second: in 1994, it won almost equal support among almost every occupational, residential, educational and age group within society. In comparison with the electorate as a whole, however, the proportion of rural-dwellers was somewhat lower and that of the middle-aged and elderly somewhat higher among those who voted for the MSZP. Meanwhile, the proportion of workers—whether measured by occupation or by self-placement—had, by 1994, increased within the socialist electorate (Gazsó and Stumpf, 1995: 9–10). In contrast to this, the MSZP was still far more successful than any other party among former MSZMP members, while it won almost no votes among the religious and church-goers. While the proportion of former party members differentiated the socialist electorate from that of every other parliamentary party, the lack of church-goers distinguished it mainly from the right-wing parties.

The MSZP electorate retained its basic character in 1998, though the ageing of that electorate continued and the proportion of former Communist Party members declined in parallel with the natural process of generational replacement. In regional terms, the party is strongest in the towns and industrial districts that were developed and given preferential treatment during the decades of communism—that is, in Budapest and the industrial towns of northern and southern Hungary.

At the beginning of the 1990s, the electoral base of the *Federation of Young Democrats* displayed strong generational traits: as a former youth organization, the party was able to win votes above all among those aged between eighteen and thirty-five years. Fidesz voters are also somewhat characterized by higher levels of education and by urban place of residence. The youthful character of the Fidesz electorate faded temporarily when the party became very popular in 1991 and 1992, but it had already returned by the time of the 1994 elections. That character remained strong in 1998, but the proportion of the young among the party's voters is no longer as strikingly high as it had previously been.

The second, cultural feature of Fidesz voters in the 1990 and 1994 elections was that among them, as among MSZP voters, the proportion of church-goers is very low and that of the non-religious very high. In contrast with the MSZP's electoral base, meanwhile, the proportion of former party members is low. Following its shift to the right, Fidesz has, in the second half of the 1990s, won over a significant proportion of former MDF and KDNP voters, in consequence of which its electorate has gradually changed in socio-cultural character and taken on a more 'catch-all' character. From the point of view of religiosity, it has become more mixed (Tóka, 1998: 24; Marián, 1998: 674; Gazsó and Stumpf, 1998: 643). In regional terms, Fidesz gained the most votes in 1998 in the traditionally more developed, more urbanized counties of western Hungary that were previously the strongholds of the SZDSZ, and in some agricultural areas.

The electoral base of the *Christian Democratic People's Party* was related most closely to the core electorate of the Smallholders' Party:

within it, the proportions of the elderly, the less educated, blue-collar workers and those of low social status and low income were high. Its voters came primarily from rural communities and, to a lesser extent, from provincial towns. Its electorate did, however, differ in some respects from that of the Smallholders' Party: it had more female voters than male; its base was not confined to the agricultural population; and it did also gain support among the more educated. The most characteristic feature of the Christian-democratic electorate—which differentiated it from that of every other party, including the Smallholders—was the exceptionally high proportion of active, church-going Christians. This also gave a slight regional bias to the KDNP electorate: the party was strongest in the overwhelmingly Catholic counties of the north and west of the country. By the time of the 1998 elections, however, the KDNP electorate had shrunk to such an extent that the party was unable to gain the 5 per cent of the votes necessary for entry into parliament.

In terms of the social composition of its voter base, the *Hungarian Party of Justice and Life* displays the hallmarks of a middle-class protest party. Its electorate is characterized by high proportions of the young and middle-aged and of those with intermediate to high levels of education, though the religious are also over-represented. In regional terms, support for MIÉP is highest in Budapest—particularly in the élite districts of Buda traditionally occupied by the middle classes—and its environs.

In summary, it is clear that the parties that have entered the Hungarian parliament during the 1990s differ widely in the nature of their voter appeal. It is possible to find among them a programmatic party (the SZDSZ), a catch-all party (the MDF), sectoral parties (the FKGP and the MSZP), a denominational party (the KDNP) and even a generational party (Fidesz). By 1994, the earlier catch-all electorate of the MDF had narrowed to that of a sectoral party, based upon the more elderly, religious middle class. Meanwhile, the MSZP's support had broadened to that of a catch-all party. By 1998 most of the KDNP and MDF electorates and a significant part of the SZDSZ electorate had switched to the Fidesz camp. Close to two-thirds of the votes cast in the first round of the 1998 elections were won by Fidesz or the MSZP. The socio-cultural factors most clearly differentiating the electorates of the parties were age, religion, former membership of the Communist Party and place of residence.

These factors are more than mere statistical variables: as was seen in Chapter Four, they constitute politically important *cleavages* cutting through Hungarian society.

3. Political Camps: The Value Systems, Political Attitudes and Ideological Self-Placements of the Voters

As can be seen from empirical investigations conducted in Hungary since the late 1980s, the ideological triangle that is articulated at the level of the political élite is perceptible among voters too. Though one-half of the electorate displays no coherent ideological disposition or orientation, within the other half three clear attitude combinations are to be found. Furthermore, this was true even before the influence of the emerging parties took effect. Whether we examine self-placement in terms of a range of political or ideological concepts (national, conservative, liberal, left-wing, socialist and so on[2]) or attitudes in respect of particular issues that have been the subject of political debate (attitudes to, for example, the communist system, the ethnic Hungarians living in neighbouring countries, equal income distribution, the justice of social differences, the role of the government in creating social equality, tolerance towards minorities, and whether crimes committed under the communist system should be punished), three characteristic attitude systems or 'position bundles' emerge—the '*liberal*', the '*socialist*' and the '*conservative*'. The relationship of these to one another can be represented by the three corners of an equilateral triangle (Figure 1). Each opinion bundle is correlated with party preference: those in the 'liberal' corner support primarily the SZDSZ or Fidesz; those placed around the 'conservative' position for the most part choose the MDF, the KDNP or the FKGP; and the preferred party of those in the 'socialist' corner is the MSZP.

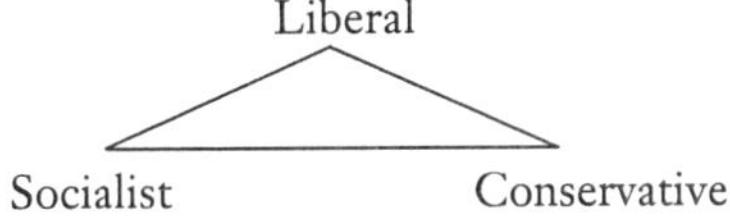

Figure 1 The three political camps

Source: Angelusz and Tardos, 1994: 132; cf. Lázár, 1996.

Connections between Concepts: The Semantic Level

We know from the results of other studies that the value preferences and ideological orientations of the voters are linked in such a way as to raise a single principal axis to prominence, integrating the other axes within it. The development of the axis of *belief in progress versus protection of the existing model* into such a principal axis (Angelusz and Tardos, 1992) shows that the liberal/conservative and left-wing/right-wing dichotomies are not entirely independent from each other in voters' value preferences. Liberal values lie closer to the 'progressive' values of the left and are associated with the left also at the conceptual level, while conservative values are linked more to the concept of the right. This matches similar tendencies seen in the political spectrum. In consequence of this, the concepts of left and right in Hungarian politics primarily signify not preferences as to economic policy and the distribution of income, but rather a cultural-ideological scale. At one end of this, the left is linked to liberalism; at the other end, the right is linked to conservatism. A further consequence is that, within this conceptual-semantic space, the 'right-wing liberal' position has remained weak (Table 7).

Table 7. Self-placements on the liberal/conservative and left/right scales, by party choice, 1995 (percentages)

	MDF	SZDSZ	FKGP	MSZP	Fidesz	KDNP
Left-wing	13	30	11	60	14	11
Right-wing	34	12	14	3	26	20
Neutral, don't know	53	58	75	37	60	69
Liberal	11	46	13	31	34	19
Conservative	44	11	23	21	7	25
Neutral, don't know	45	43	64	48	59	56

Source: Marián, 1996: 583, 585.

The Issue Level

This does not mean, however, that there are no systematic differences between the parties or party electorates in respect of economic-policy attitudes and positions on concrete economic-policy questions. A general tendency in the economic-policy attitudes of Hungarian voters between 1990 and 1998, and one independent of party choice, was a significant shift to the left. In 1990 only 44 per cent of those questioned agreed that the state should control prices through laws and decrees. By 1994 this had increased to 67 per cent, and in 1998 it stood at 65 per cent. In 1990 48 per cent, in 1994 69 per cent and in 1998 66 per cent agreed that economic crisis sectors should be supported in order to protect jobs. In 1990 24 per cent and in 1994 60 per cent considered the fight against unemployment to be more important than the fight against inflation. In both 1990 and 1994 63 per cent and in 1998 67 per cent considered the influence of trades unions to be too little. Finally, the proportion opposing the purchase of Hungarian companies by foreigners more than doubled in the same period (Tóka, 1994: 476; Tóka, 1998: 6). Alongside this general leftward shift, large differences remained between the party electorates in their attitudes on economic policy, and the characteristic left- and right-wing images have remained unchanged. KDNP, FKGP and MSZP voters possess (in that order) progressively more left-wing attitudes on economic and social policy, while SZDSZ and, to a somewhat lesser extent, MDF voters, have more right-wing attitudes (Table 8).

The general leftward shift that occurred between 1990 and 1994 was strongest among MSZP voters. Whereas in 1990 there was a roughly even split between left- and right-wing attitudes among MSZP voters—in three of the seven questions listed, more took a right-wing economic position than a left-wing position—by 1994 there was a left-wing majority on every question. In 1998, that left-wing majority remained on most questions. That is, the growth in support for the MSZP was much greater among left-wing than among right-wing opinion groups (Tóka, 1994: 469–476). This is tied also to the fact that, while in 1990 the MSZP was above all the party of the former *nomenklatura* (leaders and middle strata), by 1994 its support base had become diluted through the arrival of the lower middle strata, low status groups and the working class. Similarly, as the Fidesz voter base widened between 1994 and 1998 it too took a more left-wing character.

Table 8. Economic-policy attitudes, by party preference, 1994 and 1998 (percentages)

	MDF	SZDSZ	FKGP	MSZP	Fidesz	KDNP	MIÉP	Other	Total
State price controls:									
1994 support	10	17	10	39	6	8	-	10	100
oppose	13	25	6	33	8	5	-	11	100
1998 support	3	7	14	36	30	-	4	7	100
oppose	3	14	11	35	26	-	5	6	100
Support of crisis sectors for protection of jobs:									
1994 support	10	19	9	40	5	8	-	9	100
oppose	13	26	7	24	11	7	-	11	100
1998 support	2	7	16	34	30	-	3	8	100
oppose	4	11	9	33	33	-	7	3	100
Influence of trades unions:									
1994 too little	8	21	8	43	7	6	-	8	100
too great	26	26	11	14	2	8	-	14	100
1998 too little	2	11	12	34	29	-	5	7	100
too great	0	9	22	35	23	-	0	10	100
Privatization:									
1994 oppose	7	16	10	43	4	8	-		100
faster the better	23	23	8	30	6	8	-		100
Hungarian companies that foreigners should be allowed to buy:									
1994 none	8	16	11	42	6	7	-	11	100
only loss makers	9	20	8	39	7	8	-	9	100
any, if they pay most	18	24	6	32	6	6	-	8	100
1998 none	4	4	19	28	30	-	6	10	100
only loss makers	1	10	11	34	35	-	4	5	100
any, if they pay most	3	16	9	46	20	-	1	6	100

Note: We have omitted various intermediate answers from the table, with the result that the numbers do not add up to 100 per cent.
Source: Tóka, 1994: 469–475; Tóka, 1998: 17–21.

Notes

1. The value of Pedersen's index gives the total change between elections in the votes cast for parties whose support fell and for parties that ceased to exist between those elections.

2. For example, the proportions of the various groups found in a survey from early 1995 based upon self-characterizations were the following: socialist, 22 per cent; liberal, 17 per cent; national, 14 per cent. Fourteen per cent, meanwhile, did not give a self-description, while 32 per cent said they could not place themselves in any of the categories (Marián, 1996: 582).

Chapter Seven

The Electoral System and Elections

Elections are among the most important events in any democratic political system: their results have a large bearing over—and often determine—the composition of government during the years that follow. In this chapter we therefore consider the three parliamentary elections that have taken place since the régime change in Hungary (a short overview of the results is given in Appendix B). A large part of that analysis will concern the electoral system—which, of course, has a powerful impact upon the final outcome in terms of the distribution of parliamentary seats. Hungary's electoral system is an unusually complex one. We will begin by describing its mechanics in detail. We will then survey the distribution of votes in the three parliamentary elections to date. Finally, we will consider the effects the system has had in these three elections upon the results produced.

1. The Mechanics of the Electoral System

The parliamentary electoral system employed in Hungary is the product of a political compromise reached at the time of the régime change in 1989. The historical parties (the Smallholders, the Christian Democrats and the Social Democrats) favoured the county-based list system used in the elections of 1945 and 1947. The Socialists and the Free Democrats, meanwhile, supported a system of single-member districts, and Fidesz advocated the introduction of a mixed system. Because of the opinions of the parties, but also because of the weakness of mass support for the parties and the uncertainty already perceptible in public opinion towards the parties, it was not possible to eliminate single-member districts—which offer a more direct relationship between voter and representative and greater accountability of politicians—from the electoral system. In the end, the compromise that was agreed between the parties negotiating over the institutional form of the democratic system involved a mixed electoral system. This was enshrined in law before the end of 1989, and it has continued to operate, with minor modifications, since that time.

This *mixed electoral system* distributes the 386 seats in the Hungarian parliament by means of two principles and three institutional mechanisms. One hundred and seventy-six seats are distributed on the basis of the majoritarian principle using a two-round single-member-district system. At most a further 152 seats are distributed using regional party lists according to the principle of proportional representation. The voters have two votes: one for the candidates in their single-member district and one for the regional party lists. The remaining seats—at least fifty-eight—are distributed using national party lists in a compensatory system based upon the principle of proportionality that employs surplus votes from the single-member and regional-list contests. We will consider each of these three mechanisms in turn.

The electoral law divides the country into 176 *single-member districts*, each containing approximately sixty thousand eligible voters. Strict nomination requirements must be passed before a candidate can run for election in these districts. The electoral law stipulates a two-month official electoral campaign, the first month of which is devoted to nominations, and in order to stand in a single-member district, a candidate must gather the signatures of 750 eligible voters living within that district.

The first round of the election in any given district is valid if the turnout exceeds 50 per cent. If this requirement is fulfilled and one candidate wins more than 50 per cent of the votes cast, that candidate is declared the winner. This, however, happens only rarely—in five of the 176 districts in 1990, two in 1994 and one in 1998. If the turnout requirement is met but no candidate wins more than 50 per cent of the vote, a second round is held two weeks after the first. The first three candidates from the first round plus any further candidates winning more than 15 per cent of the first-round vote are entitled to run in the second round, though they may withdraw between the rounds if they wish. The turnout requirement at the second round is only 25 per cent, and only a relative majority is needed for victory. If the turnout requirement at the first round is not met (as was the case in several districts in 1998) the same procedure is followed, except that all the candidates are able to run in the second round.

For the purposes of the *regional-list* part of the election, the country is divided into twenty multi-member districts. These match the units of regional administration—the nineteen counties and the capital city. These districts return differing numbers of deputies, ranging from four to twenty-eight, depending on size. A party can put forward a regional list in any given region only if it is successful in having its candidates nominated in at least one-quarter of the single-member districts—but not less than two districts—within that region.

Provided turnout exceeds 50 per cent, the distribution of the regional-list seats is determined at the first round of the election. (If turnout is below 50 per cent, as was the case in two counties in 1998, a second round is held with a lower turnout requirement.) The parties are able to enter parliament through the lists only if they pass a *minimum threshold*—in 1990, 4 per cent of the national total of votes cast in the regional list elections, and since 1994 5 per cent of the same. The seats are distributed in each county on the basis of the principle of proportionality using the largest-remainder system and the Hagenbach-Bischoff quota.[1]

No votes are cast specifically for the *national lists*. Rather, the national-list seats are distributed on the basis of a national pool of votes that is created from two sources. First, fractions of the full quota of votes in the regional-list elections that remain after the distribution of seats are transferred to the national pool. Second, all votes for losing candidates in the second round of the single-member district election are transferred. These pooled votes are translated into seats using the d'Hondt version of the highest-average system.[2] The minimum number of seats available for distribution on the national lists is fifty-eight. In addition, however, any seats that cannot be distributed on the regional level (that is, any seats for which a full quota of votes does not exist at that level) are transferred to the national level. As a result, the number of seats distributed at the national level was ninety in 1990, eighty-five in 1994 and eighty-two in 1998. These seats are available only to parties that pass the threshold for entry into parliament in the regional-list election.

The condition for putting forward a *national list* is that the party successfully put forward regional lists in at least seven of the regional districts. The parties that are able to put forward a national list can participate in the campaign programmes during the second month of the campaign on national state television and radio. The system of nominations acts as an important selection mechanism before the elections have even begun. Twelve parties were able to put forward national lists in 1990, fifteen in 1994 and twelve in 1998 (Körösényi, 1990: 39; Szoboszlai, 1995: 45; *Magyar Közlöny*, 1998, no. 47).

2. Elections and the Distribution of Votes

One question concerning elections is always that of the level of *turnout*. Turnout has fluctuated in parliamentary elections in Hungary during the 1990s between 45 and 69 per cent (Table 1), which, by European standards, is rather low. Attention is paid to turnout not only because it is considered by many to be a measure of the popular acceptance of the parliamentary system and the parties, but also because different levels of turnout affect the parties differently in terms of their chances of winning votes. In the 1998 elections, for example, the outcome of the battle between Fidesz and the MSZP was linked to the level of turnout: high turnout favoured Fidesz and low turnout the MSZP. The MSZP could put its first-round lead down to the low level of turnout. One factor in its defeat at the second round, meanwhile, was that—unlike in the previous two elections—the level of turnout did not fall between the rounds.

Table 1. Electoral turnout, 1990–1998

	1990	1990	1994	1994	1998	1998
	first round (25th March)	second round (8th April)	first round (8th May)	second round (29th May)	first round (10th May)	second round (24th May)
Eligible voters	7,798,018	7,613,128	7,959,206	7,873,937	8,062,708	8,016,397
Actual voters	4,900,960	3,459,798	5,485,618	4,339,896	4,536,254	4,570,386
Turnout	65.8%	45.4%	68.9%	55.1%	56.3%	57.0%

Sources: Angelusz and Tardos, 1996: 14; *Magyar Közlöny*, 1998, no. 47: 3889.

In the first two elections, the first round not only gave a general picture of the distribution of seats in the new parliament, but also determined which of the parties would enter that new parliament. The fact that it was the same six parties that entered parliament on both occasions pointed to a certain stabilization of the party system. The 1998 elections were different in several respects. The low level of turnout in two eastern counties meant that the first-round regional-list election there was invalid. In consequence of this, the regional-list seats could not be distributed after the first round, and the final list of parties passing the 5 per cent threshold could be ascertained only after the second round, when the list election was repeated in the two eastern counties.

Huge swings have occurred in the proportions of votes, and even more the proportion of seats, won by the various parties (Table 2). In 1990, the MDF won the elections with 25 per cent of the list votes; in 1994 it was the MSZP that won, with 33 per cent of the vote. The former won a relative majority of the seats (164) and the latter an absolute majority (209). In 1998, Fidesz lagged behind the MSZP by 3.5 percentage points in terms of list votes. It was nevertheless able to become the largest party in parliament as a result of its landslide second-round victory in the single-member districts (Table 3).

Table 2. Distribution of list votes among the larger parties, 1990–1998

Parties	1990 votes	1990 %	1994 votes	1994 %	1998 votes	1998 %
MSZP	535,064	10.89	1,781,504	32.99	1,497,231	32.92
SZDSZ	1,050,799	21.39	1,065,889	19.74	344,352	7.57
MDF	1,214,359	24.73	633,770	11.74	127,118	2.80
FKGP	576,315	11.73	476,272	8.82	597,820	13.15
KDNP	317,278	6.46	379,523	7.03	104,892	2.31
Fidesz	439,649	8.95	379,344	7.02	1,340,826	29.48
MIÉP	–	–	85,735	1.59	248,901	5.47
MSZMP/MP	180,964	3.68	172,109	3.19	179,672	3.95
MDNP	–	–	–	–	61,004	1.34

Sources: Szoboszlai, 1995: 25, 28; *Magyar Közlöny*, 1998, no. 47.

In 1990, the victorious MDF formed a centre-right government coalition with the FKGP and the KDNP. In 1994, the MSZP formed a centre-left coalition with the SZDSZ. In 1998, it was the turn of the centre-right again to enter government, through the coalition of Fidesz with the MDF and the FKGP. In 1990, the voters voted against the MSZP—the successor party to the communists—and among its rivals favoured the parties of the moderate centre-right. In 1994, the opposite occurred: the voters cast their votes not only against the centre-right government but also in favour of the party bearing the legacy of the Kádár era. In 1998, again, the same pattern was reversed. The level of change is shown, for example, by the fact that in 1994 the MDF won barely half of the votes it had secured four years earlier, while the MSZP won more than three times as many. The support for the other parties did not change so dramatically—they obtained around the same number of votes in both elections (Table 2). In 1998, by contrast, while the SZDSZ lost two-thirds of its electorate, support for Fidesz more than trebled. The party composition of parliament also changed, with the KDNP being replaced by MIÉP.

3. The Three Channels and Two Rounds of the Elections and the Distribution of Seats

The operation and political effects of the electoral system can be more easily understood if we consider individually the two electoral rounds and the three channels through which seats are distributed. In this section, therefore, we assess how the three branches of the electoral system have operated in practice during the 1990s.

Table 3. Seats won through the three channels of the electoral system, by party

(a) 1990

Parties	Single-member districts	Regional lists	National lists	Total Seats	Total %
MDF	114	40	10	164	42.49
SZDSZ	35	34	23	92	23.83
FKGP	11	16	17	44	11.40
MSZP	1	14	18	33	8.55
Fidesz	1	8	12	21	5.44
KDNP	3	8	10	21	5.44
Agrarian Alliance	1	–	–	1	0.26
Independents	6	–	–	6	1.55
Joint candidates	4	–	–	4	1.04
Total	176	120	90	386	100.00

(b) 1994

Parties	Single-member districts	Regional lists	National lists	Total Seats	%
MSZP	149	53	7	209	54.14
SZDSZ	16	28	25	69	17.88
MDF	5	18	15	38	9.84
FKGP	1	14	11	26	6.74
KDNP	3	5	13	20	5.70
Fidesz	–	7	13	20	5.18
Agrarian Alliance	1	–	–	1	0.26
Joint candidates	1	–	–	1	0.26
Total	176	125	85	386	100.00

(c) 1998

Parties	Single-member districts	Regional lists	National lists	Total Seats	%
Fidesz-MPP	90	48	10	148	38.34
MSZP	54	50	30	134	34.72
FKGP	12	22	14	48	12.44
SZDSZ	2	5	17	24	6.22
MDF	17	–	–	17	4.40
MIÉP	–	3	11	14	3.63
Independent	1	–	–	1	0.26
Total	176	128	82	386	100.00

Sources: Gábor, Levendel and Stumpf, 1995: 474; *Magyar Közlöny*, 1988, no. 47.

Single-Member Districts

The single-member districts form the branch of the electoral system where the electoral victor—the party winning the most votes nationally—can most efficiently translate the votes it wins into seats. Since it is rare for a seat to be won at the first round, the second round is decisive. Here the important factors are the size of the lead of the first-placed candidate in the first round and the strength of the electoral 'coalitions' that come into being between the two rounds. The order of candidates can be changed by the second preferences and electoral participation of the supporters of the candidates who do not run in the second round.

a) If the lead of the first-placed candidate is large—if he or she wins 30 to 40 per cent of the votes in the first round—the significant drop in turnout that generally occurs before the second round means that, provided the candidate is able to retain his or her first-round voting base, he or she can, without gaining further supporters, count on at least 40 per cent of the second-round vote. With at least three candidates in the contest, this is enough for victory. This was the experience of many MSZP candidates in 1994.

b) If the advantage of the leading candidate is smaller—if he or she wins only 20 to 30 per cent of the vote—the result of the second round depends heavily upon, first, the second preferences of the supporters of the candidates who drop out of the contest and, second, electoral coalitions agreed with rival parties, as well as the extent to which the supporters of those rivals follow the party lead.

In 1990, the MDF was the first-round victor in eighty districts. In the second round, in addition to these seats, it won a further thirty-four through vote transfers from other parties (Table 4). The party won 26 per cent of all single-member-district votes in the first round and 41 per cent in the second round, and on the basis of this it was able to secure 65 per cent of the single-member-district seats. The second largest party, the SZDSZ, was placed first in sixty-three districts after the first round. But, because it was less successful than the MDF in gaining votes from among the supporters of the candidates who had dropped out, it lost twenty-eight of these districts at the second round. In the 125 districts where MDF and SZDSZ candidates confronted each other head on in the second round, the SZDSZ candidates were able to increase the number of votes they won by an average of just 5 per cent between the rounds, while the MDF candidates could increase their vote by 29 per cent (Körösényi, 1990: 43). The explanation for the MDF's landslide second-round victory in 1990 was thus that it was the second preference of the greatest number of supporters of candidates who did not reach the second round. The supporters of the KDNP, the FKGP and the other smaller parties saw their 'natural ally' in the MDF rather than in the SZDSZ.

The sweeping victory of the MSZP in the single-member districts in 1994 showed that a first-round lead of 10 to 15 percentage points—and often 20 percentage points—is generally enough to secure victory at the second round. As the loss of ten districts showed, however, a smaller advantage than this is often not enough, particularly where (as was the case with the MSZP) the party cannot count, or can hardly count, upon the second preferences of the supporters of the smaller parties. The SZDSZ, the MDF and the KDNP were able to turn a first-round deficit into victory at the second round in around a dozen districts because their candidates could count on the second preferences of the supporters of their 'allies'.

At this time it was relatively rare for parties belonging to the same political camp to take advantage of the possibility of withdrawing their candidates in each other's favour and calling upon their voters to support those other candidates at the second round, thereby increasing their chances of securing election. In 1994 a total of twelve such withdrawals took place, of which ten were among the four parties of the so-called liberal block. In 1998, by contrast, the large number and the political efficacy of mutual candidate withdrawals at the second round turned the outcome of the elections around.

The possibilities for political change at the second round of the single-member-district elections manifested themselves dramatically in 1998. In the first round, the Socialists came first in 113 of the 176 districts, and their coalition partners, the Free Democrats, gained the most votes in a further two. The candidates of the opposition won in only sixty-one districts (one of which they won in the first round by securing over 50 per cent of the vote). Thus, the MSZP, just as in the results of the list election, was in the lead. In the second round, however, it lost over half of those 113 districts, and in the end it had to be content with a total of fifty-four single-member seats. By joining forces for the second round, the opposition parties were able to turn an initial second place into victory in fifty-nine districts; they thus doubled the number of their successes, and secured a total of 120 single-member seats.

Table 4. The single-member-district competition: first- and second-round results

(a) 1990

Parties	No. of seats where first in first round	No. of seats won in second round	% of seats where first in first round	% of seats won in second round
MDF	80	114	45.45	64.77
SZDSZ	63	35	35.79	19.88
FKGP	11	11	6.25	6.25
MSZP	3	1	1.70	0.57
Fidesz	3	1	1.70	0.57
KDNP	4	3	2.27	1.70

(b) 1994

Parties	No. of seats where first in first round	No. of seats won in second round	% of seats where first in first round	% of seats won in second round
MSZP	160	149	90.90	84.66
SZDSZ	12	16	6.82	9.09
MDF	1	5	0.57	2.84
FKGP	0	1	0.00	0.57
KDNP	1	3	0.57	1.70
Fidesz	0	0	0.00	0.00

(c) 1998

Parties	No. of seats where first in first round	No. of seats won in second round	% of seats where first in first round	% of seats won in second round
MSZP	113	54	64.20	30.68
SZDSZ	2	2	1.14	1.14
Fidesz-MPP	41	90	23.30	51.14
MDF	13	17	7.39	9.66
FKGP	6	12	3.41	6.82
Independent	1	1	0.67	0.67

Note: Joint candidates are not included in the figures for 1990 and 1994.
Sources: For 1990 seat numbers, Körösényi, 1990: 41; for percentages, Kiss, 1991: 537; for 1994, author's calculations based on Tóth, 1995: 443; for 1998, *Magyar Közlöny*, 1998, no. 47.

Besides the factors that had already been present previously,[3] the extent of this difference in the results of the two rounds is explained in part by the fact that the Hungarian political spectrum had, by the time of the 1998 elections, become bipolar. The position of anti-clerical, anti-communist and anti-nationalist liberalism that was occupied in the early 1990s by Fidesz and the SZDSZ had, by the middle of the decade, become empty. The SZDSZ shifted left and Fidesz right, and thus the liberal centre disappeared from Hungarian politics. Following the establishment of the socialist-liberal coalition in 1994, the logic of bipolar competition gave an incentive for the opposition to organize into a 'civic' block (*bürgerliche Koalition*). The emerging dichotomy of left and right, government and opposition, was the political precondition for the mutual candidate withdrawals that occurred among the opposition parties and for the left- and right-wing 'block voting' that was seen.

Summing up the character of the single-member-district contest, we can state that it is here that the competition between the two leading parties is decided (Table 4). Here the leading party can translate most effectively its advantage in terms of votes into an advantage in the distribution of seats: in 1990 the MDF won 65 per cent of the single-member seats; in 1994 the MSZP won 85 per cent; and in 1998 Fidesz won 51 per cent. The second largest party can convert votes into seats much less effectively: in 1990 and 1994, the SZDSZ won in, respectively, 20 per cent and less than 10 per cent of the single-member districts, and in 1998 the MSZP won in 31 per cent. All other parties combined won just 15 per cent of these seats in 1990, less than 10 per cent in 1994 and 18 per cent in 1998. These parties are able to win a greater number of seats in the proportional parts of the electoral system—the regional and national list contests. It is these that we turn to now.

Regional List Seats

The competition in the multi-member districts decides two issues: first, which parties enter parliament; and, second, how the regional-list seats are shared among those parties.

The question of which parties enter parliament is in practice determined by which are able to pass the 4 or (since 1994) 5 per cent vote threshold required for winning seats in the list election. In theory, the small parties that do not pass the threshold can enter parliament through the single-member-district contests. However, their chances of doing so—unless they put forward joint candidates with one of the larger parties—are minimal. The threshold thus acts as a strongly selective device: only six parties passed it in the first two elections and five in the 1998 election (Körösényi, 1990: 39; Szoboszlai, 1995: 45; *Magyar Közlöny*, 1998, no. 47). This selectivity not only reduces the fragmentation of parliament; it also alters the character of the entire party system, favouring nationally organized parties while in practice giving no chance to regional parties or regional electoral groupings. One of the novelties of the 1998 elections was, however, that the MDF, which obtained significantly less than 5 per cent of the list vote, was, through a pre-election agreement for mutual candidate withdrawals with Fidesz, able to win seventeen single-member districts and thus form an independent party group in parliament. The co-operation of the right-wing parties in the single-member districts resulted in a greater difference between the single-member and list votes than had previously been the case.

Though the distribution of regional-list seats is performed on the basis of the principle of proportionality, two factors lead to a deviation from proportionality. One stems from the fact that the parties not reaching the 4 or 5 per cent threshold are excluded from the distribution of seats. In itself, this has the effect of giving every other party a proportion of the list seats greater than its share of the vote. The second factor is that of district magnitude. This produces differential effects upon the parties' chances of winning seats, increasing those of larger parties, while reducing those of smaller parties. While the number of seats available for distribution varies greatly—from four in three of the counties to twenty-eight in Budapest—in most of the districts (fourteen of them), the number is between four and six. In these districts, clearly, only a very disproportionate distribution of seats is possible. In thirteen of these fourteen districts, no more than four parties were able to win seats in 1994, though, as we have seen, the distribution of votes was relatively broad. In 1998 this concentration became still greater—in not one of the smaller counties did more than three parties gain parliamentary representation. In these counties the smaller parties can win seats only if they perform much better locally than they do nationwide, or through the transfer of their votes to the national level.

The influence of these non-proportional factors upon the number of seats gained by the parties passing the threshold can be seen from Table 5. The system has given the first- and second-placed parties a significant advantage—their share of the regional-list seats has been three to ten percentage points greater than their vote share. Meanwhile, it has given an advantage of one to four percentage points to the third and fourth parties, while the remaining parties have generally been disadvantaged, by up to three percentage points. In 1990 and 1998, both of the top two parties gained a significant advantage of six to nine percentage points. In 1994, when the MSZP won a greater proportion of the seats and led the second party by a greater margin, its seat share (at 42.4 per cent) was almost ten percentage points greater than its vote share (33.0 per cent), while the advantage of the second-placed SZDSZ was only around three percentage points.

Table 5. Votes and seats won in the regional- and national-list elections

(a) 1990

Parties	Regional list votes (%)	Regional list seats (no.)	Regional list seats (%)	National list seats (no.)	National list seats (%)	Total list seats (no.)	Total list seats (%)
MDF	24.73	40	33.33	10	11.11	50	23.80
SZDSZ	21.39	34	28.33	23	25.55	57	27.14
FKGP	11.73	16	13.33	17	18.88	33	15.71
MSZP	10.89	14	11.66	18	20.00	32	15.23
Fidesz	8.95	8	6.66	12	13.33	20	9.52
KDNP	6.46	8	6.66	10	11.11	18	8.57
Other	15.81	–	–	–	–	–	–
Total	100.00	120	100.00	90	100.00	210	100.00

(b) 1994

Parties	Regional list votes (%)	Regional list seats (no.)	Regional list seats (%)	National list seats (no.)	National list seats (%)	Total list seats (no.)	Total list seats (%)
MSZP	32.99	53	42.40	7	8.23	60	28.57
SZDSZ	19.74	28	22.40	25	29.41	53	25.23
MDF	11.74	18	14.40	15	17.64	33	15.71
FKGP	8.82	14	11.20	11	12.94	25	11.90
KDNP	7.03	5	4.00	14	16.47	19	9.04
Fidesz	7.02	7	5.60	13	15.29	20	9.52
Other	9.47	–	–	–	–	–	–
Total	100.00	125	100.00	85	100.00	210	100.00

(c) 1998

Parties	Regional list votes (%)	Regional list seats (no.)	Regional list seats (%)	National list seats (no.)	National list seats (%)	Total list seats (no.)	Total list seats (%)
MSZP	32.92	50	39.06	30	36.59	80	38.10
Fidesz-MPP	29.48	48	37.50	10	12.20	58	27.62
FKGP	13.15	22	17.19	14	17.73	36	17.14
SZDSZ	7.57	5	3.91	17	20.73	22	10.48
MIÉP	5.47	3	2.34	11	13.41	14	6.67
MDF	2.80	–	–	–	–	–	–
Other	8.61	–	–	–	–	–	–
Total	100.00	128	100.00	82	100.00	210	100.00

Sources: For 1990, Szoboszlai, 1994: 53; Gábor, Levendel and Stumpf, 1994: 474; for 1994, Szoboszlai, 1995: 44; for 1998, *Magyar Közlöny*, 1998, no. 47.

National List Seats

The rule that has operated in practice in the distribution of the national list seats has been that the more seats a party has won in the regional-list and (particularly) single-member-district elections, the fewer surplus votes it has had, and so the fewer seats it has won on the national lists. The MSZP and the SZDSZ can attribute the large number of compensatory seats they won from the national lists in 1998 (respectively, thirty and seventeen seats) largely to the surplus votes transferred from the single-member districts in which they lost. Besides the SZDSZ, MIÉP too gained most of its seats (eleven out of fourteen) from the national list. By contrast, for Fidesz, which won the highest number of regional-list seats and which was able efficiently to translate its votes into seats in the first two branches of the electoral system, the national list brought only a proportionately small number of additional seats (see Table 5). We can state in general that the national list is most important for the smallest parties that pass the parliamentary threshold.

4. The Impact of the Electoral System upon the Political System

The rules of parliamentary elections are of interest not only because of their direct effects on the party-political balance of power. The nature of the electoral system also influences the role played by parliament in the general operation of the political system—namely, whether parliament serves primarily *political representation* or *governance*.

Hungary's mixed electoral system, combining single-member and party-list branches that are based upon differing principles, fills two different functions. In the single-member districts it is decided which party will form the government (or government coalition), while in the regional- and national-list contests political representation is guaranteed for the important political forces—the large and medium-sized parties. In the interests of reduced parliamentary fragmentation and greater governability, the electoral system excludes the small parties from representation in the legislature. Thus, the single-member-district branch of the electoral system and the administratively determined threshold for entry into parliament serve the interests of *governance*, while the regional lists and the national compensatory list promote political *representation*.

Through the single-member-district contest, the electoral system has the effect of increasing the lead of the largest party when the votes are translated into seats. Thus, in 1990 the MDF won 1.72 times more seats than it would have won with perfectly proportional representation, while in 1994 the MSZP won 1.64 times as many and in 1998 Fidesz won 1.30 times as many.[4] Of the three elections, it was in 1998 that the competition between the two largest parties was most even, and therefore then that the preferential effect for the largest party was smallest.

These numbers point to a feature of the Hungarian electoral system that is seen also in more precise indicators of proportionality—that, despite the mixed nature of that system, in terms of the proportionality of representation, it is closer in its final result to the majoritarian systems than it is to the proportional systems (Fábián, 1994). Putting it another way, the system favours governability over representation (Szoboszlai, 1994: 55). Nevertheless, while it reduces the number of parties entering parliament and gives a significant advantage to the electoral victor, it also secures parliamentary representation for every major political orientation—for six parties in the three parliaments to date. We can thus state on the basis of experience to date that it does achieve a level of compromise between the two principles.

Notes

1. The quota determines the number of votes required to obtain one seat. The Hagenbach-Bischoff (or Droop) quota equals the total number of votes cast divided by the number of seats plus one (votes/[seats + 1]) (Electoral Law [1994, Act XXV]; Mészáros and Szakadát, 1993: 52; in English, Farrell, 1997: 64).

2. For further details see Mészáros and Szadadát, 1993: 58–62, or, in English, Farrell, 1997: 64–65.

3. In the second round, of the two first-placed candidates the one more popular in terms of voters' 'second preferences' has the greatest chance of winning votes from other candidates, thus improving his or her chances of election.

4. Calculated from Tables 3 and 5.

Chapter Eight

Economic Interest Groups and Interest Reconciliation

During the democratic transition, besides the parties, organized interest groups also appeared spontaneously in Hungarian politics. Tens of thousands of associations, foundations and interest-representative organizations emerged during the first half of the 1990s. In what follows we will consider only a few of these, focusing upon economic interest-representative organizations that possess political weight, and in particular upon the role of trade unions and institutional interest reconciliation.

1. Trade Unions

The processes of economic and political transformation have changed fundamentally the structural position and operational conditions of the trade unions. Institutions of plant-level worker participation and of macro-level interest reconciliation have both developed. With the collapse of the communist system, the privileged power position of the unions came to an end, and between 1988 and 1992 the unions were weak, politically defensive actors in Hungarian politics. In consequence of the régime change, the monopoly of the official trade unions of the communist system ended, and the National Council of Trade Unions (*Szakszervezetek Országos Tanácsa*, SZOT), the alliance of unions under Communist Party control, disintegrated. New unions, independent of the party-state, were formed and the communist union alliance was also transformed. Unlike the Communist Party, however, the party-state trade unions did not dissolve themselves; only their alliance (SZOT) was dissolved and replaced by four large confederations. At the same time the nineteen sectoral unions were divided into fifty-nine sectoral or craft unions. In some sectors (such as iron-working, mining, textiles and building) the unions retained their sectoral character, while in others they were divided by profession (Kőhegyi, 1995: 11). The *successor unions* inherited the four-million-strong membership and all of the assets of the former party-state unions. (The assets of SZOT, meanwhile, were distributed among the new unions during the early 1990s.)

The structural consequences of the economic transition also weakened the position of the unions. The reduction in unemployment, the downscaling of sectors with traditionally strong union activity and high levels of unionization (such as coal mining and iron smelting), the privatization of state companies, the division of large enterprises into small units, the transformation of company structure, the reduction in the role of large enterprises and a range of other factors all had the effect of reducing the level of unionization and weakening the bargaining position of the unions.

The old unions had to face declining membership, a legitimacy crisis, problems in leadership and organization and the challenge posed by the new unions. The creation of new unions could not counterbalance the huge decline of membership in the old unions. Total union membership—and thus also the level of unionization within the working population—began to fall slowly in 1987, and from 1989 it plunged dramatically. While the level of unionization in Hungary in the mid–1980s—at almost 70 per cent—exceeded that found even in the model neo-corporatist countries of Western Europe such as West Germany and Austria, by the mid–1990s official union sources put the unionization level at around 30 per cent, and the downward trend was continuing.

The decline in union membership and the level of unionization was linked also to other structural changes in the economy. Before the régime change, the company structure of the competitive sphere in industry was characterized by the dominance of large enterprises. By contrast, by the mid–1990s, in an economy which was already predominantly capitalist and privately owned and whose sectoral structure had changed greatly, around one-half of all those employed in industry worked in firms employing less than fifty people. In some privately owned firms and a great many small businesses, the trade unions are not present at all.

Despite their policy and organizational reforms, the prestige of the trade unions among the public remains very low: of the political institutions, only the parties are trusted less (see Chapter One, on political culture). Yet despite the lack of trust, the initial legitimacy crisis of the union leaders and the decline in membership, the successor unions have as a whole consolidated their position. They have retained the bulk of their assets, including their holiday, sport and social institutions, thereby giving them the means for providing 'selective incentives' to encourage their members to stay (Tóth, 1993).

Despite a favourable political environment and supportive legislation during the first parliament, the new unions were not able to break the advantage of the successor unions. Though the old unions lost over one million of their members, the largest of the four confederations that took over from SZOT—the National Association of Hungarian Trade Unions (*Magyar Szakszervezetek Országos Szövetsége*, MSZOSZ)—retained more than one million members in 1993, and the other three successor confederations combined also had a membership exceeding one million. By contrast, the total membership of the new unions at the same time was only 400,000–500,000. Thus, by 1993, the new unions could claim only a sixth of total union membership (Table 1), a proportion that did not change significantly later.

As we have seen, a *pluralistic* system of trade unions operates in Hungary, with no single national peak organization. There is a tendency towards organization based upon ideology, with socialist, liberal, Christian and radical union confederations all present. During the first half of the 1990s, most of the union confederations fostered links with one of the political parties.

Most of the successor unions were characterized by continuity of the leadership recruited under communism. As the membership figures show, those dissatisfied with these unions and their leaders generally left them and stayed outside the union movement, while the more radical minority joined the new unions. There was no fundamental internal transformation that would have resulted in élite change. The natural point of political orientation for the leaders of the successor unions—particularly the MSZOSZ and the unions within it—thus became the MSZP. This was symbolized in both 1994 and 1998 by electoral agreements between the MSZP and the MSZOSZ and the appearance of union leaders on the Socialists' electoral lists. (In addition, in 1998, union activists from the MSZOSZ took part in the Socialist Party's electoral campaign.)

By contrast, the leaders of the new unions rose almost from nowhere to take the helm of rapidly institutionalizing organizations in control of huge political, organizational and financial resources. This, together with the rapid development of party orientations and party links, laid the foundations for party-political careers for several of these leaders. These rapid career moves led to personal rivalries and conflicts among the leaders of the new unions, contributing to their internal leadership crises and their loss of prestige.

Table 1. Union membership and the 1993 union election results, by type of union

	Membership (1000s of persons)				Election results, 1993 (% of votes won)			
	1990	1991	1994	1995*	works councils	civil-service councils	pensions self-govt.	health-insurance self-govt.
Old unions	3,676	3,190	2,180	1,860	91.0	66.2	71.7	65.7
New unions	311	445	208	140	9.0	31.7	28.3	34.3
Total	3,988	3,635	2,388	2,000	100.0	100.0	100.0	100.0

* Membership figures for 1995 are approximate.
Sources: For membership figures, *HVG*, 14th September 1991: 6; *HVG*, 5th November 1994: 11; *Magyar Hírlap*, 18th May 1995: 5; for election results, *Szakinfo* 49 (16th September 1993).

The balance of power among the unions was reflected in 1993 in the elections to works councils, civil-service councils and the social-security functional self-governments, all of which were held with the participation of the unions.[1] The elections for functional self-governments were, in essence, general 'trade-union elections', in which 39 per cent of the national electorate participated. The elections—particularly those for the works councils—brought a landslide victory for the MSZOSZ and the other three confederations of communist successor unions. By obtaining the majority of the employees' seats on the social-security self-governments, the successor unions gained the power to intervene in the control over institutions that had powers over a substantial part of the state budget as well as significant funds of their own. This was maintained until the summer of 1998, when the new Fidesz-led government abolished the social-security self-governments and re-established government control.

The intense competition that developed between the unions during the first half of the 1990s weakened from the middle of the decade as the advantage of the successor unions—and particularly of the MSZOSZ—stabilized. In 1997, as a result of a political bargain between the Socialist-led government and the MSZOSZ (which fostered good relations and personal links with the prime minister and the MSZP), the use of elections to fill the trades-union posts on the social-security self-governments was ended, and representation by delegation—which had earlier secured dominance for the MSZOSZ—was restored. Thus, the marginalization of the new unions formed at the time of the régime change continued.

2. *Economic Conflicts of Interest*

The trades unions and associations of independents such as hauliers and farmers occasionally go beyond the institutional interest reconciliation system and employ such means of protest as demonstrations, strikes and road blockages. By contrast, the employers' organizations and large companies prefer to operate behind the scenes using the techniques of lobbying. The unions' most important source of power is their organized membership and the potential for mobilization, while that of business and the employers' organizations is given by their economic weight. Certain groups of the self-employed—such as the hauliers and farmers—also possess considerable mobilizational and protest potential. The leaders of unions and of employers' organizations have sought to broaden the range of instruments of pressure available to them also by gaining positions within the political parties.

Conflicts between employers and workers are played out primarily on the factory or company level. These disputes typically concern wages, work conditions and collective agreements, and in cases of more intense conflict can lead to strike action by the workers. But no culture of workplace protest has developed in Hungary comparable to that found, for example, in Poland. The first strike—the coal miners' strike of August 1988—took place during the early stages of the régime change. Strike action was legalized by the 1989 law on strikes. The liberalization of employment law, the privatization of state enterprises and the marketization of the economy all weakened the position of employees. Only a small fraction of the enterprises sign factory or company collective agreements. Though the 1990s have been characterized for the most part by declining real wages, this has not been accompanied by any pronounced strike wave. Only in a small number of cases have workplace protest actions, demonstrations or strikes occurred, and the union confederations have organized marches, attracting 20,000 to 30,000 participants, in only a small number of cases. Most of the strikes that have occurred have been spontaneous factory- or company-level strikes or warning strikes organized by sectoral unions and lasting in general for only two hours (Table 2). Most strikes have occurred in the transport sectors or in mining. The willingness of workers to engage in strike action is reduced also by the fact that the unions have no strike funds that could be used in order to compensate for wages lost through strike action. The data on strike action point to a level of union protest potential that is exceptionally low by international standards.

Table 2. Number of strikes

	1989	1990	1991	1992	1993	1994	1995*	1996*
Warning strikes	11	8	12	8	13	7	n.a.	n.a.
Strikes	8	6	5	5	7	4	10	7

* No separate data were available for warning strikes in 1995 or 1996. The figures given refer to all strikes, including warning strikes. The 1996 figure refers only to the period from 1st January to 20th June.

Sources: For 1989–94, Ladó and Tóth, 1996: 392; for 1995–96, *Népszabadság*, 5th November 1996: 13.

3. Macro-level Interest Reconciliation

The organ of national-level institutional interest reconciliation in the competitive sector in Hungary is the *Interest Reconciliation Council* (*Érdekegyeztető Tanács*, ÉT). Representatives from three sides—the union confederations, the employers' organizations and the government—sit on the council. The ÉT acts as a consultative and decision-making forum and also as a channel for the flow of information between the actors in the sphere of industrial relations. Its competence covers primarily wage and employment questions, but—depending on the efforts of the participants—it can also extend to the most wide-ranging parts of government economic policy. The Hungarian Interest Reconciliation Council is a clearly *neo-corporatist* institution, with a mandate extending beyond the customary role of consultation to include actual powers of co-decision in various spheres.

The political weight of the ÉT, which operates according to the principle of consensus, increased as a result of the role it played in ending the taxi drivers' blockade (the most serious protest action in post-communist Hungary) in the autumn of 1990. From 1992 onwards it became a quasi-governmental institution, and through its decisions it became involved in the process of governmental and legislative decision-making.[2] The government is required to take issues of employment policy before the ÉT and to ensure that the agreements reached there are enacted in government policy and in legislation. (For example, agreements reached in the ÉT on minimum wages or the maximum duration of work are made binding upon all employers by the employment minister's decree.) Each of the three sides in the ÉT committees that discuss these issues possesses the *right of veto* (Tóth, 1993: 53).

Between 1990 and 1994, one-third of the issues on the agenda of the ÉT's plenary session concerned *economic policy*, while more than half involved *social economic* questions. Thus, two different spheres had equal weight in Hungarian macro-level interest reconciliation from its very beginnings: employment relations and social-economic interest reconciliation (Ladó and Tóth, 1996: 82, 84). The broadest areas of economic policy—tax and incomes policy, social benefits, pensions and so on—are also considered by the ÉT, and the decisions it reaches over these issues have considerable influence over governmental and parliamentary decision-making.

The powers of the ÉT extend beyond interest reconciliation to the exercise of classical governmental, executive power: the Labour-Market Committee of the ÉT has at its disposal around HUF 100 billion (about 5 per cent of the Hungarian state budget) coming from the Employment Fund and other sources (Ladó and Tóth, 1996: 70).

Table 3 shows that, despite the employment of the principle of consensus in its activities, the ÉT is able to reach decisions over a high proportion of the issues it considers.

Table 3. Plenary sessions and decisions of the Interest Reconciliation Council

Year	Number of sessions	Employment relations		Social economic questions		Total	
		(A)	(B)	(A)	(B)	(A)	(B)
1990	11	3	100	14	50	17	58
1991	29	22	72	31	45	53	56
1992	14	12	41	34	47	46	45
1993	12	8	12	16	43	24	33
1994	7	12	92	45	62	57	68
Total	73	57	63	140	51	197	55

(A): number of issues discussed by the ÉT under the given heading.
(B): percentage of those issues in which agreement was reached.
Note: The table does not include the discussions over the Social Economic Agreement.
Source: Based on Ladó and Tóth, 1996: 81 and 87.

The bargaining power of the unions on the macro-level is further weakened by their weak representativeness (they represent only the minority of employees), their weak mobilization potential (low strike readiness) and the low level of willingness among their members to follow the unions' lead. Nevertheless, their bargaining power in national-level interest reconciliation remains greater than it is at the factory level.

4. Lobbying

The larger firms, multinational companies and financial and investment groups prefer to use informal methods in order to satisfy their interests. In many cases—such as those of Opel, Suzuki and Audi in the car industry—the arrival of multinational investors and companies in Hungary has been preceded by individual, government-level talks at which tax concessions, risk-reducing state guarantees and other favourable arrangements have been agreed. The representatives of these firms have often been able to gain direct access to the prime minister himself.

Alongside the institutionalized nationwide economic interest-reconciliation system, a process of informal political consultations has developed. This was particularly strong during the period of government led by the Socialists, with their strong ties to the unions. At times, such as during the discussions on social and economic relations in the autumn of 1994, attempts have been made to achieve progress in deadlocked institutional-level talks through informal meetings shielded from the glare of publicity. During the first half of 1997, the union leaders too gained direct access to the prime minister's office. In 1996, shifts in the balance of forces in the battle between the lobbies of two different kinds of collective farms—the agricultural productive co-operatives and the state-owned estates, both of which had good relations with the MSZP and thus, after 1994, with the government—resulted in a change of personnel at the very top of the Ministry of Agriculture.

5. The Direction of Change: From Pluralism towards Corporatism?

The first half of the 1990s was characterized by free competition between interest representatives in the workplace. Nevertheless, the bargaining power of the unions and the level of unionization fell at the plant level and, in most sectors, at the medium level too. Labour relations were liberalized, the co-decision rights of the unions at the plant and company levels were reduced, and the place of the employers was strengthened. At the same time, at the macro-level a national institution of three-sided interest reconciliation was established. This was given powers not only of consultation but also of co-decision, thus giving it classical governmental, executive functions. The ÉT was also able, particularly during the first half of the 1990s, to bring questions of general economic policy into its domain. Besides the ÉT, the national interest-representative organizations were represented also on the social-security self-governments and on a string of other state and semi-state decision-making organs, including the directorate of the Labour-Market Fund, the National Training Council, the councils for labour affairs and regional development, the supervisory committee of the state privatization agency and the board of trustees of the National Holiday Foundation. Thus, a neo-corporatist system emerged (Ory, 1997).

What emerged in the early 1990s was a combination of a pluralistic, competitive interest-representation system and a centralized, neo-corporatist system. However, by the mid–1990s the latter elements had already begun to strengthen. The organizations that entered the ÉT on the employers' and employees' sides at the time the council was formed gained a monopoly over interest representation. The ÉT was in practice closed—new organizations were not admitted into the process of interest reconciliation. Furthermore, the stronger organizations began to push the weaker groups off the council.

The trend in the balance of power between interest-representative organs during the 1990s was that the elements of pluralistic interest representation and competition weakened, while the largest peak organizations—for employees the MSZOSZ and for employers the Hungarian Employers' Association (*Magyar Munkaadói Szövetség*, MMSZ)—moved towards a position of hegemony. The bargaining power of the ÉT *vis-à-vis* the government and the prime minister decreased: since 1995 it has been less able to exercise influence over general economic policy (such as tax and social-security rules). The pluralism of interest representation—at least for employees—weakened on both the local level (that of companies and factories) and the national level (that of the ÉT and the social-security self-governments). Meanwhile, the hegemony of the successor unions—particularly the MSZOSZ—increased on both levels. This tendency is the product of the following factors, among others. First, the decision-making system within the ÉT changed in 1996, such that consensus was no longer required within the employees' side. Second, the process by which the smaller unions were pushed off, or themselves dropped out of, the ÉT began. Third, the Socialist-led government between 1994 and 1998 often negotiated with selected partners outside the institutionalized organs of interest reconciliation. Thus, for example, they often circumvented the ÉT and dealt directly with the MSZOSZ. The MSZP-led government favoured the peak organizations that already existed prior to the régime change, thus promoting the hegemony of the MSZOSZ and the MMSZ.

The result of all of this was that during the 1990s the neo-corporatist character and the monopolization of interest representation in Hungary that could already be seen during the early part of the decade further strengthened. The strengthening of the MSZOSZ is tied also to the strong position that it holds within the MSZP.[3] The so-called trade-union wing of the party leadership and the party's parliamentary group acts as a counterweight to the 'liberals' within the party. Prime Minister

Horn leaned on it when rejecting the restrictive economic programme of the finance minister László Békesi in 1994, and later when removing the minister himself. The MSZP has good relations not only with the MSZOSZ, but also with the employers' MMSZ, which emerged out of the communist-era Hungarian Economic Chamber (*Magyar Gazdasági Kamara*, MGK). Etele Baráth, who was vice-president of both the MGK and the MMSZ, became an MSZP parliamentary deputy in 1994 (Kőhegyi, 1994: 8; Kiss, 1996: 30–31).

In late 1994 and early 1995, the MSZP-MSZOSZ-MMSZ version of the so-called Social Economic Agreement (*Társadalmi Gazdasági Megállapodás*, a plan for a comprehensive economic and social pact) proposed an even stronger tripartite, neo-corporatist structure than existed already.[4] The failure of the agreement and later the monetarist economic policy pursued between 1995 and 1997 significantly weakened the influence of the ÉT over economic policy. Meanwhile, the neo-corporatist infiltration of the interest representatives into the state institutions and organs of decision-making continued.

Notes

1. For further details on the social-security self-governments, see Chapter Five ('Political Elites'), footnote 14.

2. While in the first years of the ÉT's operation, the employers' and employees' organizations formed a single front against the government, following the privatization of many state companies, the ending of state controls over wages and the 1992 liberalization of employment law, the conflict of interests between employers and employees came to the fore and the government became a 'neutral' arbiter on many issues (such as that of the minimum wage).

3. In the parliament elected in 1994, nine leaders of unions belonging to the MSZOSZ sat in the MSZP's parliamentary group (*Magyar Hírlap*, 18th May 1995: 5).

4. In the autumn of 1994, during the negotiations on the agreement, both the employers and the trade unions presented the government with detailed lists of demands that amounted to alternative economic policies (Bossányi, 1994: 13).

Chapter Nine

The Constitutional and Governmental System

1. Constitutional and Governmental Traditions

One of the most important historical features of the Hungarian constitution is that for centuries it was based upon *customary law*. The common law 'selected' from the corpus of written and unwritten law those laws that were to have constitutional strength and to become constitutional traditions. The so-called historical constitution that developed in this way remained in force until the middle of the twentieth century. The continuity of the historical constitution—discounting the short period of 1918–19—was broken only with the end of the Second World War. Act I of 1946 brought to an end the monarchy that had existed for over one thousand years and introduced a republican form of government. Then, in 1949, the introduction of the Soviet-style constitution gave Hungary its first written constitution, which was to remain the basic law of the country for four decades. The 1989–90 democratic transition did not, in formal terms, lead to the adoption of a new constitution. Rather, in broad continuation of the second important characteristic of the development of the historical constitution—that of gradualism—a new constitutional order was created through the fundamental reform of the existing document. Thus, the legal basis of the democratic transition was not created by a constitutional assembly, and the constitution that came into existence as a result of the reforms was not ratified by a referendum. The continuity of the constitution and of the legal system, and the absence of the symbolic moment of constitution-making, weakened the legitimacy of both the constitution and the governmental system that emerged (Paczolay, 1993: 28–33).

Before 1946, the continuity and legitimacy of the monarchy were interrupted only briefly. In this regard Hungarian development deviated from the main direction of French and continental progress: there was no genuine breakthrough for the principle of the sovereignty of the people—or, at least, such breakthroughs as there were were very short (in 1918–19 and in 1945–46). As a result, the parliamentarism that was constructed in Hungary during the nineteenth century was built not upon the principle of popular sovereignty—and the 'empirical popular will' connected with this (Fraenkel, 1991)—but, reflecting the tradition of representation by estates, upon the representative principle.

Thus, the governmental system of the Hungarian state between 1867 and 1944 was characterized by parliamentary government that fell far short of contemporaneous arrangements in Germany or France. It may be better compared to the British parliamentarism of the eighteenth and nineteenth centuries. All the same, parliamentarism it was. Beginning in 1867, the parliament became the location of the search for political compromise, and it was there that the government's political majority was created. In addition, as a result of Habsburg control, the formation of the modern, centralized public administration characteristic of a nation-state occurred relatively belatedly, following the creation of the independent, representative Hungarian parliament in 1867. The public administration formed in this way could not become the exclusive repository of the public interest, and it could not question the primacy of parliamentary government (Magyary, 1942: 133, 380).

The democratic transition of the late 1980s and early 1990s brought a revival in this Hungarian parliamentary tradition. But now the tradition operated, on the one hand, within a republican framework and, on the other hand, under the strong modifying influence of the constitutional and governmental system of the Bonn Republic. The principle of popular sovereignty was established, but only within numerous limiting institutions created according to the model of the German *Grundgesetz* (Basic Law). The changes of 1989–90 brought the victory of liberalism rather than of democratic radicalism: the Rousseauist principle of popular sovereignty—if it appeared at all—did not become dominant; rather it remained subordinate to the liberal concept of the *Rechtsstaat* and the corporatist concept of technocratic self-administration. This pushed the developing governmental system and conception of the state towards the splitting of the internal sovereignty of the state, the narrowing of the institutions of parliamentarism and responsible government, and the extension of the vertical and horizontal separation of powers—particularly during the first half of the 1990s.[1] In this way, the Hungarian conception of the state came to differ markedly from the British conception built upon parliamentary sovereignty and centralized government. It continued to be very different from the *étatiste* French conception, based upon the principle of popular sovereignty. Rather, it came to resemble—and in a certain sense to outstrip—the German conception of the state founded upon divided sovereignty (the 'semi-sovereign state') and on the institutional model derived from it.[2]

From among the three basic governmental systems found in modern democracies—the presidential, the semi-presidential and the parliamentary—the system formed in Hungary with the democratic transition belongs unambiguously to the last. As we shall see, however, Hungarian parliamentarism in the 1990s is a *limited parliamentarism* possessing many unusual characteristics. In order to understand these characteristics, we must outline briefly the principal features of European parliamentarism. It is to this that the next section now turns.

2. *The Development of Parliamentary Government in Europe*

The constitutional monarchies of the eighteenth and nineteenth centuries were built upon the principle of the separation of powers and the *dualism* of the legislature and the executive. The government was responsible not to the parliament but to the ruler who appointed it. The king could dismiss his ministers, while the parliament could not. On the other hand, the members of the parliament—or at least of the lower house—were chosen independently of the executive, and the assent of the majority of parliament was necessary for the passage of laws. All of this corresponded to the contemporaneous conception of the division of power. For the day-to-day operation of the government—if the government did not wish to pass new legislation—the support of parliament was not required. On two points, however, the government was always obliged to secure the support of the parliament: in respect of the budget and of the military. The introduction of new taxes or the recruitment of new draft soldiers was not possible without the assent of the representatives of those bearing the burden—that is, of the parliament.

During the nineteenth century, parliamentarism—that is, the concept, and later the practice of government *responsible* to parliament—gradually gained ground. This was the consequence of two pressures. First, the balance between the parliament that represented the political community (the legislature) and the government of the ruler (the executive) gradually destabilized. Since the parliament represented the entire political community, belief in the rightfulness and legitimacy of government lacking the confidence of parliament—the support of the parliamentary majority—waned. Second, during the second half of the nineteenth century, the building of the modern state began. The tasks of the state multiplied immeasurably, making necessary the acceptance of a growing number of new laws. Likewise, the expenditures of the state experienced extraordinary growth. All of this meant that it became difficult to govern without parliamentary support, and thus the system of parliamentary government gradually emerged. The third change was the extension of the franchise that took place during the nineteenth century, and later the introduction of universal, equal suffrage and the secret ballot. These processes had concluded in Europe—above all in the north and west of the continent—by the 1920s. With the development of parliamentary democracy, the modern political parties became central to political life. That is, modern democracy is, at one and the same time, mass democracy and party-based democracy. Parties create a linkage between the millions of voters and political decision-makers. They mobilize the voters at the time of elections, and they compete for power. The politician in a mass democracy is a party politician: without party support, it is not possible to win elected office. The parties put forward candidates during elections, and it is their representatives who sit in the parliaments. Once the government is unable to secure the *confidence* of the parliamentary majority, the party or parties possessing that majority (50 per cent plus one vote) can form a new government. As these characteristics of the system emerged, the political rule of the party leaders began.

With the development of modern, party-based parliamentary democracy, the relationship between the legislature and the executive that emerged during the eighteenth and nineteenth centuries also changed. Since the party (or parties) winning a parliamentary majority in the elections forms the government, control of the legislature and of the executive both fall into the hands of a single political force or coalition. A *unity of political action* between the government and the governmental majority in parliament has thus arisen. With this, the relative balance that had previously existed between the legislature and the executive has been weakened, and the principle of the separation of powers has—at least in a political sense—been damaged. The political party has become the central institution of politics. The relationship of government and parliament has developed as a function of the emerging *party system.*

Since the appearance of modern parties in parliament, consideration of Montesquieu's formula concerning the separation of the branches of power has been justified only from the point of view of constitutional law; in a political sense it is more likely to mislead (King, 1990: 208). While the presidential system is characterized by the separation of the branches of power, parliamentary systems are marked by the *intertwining* of the legislature and the executive. The principal characteristics of twentieth-century parliamentarism may be summarized in the following (Alemann, 1989: 652–653; Bogdanor, 1987: 408–409).

1. Members of the government are usually chosen from among the parliamentary deputies. Ministers themselves sit in the parliament—that is, the politicians leading the executive are, at the same time, legislators. Unlike in the presidential system, the notion of the *incompatibility* of these functions that stems from the separation-of-powers principle does not operate.[3]

2. The government (and its various members) must carry the confidence of the parliamentary majority—that is, the government becomes dependent upon the parliament. This is the basis of the principle of *responsible government.* In the event of the withdrawal of this confidence, the government falls; a new government is formed, or the parliament is dissolved and new elections are called.

3. A reverse dependency is created by the fact that *at any time* the head of government can—through the head of state—dissolve the parliament and call new elections. Government and parliament are thus mutually dependent upon each other.

4. In parliamentary government, unlike in the presidential system, the posts of head of state and head of government are separated. In the nomination of the head of government, the head of state in general has some legal leeway, though this cannot be used in opposition to the majority in parliament.

5. Within government, the *cabinet principle* operates: the head of government normally rises above the other members of the government, but the various ministers have their own policy competences and in consequence are personally responsible before the parliament. While in the

presidential system the members of the government are responsible only to the head of the executive, in parliamentary government, their responsibility extends also to the legislature, and through a motion of no confidence it is possible for their mandates to be withdrawn.

6. Members of the government are members of the parliament not only in person: in addition, the *government* as an institution is a *privileged participant in the parliamentary legislature*. This role is guaranteed under public law—for example, through the rights to initiate bills and propose the agenda, and the privileged position of government members in the proceedings of parliament. This is a newer element in the fusion of legislature and executive that is characteristic of the parliamentary system.

7. Adherence to the *majoritarian principle* is equally strong both in parliamentary decision-making and with regard to the political responsibility of the government before parliament. It is the basis of responsible government that identical decision-making rules should operate in both cases.

8. A large part is played by the political parties in the creation of political unity between government and parliament: the representatives of the nineteenth century who possessed a free mandate to follow their own beliefs have been replaced in the parliaments of the twentieth century by *disciplined party groups in parliament*. The government is able politically to control the legislature through the party groups that give it its majority.[4]

9. The government and the parliamentary majority co-operate closely and are politically intertwined. The traditional division of power between the branches of the state is replaced by the conflict between the government (the governmental majority) and the opposition—by a new form of the division of powers (a *new dualism*).[5] The confrontation of government and opposition is the basic structuring factor of the modern parliament and political life.

On the basis of all of this, we can state that in modern party-based parliamentarism, in contrast to the former separation of the branches of power, precisely the fusion of those branches has now occurred.

The tradition of Hungarian parliamentarism following 1867 has also conformed to the general trend in European parliamentarism, and this parliamentarism was revived with the democratic transition of 1989–90. The central legislative organ in Hungary, too, is the government—the *functional* intertwining of executive and legislative power has now been carried to the constitutional level. As with most governments operating within parliamentary systems, the Hungarian government and parliament are also intertwined at the level of individuals: in general, the members of the government are at the same time parliamentary deputies. Thus, in Hungary as in other parliamentary systems, the government/parliament conflict has been superseded by the confrontation of *government* (government parties) and *opposition*. This change has already been observed in domestic parliamentary law for more than one hundred years. In two senses, however, today's governmental system in Hungary exhibits limited parliamentarism. In a narrower sense, the features of the system that deviate from the general characteristics of parliamentarism lead to the limitation of the fusion of the executive and the legislature. In a broader sense, the vigorous development in the institutions of the division of power in other parts of the governmental system place further limits upon the operation of parliamentarism.

Before sketching out the principal features of the constitutional and governmental system formed as a result of the democratic transition, the next two sections will, in the interests of understanding those features, consider briefly the pre-conditions of their development. First, we will assess the *political thinking* of the régime change and of the years following it—the ideas and approaches that helped to form the constitutional and governmental system. Second, we will consider the nature of the democratic transition, and within that the political conditions for constitutional reform and the strategies of the political actors who participated in the 'constitution-making' process.

3. Political Thought on the Relationship between State and Society and on the Government

Regarding many of the main goals of the democratic transition, there existed in Hungary a consensus among the political actors who brought the régime change to fruition. In respect of the relationship between state and society, and of the interpretation of the constitution and the governmental system, however, there emerged from the end of the 1980s onwards a range of—partly complementary, partly contradictory—conceptions. In what follows, we restrict ourselves to those conceptions that we consider to have played a formative role with regard to the thinking of the political élite and to public opinion, and thereby to have influenced the formation and operation of the constitution and the governmental system, as well as judgements in respect of that operation.

1. The first is the *parliamentarist* conception of politics, which exercised a considerable influence over the formation of the governmental system, showing the rejuvenation of one of Hungary's most important political and legal traditions. This conception divided, and continues to divide, the political élite that came into being with the régime change. It is perhaps connected also to the fact that parliament, the parliamentary parties and government responsible to parliament entered the centre of political life at this time. The parliamentary tradition fits into the *gouvernementale* and institution-oriented conception of politics (see below and Körösényi, 1996: 81). It is perhaps enough for us to note this well-known characteristic of the Hungarian political system in passing, and in what follows to outline the other tendencies that are visible.

2. The second characteristic of Hungarian political thought is that the ruling ideological current of the régime change was that of *liberalism*. The conversion of liberalism into a ruling concept occurred as a backlash against the communist system, but was at the same time also an effect of broader international forces operating at the time. In contrast to the almost half-century of experience of a centralized party-state that ended the separation of powers and nationalized the economy, liberalism provided a comprehensive ideological framework for shaping the political and economic aims of the transition. The programme of limiting the state; separating the branches of power; depoliticizing the economy, the public administration and other spheres; protecting individual freedoms and creating a constitutional state; as well as creating a capitalist market economy, was formed on the basis of the classical corpus of ideas that had emerged since the eighteenth and nineteenth centuries under the title of liberalism. The setting of these political goals signified a return to the strand of European constitutional and political development that Hungary had sharply deviated from in the 1940s and that had become universal in Western Europe after 1945. As part of the main current of liberalism in Hungarian political thought, the concept of the *constitutional state* was the first to gain the centre ground. The constitutional reforms created a succession of institutions corresponding to those of the modern constitutional state that had emerged internationally after 1945—the constitutional protection of basic rights, a Constitutional Court and a

parliamentary commissioner for citizen rights. These institutions became a part of the constitutional and political system.

3. The third major current of thought behind the democratic transition was that of *nationalism*, which appeared in various forms concerned with the national idea, national independence and the question of the ethnic Hungarians living outside Hungary. The first mass protest of the transition took place in 1988 over the fate of the Hungarians living in Transylvania. The 'national feeling' and its various forms were tied to different party-political orientations, such that, in place of political integration, they at times fed polarizing tendencies that could set liberalism and nationalism against each other. The radical, collectivist current of nationalism represented by the so-called *népi-nemzeti* and national-radical intelligentsia and movement came into conflict with the concept of pluralistic political society and the democratic state built upon the institutional division of power.[6] National radicalism is characterized not by the *gouvernementale* but by the anti-political conception of politics and the state (see below).

4. Alongside the conception of *gouvernementale* liberalism that ended political dictatorship and sought a constitutional state with limited, divided powers, an emancipatory-radical conception of liberalism (which went well beyond liberalism) also appeared and, through the opinion-leading intellectual élite, exercised considerable political influence. The most important concepts of the *gouvernementale* view—hierarchy, power, division of power, the state, government, leadership and governance—are connected above all with the institutions of power and with the mode of the exercise of power. By contrast, at the heart of the emancipatory concept of politics stand the limitation of power, democratization, participation, equality and human rights, which serve the creation of the foundations of a normative-critical approach in political thought and the criticism of every kind of power and power institution. For the emancipatory view, power and politics are somewhat external or 'artificial' things from beneath which it wishes to free the individual and society. It wishes to place politics beneath individual liberty and society. In the emancipatory strand of Hungarian political thought, the concepts of the *gouvernementale*, institution-oriented attitude are pushed to the background and often appear only in the form of the objects of criticism. The emancipatory conception is, at the same time, of strongly normative character. While in the *descriptive* approach, politics is a type of societal activity, in

the *normative* understanding, politics is charged with the creation of proper order and a just society. Politics and morals are inseparable. One of the background assumptions of the normative conception of politics is that the common good or public interest is harmonious—from the beginning, or through individual actions and the cohesion of particularistic interests. Two versions of the emancipatory-normative conception of politics—one institutionalist and one anti-institutionalist—have appeared in Hungarian political thought and have influenced the concept of the state.

5. One of these versions forms a part of the institution-oriented tradition. It regards the bearer of the public interest, however, as being not primarily the political institutions, but rather precisely the *non*-political institutions of the state. In this *depoliticized conception* of the public interest, that public interest is represented against the parties, parliament and the government by the public administration and by technocratic bodies of experts, or the common good is supported by the institutions of the *Rechtsstaat* that control the political sphere (the courts, the Constitutional Court, the ombudsmen). The technocratic/bureaucratic and *Rechtsstaat* currents of thought also differ from each other, but what they have in common is that they detach the concept of the public interest from the democratic representative institutions and the political government, which articulate, represent or formulate the wishes of the political community. They subordinate the principle of popular sovereignty to the principle of, on the one hand, the rule of law, and, on the other hand, technocracy or bureaucracy. More generally, they deny the political character of sovereignty and the state. As regards the actors of the governmental system, this means that the common good is represented not by politicians, but by experts, public servants or lawyers—by the possessors of technical-administrative or legal-moral knowledge. This view implicitly or explicitly rejects the autonomy of politics, of the political government (or parliament) in the formulation of the public interest. A forceful example of the partition of internal and external state sovereignty and the rejection of the political character of that sovereignty is offered by the experience of the first half of the 1990s, when governmental control over the organs of the state dealing with internal order (the police) and external defence (the military) was rejected, leading, to all intents and purposes, to the withdrawal of these organs from political supervision.[7]

The depoliticized conception of the public interest and the common good was formulated by newspaper columnists, political scientists, public lawyers and technocratic reformers, and the strength of its influence is shown by the fact that it has encompassed even politicians. It is routine for politicians to put aside the 'political viewpoint' and pursue or call for 'professional' dialogue, thus seeking to show that it is not 'in reality' a political or party interest—that is, some kind of *sectional* interest—that they have before their eyes, but rather the *public* interest. At other times, where a conflict of interests emerges, the opposing sides are warned away from political influence, and generally they too wish to resolve the issue in a manner 'free from politics'. The 'politics-free' conception of the public interest—which in political theory is self-contradictory—undervalues party politicians, the parliament composed of party politicians and, in particular, the government, and against these over-values the actors and institutions that are supposedly free of political influence. As regards the institutions of the governmental system, the 'neutral' or 'depoliticized' actors—the public administration, the courts and particularly the Constitutional Court—are lauded as the bearers of the public interest. The primacy of *expertise* and *legality* over politics in the formulation of the public interest and the common good goes back in part to the view of politics and the conception of the state of the Prussian and Austrian—but not Hungarian—tradition of the eighteenth and nineteenth centuries: (party) politics and parliament are the world of sectional interests; the common good is represented by *experts* and civil servants. Thus, the common good exists in professional knowledge; it is independent from, and exists prior to, the political processes (Körösényi, 1996).

6. The *anti-political conception* that has emerged in Hungarian political thought does not simply reject the autonomy and role of political institutions in the formulation and representation of the public interest: it would prefer to exclude the whole institutional system of the state from this realm. That is, the public interest is seen not as the product of institutional processes (for example, representation); rather, it gives preexisting content to those processes. It belongs to the nature of the common good understood in this way, that that common good exists directly in society and in the nation independently from, and prior to, institutional political processes. Thus, the common good has an anti-political character. Three forms of this anti-institutional conception of Rousseau's principle of popular sovereignty appear in the Hungarian political thought of

the 1990s. Among other factors, what separates them from each other is the issue of what they regard as the bearer of popular sovereignty and of the common good, and what relationship they see that as having to the state. For one form, the bearer of popular sovereignty and the common good is *civil society*, for another it is the *nation*, and for the third it is the *community of citizens*. The first of these is represented by the social-liberal intellectuals around the Democratic Charter, the second by the national-radical intellectuals of the Hungarian Way Circles *(Magyar Út Körök)* and MIÉP, and the third by the reformers of the Smallholders' Party who seek the institutionalization of the principle of direct democracy (through direct presidential elections and referendums, and by making it possible to withdraw the mandates of members of parliament).

In consequence of the *anti-political* approach that has appeared in contemporary Hungarian political thought, along with its anti-party and anti-state features and the *depoliticized* conception of the common good, the political parties, the party-based parliament and the parliamentary government (the political executive), despite strong domestic parliamentary traditions, have not become the unambiguous repositories of the public interest. While the depoliticized view sees non-party—above all, professional—élite groups as the bearers and legitimate representatives of the public interest and the common good, the anti-political view takes an explicitly *anti-political-élite* approach. The political movements or referendum initiatives against the parliament conceived in the spirit of the anti-political view are anti-institutional and anti-élite in character. And though certain groups of the political élite have used such instruments against their political opponents in order to further their own goals—and in some cases have taken part in their organization[8]—on the whole the dominant political élite keeps its distance from these movements.

7. The radicalized conception of the *principle of the division of powers* that entered the foreground of political thought during the 1990s can also be understood as a separate approach, though it is at the same time an eclectic combination of the various approaches already outlined. It is complemented by the strong preference towards the *principle of consensus*. At the heart of this lies the concept, taken from political science, of consociational democracy *(Konkordanzdemokratie)*, which institutionalizes the principles of both consensus and the division of powers. It thus puts into practice, first, through the institutional realization of the principle of participatory democracy, the programme of 're-conquest' of politics by

society, and, second, the division of the internal sovereignty of the state between the various institutions of the governmental system. The institutions of this division of power besides—and opposed to—the government and the parliamentary majority, are the parliamentary opposition, the head of state, the Constitutional Court, the public administration, the local councils, the 'functional self-governments', the semi-state institutions, and the institution of the referendum. An institutional system that is not only functionally, but also politically, disintegrated to this extent can operate, however, only with broad agreement and co-operation among the political and institutional actors. For this reason it relies upon a *consensus-oriented* approach to politics. The consensus-oriented conception of politics, which is the common denominator for most of the strands of Hungarian political thought mentioned above, can be founded in principle upon two bases—the concept of the public interest or that of the common good. In the depoliticized and anti-political conceptions of the state, consensus rests upon the *ex ante* character of the concept of the common good, while the procedural approaches are built upon the *ex post* nature of the concept of the public interest, which emerges as the product of pluralist democracy. In the first, the common good signifies pre-existing harmony; in the second, the public interest signifies a harmony that emerges by way of a process (Körösényi, 1996).

The various conceptions of the state that have been listed here have at times pushed to the foreground and at times fallen into the background, just as the political actors and institutions carrying them have at times strengthened and at times weakened. But during the decade following the political régime change all of them have exercised an influence over the constitutional reforms, over the conception of the constitution and over the formation and operation of the governmental system.

4. The Emergence of the Democratic Constitutional and Governmental System and the Nature of the Régime Change

Alongside the reigning ideas in political thought, an important influence has been exercised upon the character of the emerging governmental system by the nature of the transition and, within that, by the nature of the constitutional reforms. The democratic constitution that lays the foundations of Hungary as a constitutional state is the result not of the work of a constituent assembly, but of the reforms that took place through a series of amendments to the 1949 constitution. Between 1987 and 1997, seventeen constitutional amendments were passed, nine of these during the two major waves of constitutional amendment in 1989 and 1990 (Kukorelli, 1995: 12). The first wave was the result of the agreements reached in the three-sided talks that were held in 1989 between the Communist Party, the opposition, and the social organizations making up the so-called third side. The second wave was the product of the agreement signed in 1990 following the first free elections by the two largest parliamentary parties—the MDF and the SZDSZ—and gained the support of the majority of the parties within the new parliament.[9] Between 1991 and 1997 a further seven constitutional amendments were passed, in most cases through consensus among all the parliamentary political forces.[10]

Comparing the two principal waves of constitutional revision, it may be stated that the first signified the introduction of *parliamentary rule*, of the minority veto (the requirement for a two-thirds majority) as a general principle of decision-making, and of other counterweights to central power (such as the Constitutional Court). The second brought the maintenance of the legal and political division of powers despite a certain limiting of the minority veto, and simultaneously brought stability for the government against parliament through the adoption of various elements of so-called chancellor democracy. As has been argued already, the prevailing conceptions of constitutionalism and the state were important influences over the course of constitutional reform. An additional influence was the *nature of the régime change*. In what follows, the effects of this will be discussed in relation to the two principal waves of constitutional reform of 1989 and 1990.

Up to the end of 1989, or at least until the self-dissolution of the Communist Party (MSZMP) in October 1989 and the success of the referendum in November of that year, the direction of the political transition remained highly unclear and the success of the democratic transformation remained uncertain. At that time the political fights that brought the régime change to a conclusion were still in full flow. The opposition (the Opposition Roundtable, or *Ellenzéki Kerekasztal*, EKA) did not trust the leaders of the MSZMP, who continued to hold power and among whom popular politicians known to be reformers could be found. Distrust developed among the parties that formed the EKA as well: the radicals feared that the moderate parties of the democratic opposition would ally with the reformers of the MSZMP. Uncertainty continued to surround the outcome of the free, multi-party parliamentary elections that were sought, as well as the possible coalition formation and the emerging political arrangements that would follow those elections. The opposition feared that the MSZMP—which ruled almost every institution of public power—would be able, despite the free parliamentary elections, to preserve its power and protect its position within the executive. It was for this reason that the opposition sought guarantees against the future government and parliament, as with the establishment of the strong Constitutional Court (Halmai, 1993: 23). The more radical part of the opposition considered particularly dangerous the strong presidency and direct presidential elections that were envisaged in the government's earlier plans for constitutional reform (the MSZMP—later the MSZP—possessed a popular reform politician in the person of Imre Pozsgay). It thus preferred the creation of a parliamentary system of government with a weak, indirectly elected head of state.

The fear of excessive governmental and presidential power was a key motivating factor behind the constitutional reforms of the autumn of 1989 that built upon the agreements reached in the three-sided political talks. Thus, the parliament (the legislature) was given exceptional strength *vis-à-vis* the government and the head of state (the executive), and the construction of other power-dividing institutions (for example, the Constitutional Court and the ombudsmen) was begun.

Two elements of the reform strengthened the legislature *vis-à-vis* the executive. One was the extension of the principle of the qualified (two-thirds) majority in parliamentary decision-making, which became almost the guiding principle of the constitution. Previously, a qualified majority had been required only for the amendment of the constitution. The constitutional reform of 23rd October 1989—Act XXXI of 1989—introduced the requirement for a two-thirds majority in three large areas of decision-making. The first was the group of laws *('laws of constitutional strength')* concerning questions of public law and basic rights considered to be of importance. Second, certain questions pertaining to individuals—such as the election of members of the Constitutional Court and the initiation of proceedings for the impeachment of the president—were placed in this category. Third, a qualified majority was prescribed for certain 'statements of fact', such as the declaration of war or of a state of emergency (*Magyar Közlöny*, 1989, no. 74: 1236). The concept of the laws with constitutional force had already played a part in proposals for constitutional and wider legal reform that were drafted by the Ministry of Justice in 1988 and published in January 1989. But we may assume that the participants in the three-sided talks of the summer of 1989 were also motivated to support the introduction of the two-thirds principle by the consideration that, in the event of their being in a minority or opposition situation within parliament, they would then still have considerable power in respect of these laws.

The second factor strengthening the parliament is its unusual degree of protection and independence from the executive. In contrast to general parliamentary practice, the executive in Hungary does not have the capacity to dissolve parliament early (Pokol, 1994: 15–20; Brettschneider, 1994: 481–485; Kovács, 1988; Alemann, 1989: 653).

The agreement between the MDF and the SZDSZ reached in the spring of 1990 was signed within a very different political environment. The political processes of the six months following the constitutional reform of autumn 1989 created a multi-party, polarized political landscape in Hungary. The elections of March and April 1990 resulted in a parliament exhibiting medium levels of fragmentation, and a majority government could be formed only through a coalition of several parties. The combination of the exceptionally strong parliament created by the 1989 constitutional reform and a weak, unstable government gave rise to the fear of *ungovernability* and '*Weimarization*'. The principal elements of the 1990 constitutional reform aimed at the avoidance of these problems; in many respects they thus strengthened the government *vis-à-vis* the parliament.

First, the range of laws requiring a two-thirds majority in parliament was reduced. This had the effect of limiting the veto power of the parliamentary opposition on governmental proposals. The laws still requiring a two-thirds majority are listed in Table 1.

Second, fearing the fragmentation of parliament and the dangers of coalition government—above all, fearing governmental instability—special constitutional mechanisms were introduced that strengthened the position of the prime minister and the whole government, as well as of individual ministers, *vis-à-vis* the parliament. The first aim was served by the introduction of the institution of the *constructive vote of no confidence against the prime minister*, while the second was promoted by the ending of the institution of the *parliamentary vote of no confidence against individual ministers*, that is, by the weakening of the responsibility of members of the government before parliament.[11]

Table 1. Laws requiring a two-thirds majority in parliament, 1996

7 (2) on the legislative process
19 (5) on referendums
19/D on rules applying during states of emergency
19/E (1) on powers immediately exercisable by the government in the event of external attack
20 (4) on allowances for parliamentary deputies
20 (6) on the legal status of parliamentary deputies
24 (3) changing the constitution, and certain decisions determined in the constitution
30 (2) on the allowances of the president of the republic
32/A (6) on the Constitutional Court
32/B (7) on the parliamentary commissioner (ombudsman)
32/C (4) on the National Audit Office
35 (3) on the powers of the government exercisable in situations of exceptional danger
40/A (1) on the responsibilities of the armed forces
40/A (2) on the police
40/B (5) on the limitation of the political activities of non-professional members of the armed forces
44/C on local government
50 (4) on the judiciary
58 (3) on the freedom of travel and settlement
59 (2) on the protection of personal data
60 (4) on the freedom of conscience and religion
61 (3) on the freedom of information of public interest
61 (3) on the freedom of the press
61 (4) on the public-service media
62 (2) on the freedom of assembly
63 (3) on political parties
63 (3) on the freedom of association
65 (3) on the right to asylum
68 (5) on the rights of minorities
69 (4) on citizenship
70/C (3) on strikes
70/H (3) on national service
71 (3) on parliamentary elections
71 (3) on local-government elections
76 (3) on the usage of emblems of the republic

Note: The numbers refer to the articles of the constitution in which the two-thirds requirement is stipulated.
Source: Based on the constitution.

These elements of the reforms clearly reduced the dependence of the government upon parliament. Not all of the changes that were made pushed in the same direction—the two-thirds requirement was *strengthened* in respect of appointments made by parliament, and it was agreed that the presidency would go to a member of the opposition SZDSZ in order to compensate for the narrowing of the two-thirds requirement over legislation. But the general tenor of the changes was clear.

In what follows we briefly summarize those features of Hungary's constitutional and governmental system that are peculiar to the Hungarian political system.

5. The Principal Features of the Constitution[12]

Hungary, both according to the constitution and in the practice of the political system, is a *parliamentary republic.* The parliament is unicameral and the head of state (the president of the republic) is elected by parliament. The government and the parliament stand at the centre of the governmental system. The constitution institutionalizes the principle of the separation of the branches of power. Alongside the *written constitution,* the examination of parliamentary and governmental legislation by the Constitutional Court further limits the power of the government and the parliament, and the institution of the referendum also exists. The stability of the constitution is protected by a minority veto. The state has a *unitary* administrative and organizational structure. It is easy to see that the strongest influence over the formation of the Hungarian constitutional and governmental system was that of the Bonn Republic. The governmental system is *parliamentary,* many features of the structure of which may be compared to the German chancellor system.

Alongside these basic features of Hungary's constitutional and governmental system, however, there exist many characteristics that differ from the practice of the European parliamentary democracies over the last 50–100 years. These peculiarities are linked to the limitation of the *majoritarian principle*—which occurs everywhere to some extent, but which is particularly marked in Hungary—and to the extent and mode of the institutionalization of the separation of the branches of power. In what follows, we will consider the main elements of these unusual features.

1. The first peculiarity of the Hungarian constitutional and governmental system is the *radicalization of the principle of the Rechtsstaat* and the extensive intertwining of law and politics. This is seen in the Constitutional Court's broad powers—by international standards, uniquely broad powers—and in its readiness to engage in activism (see Chapter Thirteen on the Constitutional Court for details). For these reasons the Constitutional Court has become one of the key institutions of the entire political system. The 1989 constitutional reform created the equally unusual institution of the *ombudsman*, which was established in practice in 1995.

2. The second feature is the *dualistic arrangement of the relationship between government and parliament*. The *fusion* of legislative and executive powers, and the intermingling of government and parliament that are characteristic of parliamentary government are found in the Hungarian governmental system too. But they have still not led to a unity of political action between the two branches of the kind seen in most European parliamentary systems. That is, the unusual feature of the Hungarian constitution is that, in many respects, both legal and political, the *dualism* of legislature and executive is maintained. It brings about a separation of the branches of power and an independence of the executive and the legislature from each other that is exceptional among parliamentary systems and that in many ways recalls the institutionalized separation of powers to be found in presidential systems of government. In Hungary, the dependence of the legislature and the executive on each other—the fusion that is characteristic of parliamentarism—is limited in both directions. As has been mentioned, the lack of a right on the part of the executive to dissolve the legislature increases the independence of the legislature from the executive, in both constitutional and political senses.[13] Meanwhile, the dependence of the executive on the legislature is limited by the weakening of the responsibility of ministers, of the prime minister, and of the government as a whole to the parliament.[14] The independence that the Hungarian legislature and executive possess in relation to each other resembles the arrangement found not in modern parliamentary systems, but in the traditional constitutional monarchies of the eighteenth and nineteenth centuries and, among today's governmental systems, in the constitutional *dualism* of the presidential system.[15]

3. The third special feature of Hungary's constitutional and governmental system is the *power of the parliament and the parliamentary opposition* created by law and the extensive veto right of the opposition against the

government and the governmental opposition. These characteristics are created by the following: the broad scope of the exclusive legislative domain possessed by parliament;[16] the limited scope of government by decree in comparison with practice in most European democracies (Kukorelli, 1995; Sári, 1993, 1994); the strong parliamentary committee system and the character of parliament as a 'working parliament'; and the so-called two-thirds laws and the requirement for a two-thirds majority for the election of leading state office-holders. On top of these can be added the absence of a right of dissolution for the head of government, which has already been discussed. All of this gives considerable institutionalized power to the legislature against the executive and to the parliamentary opposition against the governmental majority, thus limiting legally governmental action and the mode of operation of parliamentary government.[17] The introduction of the two-thirds rule—that is, the limitation of the majoritarian principle in decision-making—conflicts in principle as well as in practice with the logic of parliamentarism and weakens the parliamentary character of the governmental system.[18]

Because of the features outlined under points two and three, the Hungarian governmental system is one of *limited parliamentarism*. Table 2 summarizes the features of that system that deviate from the main pattern of parliamentarism. The limited character of Hungarian parliamentarism is shown by the fact that, of the nine features of parliamentarism that are listed, six apply to Hungary only to a limited extent.

4. The fourth characteristic of Hungary's governmental system is that the institutionalization of the principle of the division of powers goes beyond the relationship between the executive and the legislature, thereby radicalizing that principle. Further 'counterweights' to the government are created, which similarly limit the power of the parliamentary government.

a) Outstanding among the legally institutionalized counterweights is the *Constitutional Court*. The Hungarian Constitutional Court has the largest sphere of influence of any constitutional court in Europe (Takács 1996: 351), and this is further emphasized by the judges' activist understanding of their role.[19]

b) On occasion, the power of the *head of state* can act as a counterweight to the government—not so much because of the post's legally defined functions, but because of the conception of the post's functions held by its first occupant, Árpád Göncz, and because of his party affiliation. On numerous occasions, the president has interpreted his constitutional jurisdiction more broadly than either the government or the Constitutional Court. This has limited governmental power (in a political as well as institutional sense, since during the first parliament [1990–94] the president's party was in opposition to the government).

Table 2. The general characteristics of parliamentarism and the limits of Hungarian parliamentarism

	General characteristics of parliamentarism	Limits of Hungarian parliamentarism
1.	Intermingling of branches of power (individuals simultaneously ministers and parliamentary deputies)	–
2.	Executive dualism (separation of head of state and head of government)	–
3.	Government responsible to parliament (executive dependent on legislature)	Institution of constructive no confidence; no motion of no confidence against individual ministers
4.	Parliament can be dissolved at any time (head of state dissolves it on initiative of head of government)	Prime minister has no right to initiate dissolution; president has no general dissolution right
5.	Cabinet government (individual ministers responsible to parliament)	No motion of no confidence against individual ministers—they are responsible only to the prime minister
6.	Governmental dominance in the legislature	Governmental dominance limited by minority veto
7.	Decision-making by majoritarian principle	Wide use of two-thirds-majority requirement
8.	Disciplined parliamentary party groups	–
9.	Replacement of separation of executive and legislature by government/opposition dualism	Dualism of executive and legislature in many respects survives

c) The power of parliament and the parliamentary government is limited not only by the written constitution and the Constitutional Court. The power of the representative institutions of democracy is not exclusive. The principle of direct democracy is institutionalized by the *referendum*, which, in comparison with other European parliamentary systems, is an institution of unparalleled legal strength in Hungary. The referendum is an institution with a very broad competence, and it is very easily put in motion: between 1989 and mid-1997, 100,000 signatures had to be collected, and since mid-1997 200,000 signatures have been needed in order to require that a referendum be held.

d) Hungary's constitutional and governmental system is not federal but unitary. Nevertheless, the local-government law of 1990 established a system of *local councils* that are strong by European standards (Kilényi, 1997).[20]

e) Alongside the local councils (in Hungarian, 'territorial self-governments'), a number of so-called *functional self-governments* have also been created during the 1990s. The 'social-security self-governments' placed the operation of pensions and health insurance under the direction of representatives of the employers and employees, while the financial and general accountability of government and parliament over them was maintained.[21]

f) Furthermore, a corporatist economic interest-reconciliation forum—the *Interest Reconciliation Council*—has been established and given formalized, legal status. It has a consultative competence in questions of general economic policy, while in legislation pertaining to labour issues it has a right of co-decision or veto. In a certain sense it is thus equivalent to a second chamber of parliament. (See Chapter Eight for details.)

g) The autonomy of the government in economic policy is further reduced by the broad—though not unlimited—independence of the National Bank of Hungary (*Magyar Nemzeti Bank*, MNB) from the government. The independence of the Hungarian central bank is considerable by international standards: while the central banks of the United Kingdom, France and Italy stood under the direction of the finance minister and the government during the half-century after the Second World War (Grosser, 1994: 402–403),[22] the Hungarian central-bank law of 1991 followed the example of the only exception to the European norm—the German *Bundesbank*. The law made the stability of the currency's value the responsibility of the central bank, and in large measure freed the bank from government control. Nevertheless—again in correspondence with the German model—it made it the normative duty of the MNB to support the economic policy of the government of the day. The position of the MNB *vis-à-vis* the Ministry of Finance is strengthened by the fact that it can exert strong influence and has considerable political weight. In sum, we can say that a 'system of co-decision' has formed in Hungary between the government and the central bank in the direction of monetary policy, and that the MNB acts in this system with significant autonomy as a counterweight to the government (*HVG*, 21st December 1996: 145–149).

b) The replacement of governmental supervision of the public-service media by parliamentary supervision in 1996 again strengthened the system of the division of power. Since then, public-service television and radio have been supervised by the National Radio and Television Commission (*Országos Rádió és Televízió Testület*, ORTT), and the public-service news agency—the Hungarian News Agency (*Magyar Távirati Iroda*, MTI) —has also been brought under parliamentary supervision.

These institutions all increase further the constitutional and institutional division of power in the governmental and the whole political system.

6. Political Counterweights and Division of Power

The system of division of powers and of counterweights established at the level of law is complemented by further elements of power separation at the political and sociological levels. In the preceding chapters we have discussed the fact that Hungary's political élite is sharply divided, as well as the fact—which is partly tied to the first—that a fragmented, multiparty system has emerged and that this has resulted in the creation of coalition governments.

The legal separation of powers becomes a powerful political division in particular when the branches of power and institutions that are separated from each other and set in opposition to each other are in the control of different political actors and different parties. This was the situation in Hungary in particular during the *first parliament* (1990–94): at that time, in a significant number of the institutions set up as counterweights to the government, politicians from the opposition to the right-wing government were in the majority; at the same time, the government coalition did not possess a two-thirds majority in parliament. Party-political division of powers emerged at many points in the system: between the government and the opposition in parliament (because the opposition had a veto right over much legislation and over constitutional amendment); between the government and the head of state chosen from among the opposition Free Democrats; between the government and the local councils, a large number of which were under independent or opposition control; and between the government/parliament and the functional self-governments.

During the *second parliament*, in consequence of the larger government majority that exceeded the two-thirds barrier, these institutions acted as counterweights to the government to a lesser extent. The division of powers was pushed onto political structures within the governmental coalition and thus beyond the legally established institutions. On the one hand, the grand coalition between the MSZP and the SZDSZ made decision-making—or at least voting—easier on matters requiring a qualified majority—if agreement existed between the two coalition parties. Often, however, there was no such agreement.[23] On the other hand, the mode of operation of the government coalition—with a veto right for the SZDSZ within the government—often made decision-making difficult even on issues requiring only a simple majority.[24]

Despite the government's two-thirds majority, the opposition's right of veto or co-decision operated unaltered during the second parliament in many fields, because the government, in the spirit of *consensual* democracy, introduced self-limitations on many questions. Among these were the temporary moratorium on constitution-making, the rules on constitution drafting, the allocation of places on the parliamentary committees, and, through the new parliamentary standing orders, the easing of the process for establishing committees of investigation.

The difference in the political division of power between the first and second parliaments did not change fundamentally the character of the governmental system as one embodying the division of powers. Some of the laws and constitutional amendments passed by parliament after the changes of the summer of 1990 weakened this character, among them the national defence law of 1993, the police law of 1994, and the legal and constitutional changes concerning the referendum of 1997. Others, meanwhile, strengthened it, including the 1990 law on local government, the law of 1993 creating the institution of the parliamentary commissioner (ombudsman), the creation of the 'functional self-governments' in the sphere of social security, the transfer in 1996 of supervision over the public-service media from the government to parliament (through the establishment of the ORTT), and the 1997 law on the judiciary.

During both parliaments there were legal changes that increased the division of powers and changes that weakened it. Nevertheless, the 'divided-powers' character of the Hungarian constitutional republic has not changed at any point during the 1990s.

7. *Summary: The 'Shared Out Republic'*

In consequence of the separation and mutual independence of the branches of power and of the marked limitation on the majoritarian principle brought about by the so-called two-thirds laws and other mechanisms, Hungarian parliamentarism is, in terms of both constitutional law and ordinary politics, *limited parliamentarism.* Strong constitutional limits and counterweights circumscribe the power of the political majority and the government. To these are related the political constraints that depend for their importance upon the distribution of political positions between the parties.

The constitutional order formed on the basis of the constitutional amendments of 1989 and 1990 has, however, proved to be both *stable*, in that the later amendments have not touched its basic principles, and *workable*, in that it has provided genuine rules of the game for the fight between political actors and has satisfied the requirements of governability. On the other hand, its legitimacy, which was already weak at the beginning, has further weakened, and the *legitimacy deficit* has spread to the political élite. From the start, the extra-parliamentary opposition has criticized the constitution, but, increasingly, so too have some of the parliamentary parties (during the first parliament, the Smallholders, and later, because of the 'excessive power' of the opposition, the MDF). During the second parliament various attempts at constitution making were made, only to become mired in conflict, showing that neither the legitimacy of the existing constitution nor the political will to create a new constitution is particularly strong: so far, the political consensus required for this has not emerged. Nevertheless, despite the legitimacy deficit surrounding the constitution, that constitution has become a code orienting the behaviour of the political actors and the operation of the institutions. That is, it fills its basic function in the political system.

Notes

1. There was pressure for independence from the government for an audit office, a central bank, the police, the defence forces and the public prosecutor's office, as well as for independence from political control for 'functional self-governments' in health- and pension-insurance and for public-service television and radio. To a large degree—though in part only temporarily—these ambitions were fulfilled and institutionalized during the first half of the 1990s.

2. Despite the undoubted influence of the 'German model', the differences, too, remain significant. Among these, the greatest difference in the institutional system is the lack of federalism, while as regards political thought the largest difference is that of the lack of constitutional consensus—of the German *Verfassungspatriotismus* (constitutional patriotism).

3. In some modern parliaments, however, the classical dualist principle of the separation of the branches of power has been preserved. An example is the Netherlands, where a deputy appointed as a minister must give up his or her seat in parliament.

4. In order that we gain a realistic picture of the relationship between government and parliament or executive and legislature, the parties and also the *party system* must be examined.

5. Bagehot already wrote that the old separation of the branches of power had been replaced by a new separation: the division between government party and opposition party (Döring, 1994: 336). Luhmann's binary code is also built upon this (Pokol, 1992: 139–147).

6. See footnote 1 in Chapter Two ('Political Parties') for an explanation of the term '*népi-nemzeti*'.

7. Before the acceptance of the 1994 law on the police, for example, the interior minister could not give direct instructions to the national police chief.

8. During the early 1990s, certain politicians and groups within, in particular, the MDF, the SZDSZ and the FKGP, founded or supported radical, anti-institutional political movements outside their parties.

9. The legitimacy of the constitution was weakened by the fact that both waves of constitutional amendment came about as the result of agreements among closed circles within the political élite. While the three-sided talks preceding the first amendments in 1989 took place with the participation of all of the political parties as well as the so-called civil organizations, the MDF–SZDSZ settlement that preceded the second round of amendments was based upon an agreement between the leaders of the two parties alone. Thus, while the leaders of the other parliamentary parties accepted and supported the content of the latter agreement, they criticized it strongly. Some opinion-leaders criticized not only the mode by which the agreement was reached, but also its content, and thus the MDF–SZDSZ agreement gained its place in the political literature and memory under the pejorative title of 'pact' (*paktum*) (see, for example, Kukorelli, 1995: 23).

10. The amendments enacted by Act LXI of 1994 and Act LIX of 1997 were passed without the support of the opposition parties by the government coalition of the second parliamentary cycle, which could alone secure more than the two-thirds majority necessary in parliament.

11. We can regard the fact that parliament cannot vote no confidence in individual ministers as constituting a significant weakening in the responsibility of ministers before parliament. Individual ministers can, however, still be subject to interpellations, and they have a duty to answer questions in, and report to, parliament. Thus, their parliamentary responsibility—in our analysis, and counter to many evaluations—was not abolished *entirely*, and still exists in both constitutional and political senses.

12. For the scope and structure of the constitution, see Kukorelli, 1995: 45 and 47.

13. By contrast, the parliament is able to declare its own early dissolution.

14. According to traditional constitutional theory, the most important instrument of parliamentary control over the executive in a parliamentary system is that of the motion of no confidence, which, if the confidence of the parliamentary majority wavers, can lead to the removal and replacement of the government. In contrast to this stands the presidential system built upon the principle of the separation of powers, where the head of the executive—the president—is not dependent upon the confidence of the legislature.

15. The dichotomy of the separation versus the fusion of powers is perhaps the most important factor differentiating the presidential and parliamentary systems. That is, in the *presidential system* the head of the executive—the president—does not depend upon the confidence of the legislature; he or she obtains his or her mandate not from the legislature, but directly from the electorate, for a limited period of time. Thus, politically, the president is not responsible to the legislature, but rather independent from it. Against this, the Congress likewise receives a fixed-term mandate from the electorate: the president is not able to dissolve it. By contrast, in the *parliamentary system*, the government and the head of the government are politically dependent upon the legislature—that is, upon the confidence of parliament: they receive a mandate only for so long as this confidence is sustained. Meanwhile, this dependence has a counterpart in the right of the executive to dissolve parliament. The mutual dependency of legislature and executive in the parliamentary systems is one of the most important elements of the fusion of the two branches of power. Thus, in summary, while the presidential system is characterized by the separation of powers and the mutual independence and lack of responsibility of the legislature and the executive (that is, by dualism), in the parliamentary system, the executive and the legislature stand in mutual dependency upon each other (fusion). (The general features of parliamentarism, as shown in Table 2, indicate that almost every one of those features promotes the fusion of legislature and executive.)

16. Furthermore, there are no areas that are excluded from the competence of parliament by the constitution; that is, parliament can deprive other state organs of powers.

17. Because of the loosening of the dependence of the government on the parliament, however, none of this leads to parliamentary rule, as occurred in the French Third and Fourth Republics.

18. The *majoritarian principle* in decision-making is a fundamental principle of parliamentarism on which the whole structure of the governmental system rests. The employment of a two-thirds, qualified majority in parliamentary decision-making upsets the basis of parliamentarism. The basis of both basic features of parliamentarism—the *fusion* of legislative and executive powers, and *responsible government* (governmental accountability)—is that the responsibility of government to parliament and decision-making within the legislature are *both* based upon the *majority principle*. Where this is not so—

where the government wins office on the basis of the confidence of a simple majority of parliament while the work of parliament is based upon the principle of a two-thirds, qualified majority—the responsibility and accountability of the government to parliament lose their meaning: in this situation, the government cannot be held accountable for legislation, or for the success or failure or governance. Because of the differing majorities required for the maintenance of the government and for legislation, the unity and fusion of action of the legislature and the executive, too, are loosened.

19. The judgements of the Constitutional Court concerning the conflict between the government and president over their respective powers during the early 1990s somewhat softened the separation of powers in the governmental system and increased the political autonomy of the government and the governmental majority. That is, the Constitutional Court forms a powerful counterweight to the government and parliament within the political system, but the Court's decisions—because of their *gouvernementale* viewpoint—do not threaten to lead towards ungovernability.

20. The government could counter the strong administrative decentralization during the 1990s only with gradually strengthened financial centralization.

21. See Chapter Five ('Political Elites'), footnote 14 for further details.

22. In these countries, central-bank independence became a political question only during the first half of the 1990s, under the influence of the Maastricht Treaty and the preparations for monetary union within the EU.

23. For example, the post of president of the National Audit Office was empty during 1996 and 1997 because the coalition partners could not agree on a common candidate.

24. For example, discussion of the prime minister's recommendation on the legal status of ministers and on the internal restructuring of the government lasted from 1995 until 1997; even then, many points remained unresolved because of the veto of the SZDSZ.

Chapter Ten

The Government

In modern parliamentary systems, the government is able to exercise considerable control over all parts of the state apparatus—from the legislature through the ministries to the public administration. This applies as much to the Hungarian government as to any other. In what follows, we consider the Hungarian government first from the point of view of its legal structure, and second in light of the political factors that influence the manner of its operation. We then focus our attention in particular upon the prime minister and the sources of prime-ministerial power. Finally, we consider in detail how the Hungarian government and prime minister compare with some of their counterparts in Western Europe.

Four governments have been formed in Hungary since the régime change: in 1990, the Antall government; at the end of 1993, the Boross government; in the summer of 1994, the Horn government; and in 1998, the Orbán government (Table 1). The Antall, Horn and Orbán governments were formed following, and as a result of, parliamentary elections, while the Boross government was formed following the death of Prime Minister Antall in late 1993. Our main focus in this chapter will be upon the Antall and Horn governments. The Boross government held office for less than six months, while the Orbán government has only just been formed at the time of writing, and thus it is still too early to analyse it in detail.

1. The Internal Legal Structure of the Government

In legal terms, the internal structure of the Hungarian government is based upon three principles: those of the *prime minister*, of the *cabinet* and of the *department*. These correspond to the *Kanzlerprinzip*, *Kabinettsprin-*

zip and *Ressortprinzip* that have often been seen as lying at the heart of German government. The character and form of particular governments are determined by the priorities among these principles and the methods by which they are institutionalized.

Table 1. Governments in Hungary, 1990–1998

Government	Party composition	Period of office
Antall government	MDF-KDNP-FKGP*	23rd May 1990–12th December 1993
Boross government	MDF-KDNP-FKGP	21st December 1993–15th July 1994
Horn government	MSZP-SZDSZ	15th July 1994–7th July 1998
Orbán government	Fidesz MPP-FKGP-MDF	7th July 1998–

* The FKGP left the coalition in early 1992, though the majority of the party's parliamentary deputies continued to support the government.
Source: Kurtán, 1995: 377.

The Prime-Ministerial Principle: The Pre-eminence of the Head of Government

The legal distribution of powers and rules of political responsibility make the prime minister unambiguously the key member of the Hungarian government. The power of the Hungarian prime minister is unlike that of either his or her weak Italian counterpart, or the dominant British head of government. It may be compared rather to that found in the German system: the prime minister is legally superior to the rest of the cabinet but in reality possesses powers of intermediate strength.

1. One element of this is the particular form that the government's responsibility to parliament takes. Following the German model, the so-called *constructive vote of no confidence* is used, and it is not possible to vote no confidence in individual ministers.[1] These provisions define not only the relationship between government and parliament, but also the relationship between prime minister and ministers within the government: they strengthen the government *vis-à-vis* the parliament, and they increase the weight of the prime minister within the government. Unlike in the case of classical parliamentarism, individual ministers have sanctionable responsibility only to the prime minister, while their respons-

ibility to parliament is more limited. It is not possible to introduce a motion of no confidence against them, but parliament does have at its disposal certain means to ensure their parliamentary responsibility. These include questioning, interpellations, committee hearings and the power to require ministers to report on their activities.

2. A further aspect of the prime-ministerial character of Hungarian government is the fact that the constitution gives the prime minister the right to *formulate the programme of the government*. At the time of government formation, the parliament first votes on the candidate for prime minister and simultaneously on the governmental programme that he or she submits; only after this does the chosen prime minister select the members of his or her government (Figure 1). The prime minister continues to play the key role in the determination of the government's programme and policies after the formation of the government—both within the cabinet and in the public domain. He or she is the leader of the government and is the only person who can make statements in the name of the government concerning all aspects of government policy.

3. One of the most important sources of power for the prime minister is that he or she has a *right of discretion in the choice of ministers*. This stems from the differing methods used for the appointment of the prime minister and of individual ministers. While the prime minister is elected by parliament, the ministers are named by the president on the recommendation of the prime minister. The prime minister can also dismiss ministers (through the head of state); parliament, meanwhile, can replace the prime minister along with the whole of his or her cabinet, but it cannot dismiss individual ministers. The ministers are responsible solely to the prime minister, strengthening the position of the government and the prime minister *vis-à-vis* the parliament.

The Government as a Collective Body

As in other parliamentary systems, the *cabinet principle* acts alongside the leading role of the prime minister as a basic constitutional principle in the operation of Hungarian government. The governmental statutes prescribe that, under normal circumstances, decision-making at government sittings should be by *majority vote* following collective deliberation, and that the governmental position reached should be collectively binding. According to the cabinet principle—as in the traditional British cabinet system—the prime minister is thus only *primus inter pares*. This underlines the importance of the principle of *political loyalty*, as well as the importance of the prime minister's abilities in personnel management and of his or her selection of ministers: only with ministers personally and politically loyal to him or her can the prime minister become a genuine political leader, and only in this way can the political unity of the government be preserved.

The cabinet principle is the formal rule for decision-making at government meetings. This can severely limit the prime minister in the short run: the extent to which the prime minister is able to rise above the cabinet and become its genuine leader depends upon his or her personal leadership skills, skills in personnel management and ability to balance the interests of the various ministries. On the other hand, the prime minister chairs the government meetings, increasing the chances that he or she will be able to have his or her wishes accepted. Formal votes are taken at government meetings only rarely, when clear and sharp disputes arise. In general, the prime minister sums up the discussion, highlights the important elements and *declares* the decision. As a rule, decisions are thus taken by means of so-called *negative voting* (Bánsági, 1996: 153; Verebélyi, 1996: 200).

Despite the formal character of the government as a collective body, the prime minister, as the principal determinant of government policy, can secure his or her wishes in the setting of the agenda of government meetings too—he or she is able to move issues up or down the agenda as he or she wishes. Where conflicts arise between ministers, the opinion of the prime minister is generally decisive. For example, in the debate within the government over the 'Bokros' economic stabilization package of March 1995, once it became clear that the prime minister supported the measures unconditionally, two ministers resigned before the cabinet meeting had even ended (Kóczián and Weyer, n.d.: 143–145).

Depending upon the political balance of forces, the prime minister enjoys a greater or lesser degree of autonomy in the choice and replacement of members of the government. The *cabinet reshuffle* is an accepted and frequently used instrument in the hands of the prime minister for solving personal or political tensions within the government and for restoring or strengthening the political unity of the government. There are no legal restrictions to changes in the government line-up in Hungary:

this is a matter for the discretion of the prime minister. As we will see later, however, political restrictions must be acknowledged. These arise in part because of the coalitional character of government and in part because of party-political and general political limits.

Ministerial Independence: The Departmental Principle (Ressortprinzip)

In accordance with the traditional principle of responsible government, the heads of individual ministries have legally defined responsibilities and jurisdictions. Within their defined territories, they have independent powers and, following from this, political responsibility. Of the two types of ministerial responsibility found in the traditional parliamentary system—responsibility to the parliament and to the prime minister—in Hungary, as a result of the constructive vote of no confidence, only the second is strong (it is the only one carrying an element of sanction—that of dismissal). This strengthens the position of the ministers *vis-à-vis* the parliament, but at the same time it also increases the importance of loyalty towards the prime minister. Neither this requirement for loyalty nor the powers of the prime minister implies that the prime minister can formally dictate to the individual ministers in their own policy domains. Nevertheless, in political terms, the scope for such direction is greater. This is so particularly if the minister concerned is the personal appointee of the prime minister and comes from his or her party; in the case of a minister delegated by a coalition partner, or of a rival to the prime minister who has been integrated into the government, this possibility is more restricted. All the same, the prime minister does have the right to withdraw or restructure the jurisdiction of ministers.

Administrative and legal analyses stress the weakness of *ministerial independence* in Hungary caused by the centralization of decisions on the budget and the narrowing of the decision-making competence of ministers caused by the cabinet character of government. Political and sociological analyses, by contrast, while pointing out the dominant role of the finance minister, emphasize the wider room for manoeuvre possessed by the ministers, and often see those ministers more as the representatives of their ministries or sectors within the government than as the executors of the united policy of the government within the ministries (Lengyel, 1993: 86–94).

In sum we can conclude that in Hungary, from among the prime-ministerial principle (*Kanzlerprinzip*), the cabinet principle (*Kabinetts-prinzip*) and departmental principle (*Ressortprinzip*), in legal terms it is the first that is of greatest importance. For this reason, lawyers often characterize government in Hungary as prime-ministerial government (Sári, 1996: 307). But we can understand the real power of the government and the prime minister only after considering political as well as legal factors. That is, the relationship of the three principles discussed above depends politically to a large extent upon the nature of the party system, the relationship between the government and the parliamentary groups backing it, the career paths of the members of the government, the coalitional character of the government and the mode of operation of the coalition. As we shall now see, inclusion of these factors in the analysis causes us to modify our view somewhat.

2. The Influence of the Party System and Coalition Government

The party system is a key determinant of whether the governments that are formed are single-party or coalition governments and whether they are majority or minority governments. In Hungary, majority, coalition governments have been formed following each of the three elections since the end of the communist era. We begin this section by considering how.

Government Formation

In legal terms, the prime minister in Hungary is—on the recommendation of the president—elected, but not selected, by the parliament. The prime minister is selected by the party obtaining the largest number of seats in the elections. Following the elections of 1990, 1994 and 1998, the identity of the prime minister had already been decided before the first session of the new parliament was held.

Indeed, the parties participate in elections with a candidate for prime minister already more or less clearly determined. In consequence of this and of political conventions that have been strengthened through the actions of the president, the identity of the prime minister has been almost automatically determined by the results of the elections: following the elections, the president's request to form a government has been simply a formality conforming with convention. Since 1990, it has been an *unwritten rule* of Hungarian politics that the candidate for prime minister of the largest parliamentary party should become the actual prime minister (Figure 1). The unambiguous nature of the political situation has reduced the president's room for manoeuvre to a minimum.

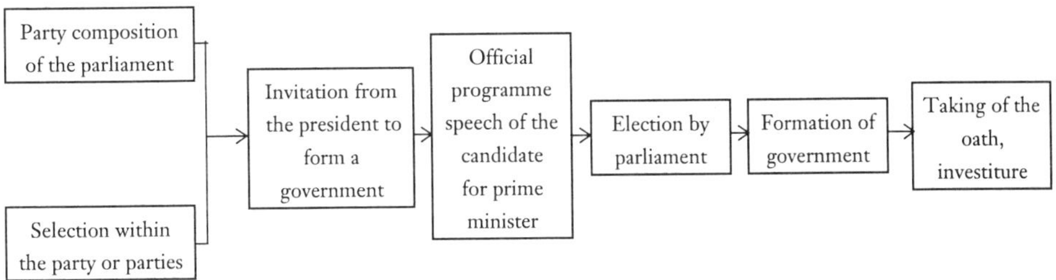

Figure 1. The process of choosing the prime minister

This means also that the choice of prime minister is—as in the formation of all four governments during the 1990s—the result of an *internal party selection* process. This again underscores the *party-based* character of the Hungarian political system.

The Recruitment, Selection and Career Paths of Ministers

Legally speaking, the prime minister elected by parliament has the right of full discretion in the choice of his or her ministers. In consequence of the political logic of the party-based parliamentary system, the most important principles in the selection of ministers are those of *political loyalty and trust*. In both 1990 and 1994, the government was formed from *party politicians* coming from the parliamentary majority. This contrasted with the expectations of a part of public opinion, of certain party politicians (in 1994, particularly from the MSZP), and of certain opinion-leading members of the intelligentsia, all of whom had expected a government of experts.[2] Surprisingly, however, around one-half of the members of the

Orbán government formed in 1998 were non-party experts and not parliamentary deputies (see Appendix C, Table 4).

An indicator of the importance of selection based upon political loyalty is provided by the prevalence of representation based upon party membership or party affiliation. The use of the political principle in recruitment to the government is shown by the fact that a large majority of government members are both party members and parliamentary party politicians, while 'civil' experts among the government ranks are exceptions. Of the fourteen ministers in the Antall government formed in 1990, for example, only two—Ferenc Rabár, the minister of finance, and Béla Kádár, the minister for international economic relations—were not politicians, but experts from the world of academia. Of the remaining twelve, all were party politicians: all were party members, and, with one exception, all were members of parliament (see Appendix C, Table 1). At the time of the formation of the MSZP–SZDSZ government in 1994, all ten Socialist ministers were members of the MSZP and MSZP members of parliament. All three SZDSZ ministers were members of the SZDSZ group in parliament, and one was also a member of the party (see Appendix C, Table 3). The changes in the line-up of ministers between 1994 and 1998 did not change these basic tendencies.

Thus, Hungarian governments are, in accordance with the principle of party-political loyalty and party government, recruited overwhelmingly from among party politicians; the typical precursor for appointment to the government is some kind of position within a political party. Even if the typical political career—with the exception of those in the MSZP—does not begin within a party (since the new parties have only recently been formed), party membership and membership of parliament comprise in the Hungarian political system an important stage that can be postponed but that cannot be dispensed with. The importance of the party principle and party support is shown by the fact that many non-party experts who become ministers—such as Béla Kádár and Mihály Kupa—have felt the need later to become party members or members of parliament. The career paths of others, such as the Free Democrat Gábor Kuncze, who entered the new political ruling class not as founding party members but, later, as experts, and who subsequently became politicians and entered ministerial office, exemplify the same point.

Prime Minister, Party President, Parliamentary Group Leader

The power of the prime minister in parliamentary systems depends in no small part upon the extent to which he or she is able to rally the support of his or her party. The British prime minister is simultaneously the leader of his or her party, and in so far as a leader of the party in parliament exists, he or she is always appointed by the prime minister and is a member of the government (Helms, 1996: 110). It follows from this that the government, the parliamentary group of the governing party, and the extra-parliamentary organization of the governing party become closely united. The German chancellor is also, in general, the president of his or her party, but the leader of the parliamentary group is chosen by the party's parliamentary members themselves. This latter point is, of course, tied to the fact that the traditional dualist conception of the relationship between government and parliament is dominant in German political thinking. In Hungary, the division of functions is similar to the German: the separation of the parliamentary group leader from the government is natural in the dualist tradition of continental parliamentarism, and it ties in with the 'divided powers' character of Hungarian political thought too. On the other hand, the group leader of the largest governing party has been the confidant of the prime minister during all four premierships to date. Still, in other parties—principally in opposition parties, but also, during 1991 and 1992, in the FKGP—it has not always been possible to achieve harmony between the party's extra-parliamentary leadership (and, in the case of the FKGP, its ministers) and the leadership of its parliamentary group.

Political rivals to the party president—or to the simultaneous party president and prime minister—have often emerged from within his own party arguing for the 'division of power'. For example, the opposition to Prime Minister Antall that emerged from within the prime minister's party under the leadership of István Csurka in 1992 wanted to obtain the post of party president; when this failed, it left the party. During the Horn government's period in office, calls for the separation of the posts of prime minister and party president were heard again and again from within the Socialist Party. These calls were aimed at removing important levers of power from the hands of the prime minister.

An important question in the party-based parliamentary system concerns *who is the real leader of a party*, or, in other words, which position bestows the genuine power of party leadership upon its occupant. In the history of European parties, following the separation of the party's parliamentary group and its extra-parliamentary organization, the question has arisen in the following form: is it the leader of the parliamentary group or the leader of the party's (extra-parliamentary) organization (the party president or party first secretary) who is the leading figure within the party, and who could form a government in the event of the party's electoral victory? The first form is exemplified by the British Conservative Party, and the second by the German Social Democratic Party.

Following each of the three parliamentary elections to date, the president of the leading party in the elections has become prime minister. But, for example, in 1990 Fidesz still did not have a single-person leadership. Following the 'collectivist' years—and collective leadership—of the transition period in Hungary, sooner or later every party appointed a single party president (Ilonszki and Punnett, 1993). By 1994 it was already generally the case that the party presidents also led their party's electoral list and campaign. This applied to Fidesz, the FKGP, the MSZP and the KDNP. But at this time the SZDSZ was still wary of such concentration of power, and it kept these two posts separate. Only following the resignation of party president Iván Pető in 1997 and the election to that post of Gábor Kuncze, the party's candidate for prime minister in 1994, did the party present the voters with a clear party leader.

A further important question within the parliamentary governmental system is that of the relationship between the party president on the one hand, and the party's parliamentary group and group leader on the other. When the party is in government, the very stability of that government depends upon this relationship. That is, the political future of the prime minister (and party president) depends upon the loyalty of the parliamentary group and the maintenance of harmony between the parliamentary group and the government. Both Antall and Horn had to confront this problem. If, as in Hungary, the identity of the party president and prime minister is not the same as that of the parliamentary group leader, a key role is played in the creation of political harmony and co-operation by the group leader, who is chosen by the parliamentary party and thus differs in his or her power base from the government members and the party president. In Hungary, particular members of the government frequently participate actively in steering the bills that they propose through parliament and in persuading their parliamentary supporters to accept them. When bills are more important, or politically delicate and disputed, the prime minister too takes part from time to time in persuading the members of the governmental majority of the merits of the government's proposed course of action. For example, in 1995 Prime Minister Horn gave a lengthy speech to a meeting of the parliamentary group of the Socialist Party in the interests of gaining acceptance for the Bokros economic stabilization package (Kóczián and Weyer, n.d.: 148).

The separation of party and parliamentary group leadership and the division of powers that accompanies it have raised the question, in relation to almost every party, of what is the relationship between the two organizations and which constitutes 'the' party (Ilonszki and Punnett, 1993: 23). Almost every party has had to confront this dilemma during the 1990s. For example, in 1993, in the MDF, when the parliamentary group, in opposition to the recommendation of the party presidency, excluded not four but six members from its ranks, one of the members of the presidency resigned his post in protest at what he saw as the deviation of the parliamentary group from the 'viewpoint of the party' (Ilonszki and Punnett, 1993: 24). In 1992 the conflict within the FKGP between the extra-parliamentary party organization and the parliamentary group led first to a split in the party, and later to party 'cleansing'. The party left the government coalition, but the majority of the party's parliamentary members—known as the 'thirty-six'—remained loyal to the Antall government. Following this, only the final means of restoring discipline remained for the party leadership—the exclusion of the thirty-six from the party. This meant that the thirty-six lost the opportunity to run under the Smallholders' banner in the elections of 1994.

The examples of the crisis in the Smallholders and of other individuals who left or were excluded from their parties show that, though the members of parliament and, collectively, the parliamentary groups, possess considerable autonomy, there remain limitations upon this created by the leaderships of the parties' extra-parliamentary organizations, which control the parties' electoral machinery. In consequence of the party-based electoral system and the high costs of entry into parliament for independent candidates and for smaller or new parties, strong or lasting opposition to the party leadership, or resignation from the party, are highly risky, potentially costly steps. A similar moral is to be drawn from the examples of the internal conflict within the KDNP during 1996 and 1997, and the experience of the members of the MDF who left the party to form the MDNP in 1996. The question of everyday politics is, of course, not this, but rather that of how to safeguard the day-to-day relationship and political harmony between the party leadership and the parliamentary group. The story of the 1994 coalition talks also gives an indication of the subordination of the parliamentary group to the extra-parliamentary party. The coalition agreement was signed not by the Socialist and Free Democrat groups in parliament, which formed the government's parliamentary support base, but by the leaders of the extra-parliamentary party organizations, with the backing of the party congresses.

The Party as a Source of, and Limitation on, the Strength of the Prime Minister

When considering the principles that define the legal framework of the operation of the government, we saw that the prime-ministerial principle is of greater importance in Hungary than the cabinet principle or the departmental principle. The most important source of the prime minister's pre-eminence over the government is, however, not legal but *political*: the prime minister enjoys the support of the largest party in parliament (Mény, 1991: 215). The Hungarian prime minister becomes the key actor within the whole governmental system because he or she is the leader of a party that is more or less united in its parliamentary behaviour and that is the election winner and the strongest party in parliament. Since 1990, every party in Hungary has gradually moved from the principle of collective leadership to leadership by a single individual (Ilonszki and Punnett, 1993). Antall, Horn and Orbán all became prime minister as the presidents of their respective parties.

In the operation of the government too, though the cabinet principle does have a legal role, the prime minister is pre-eminent. The role of the prime minister in the determination of the policy direction of the government is legally founded, despite the fact that the constitutional rules are more inclined towards cabinet government (Trócsányi, 1993: 396). The prime minister is the *political leader* and chief executive of the government, who determines and directs the policy of the government. The prime minister is the person who can act in the name of the whole government and who can represent all aspects of government policy in the public sphere and to political actors. He embodies government policy and he speaks in the name of the whole government. The members of the government either follow the policy of the government and the changes therein (which were particularly frequent during the Horn administration) or—through resignation or dismissal—leave the government. The frequent changes in the composition of Hungarian governments show the considerable attrition of personnel that those governments have experienced in consequence of personal or political conflicts within the government and of changes in government policy. Thirty-two ministers or state secretaries left the Antall government as a result of resignation or dismissal, while the number leaving during the first three years of the Horn government was sixteen.

Changes in the basic direction of government policy are in general accompanied by cabinet reshuffles, or at least by some changes of personnel. This shows the operation of the prime minister's *chief executive* function. Whereas in the presidential system the president is the head of the executive—the chief executive—in the classical parliamentary system this role is performed by the prime minister. In Hungarian politics, the prime minister is the chief executive of the government and, through this, of the whole state administration. The prime minister fills every chief-executive function:

1. he or she determines the policy programme of the government;
2. because he or she chairs government meetings and sets the agenda of those meetings, he or she is the main organizer of the activities of the government;
3. he or she issues decrees and directives between government meetings;
4. through the Office of the Prime Minister (*Miniszterelnöki Hivatal*, MEH), he or she harmonizes the activities of the ministries;
5. he or she supervises the ministers and other leaders of the public administration and can require that they report to him or her.

Legally speaking, because of the collegiate character of the government and the independent jurisdictions and responsibility of the ministers, the prime minister has no power of command over the members of the government. This differs from the situation in the presidential system and in strong chancellor democracy. But *politically*, because of the powers just listed and because of his or her patronage power, the prime minister is chief executive. Naturally, the chief-executive functions of the prime minister do not suggest that he or she personally decides all of these questions all of the time. The government programme reflects the ambitions of his or her party and of the coalition partners, the agenda of government meetings is decided largely at the administrative level, decrees may be issued by him or her only rarely, and so on. Rather, they indicate that, as a result of his or her legal powers and political weight, he or she exercises a greater or lesser degree of control in respect of these matters. (Limitations on this control will be discussed below.)

One reason that Péter Boross did not rise to pre-eminence over his government after becoming prime minister in 1993 was that he did not have the authority of party president. Of the four post-communist prime ministers to date, he is the only one to have been in this position. The position of party president is an extraordinary source of power for any prime minister. Alongside the legal factors, this party-political background gives him or her greater weight and elevates him or her to the level of genuine political leader over the cabinet-based government (Ilonszki and Punnett, 1993). It increases respect for the prime minister within the government and it provides the political background within the parliament for the stability of the government and the efficient operation of the government in the legislative process.

But the relationship also operates in reverse: prime-ministerial—or, in the case of smaller parties, ministerial—office strengthens the position of the leader within his or her party, and gives him or her considerable political authority. A governmental career can become the basis for a party career too. A good example of this is provided by the political career of Péter Boross. He entered the Antall government in 1990 as a non-party politician—who did not even have a parliamentary mandate. He was, first, political state secretary (junior minister) in the Office of the Prime Minister, then minister without portfolio with responsibility for the supervision of the secret services. Finally, though still in 1990, he became interior minister. He joined the MDF only in August 1992, but within months, in early 1993, he was elected to the national presidency of the MDF and to office as one of the party's vice-presidents. Without membership in an MDF government, this would have been an inconceivable career path. Following the death of Prime Minister József Antall in December 1993, he was chosen as his party's candidate for prime minister and, still without a parliamentary mandate, was elected prime minister by the parliament. A second example is provided by the career of the Free Democrat Gábor Kuncze. He was selected as the SZDSZ's candidate for prime minister at the time of the 1994 election campaign, though he did not hold the post of party leader. He became interior minister in the Horn government in 1994, and as (a successful) interior minister was elected to the party presidency when Iván Pető resigned from that post in 1997.

Just as a stable, united party backdrop can be an important source of power for a prime minister and for other ministers, so the absence of such a backdrop can act as a political limitation. For example, Prime Minister Antall's stable parliamentary majority was weakened by two developments: first, the departure from the coalition of the Smallholders' Party in February 1992; and second, the political challenge posed within the MDF by the national-radical opposition led by István Csurka. The success of the latter would have endangered not only the prime minister's post as party president, but also the government's majority in parliament.

The support of the party and of the party group in parliament is important—particularly during times of conflict—not only for the prime minister, but also for individual ministers. The lack of the necessary basis in the parliamentary group of the leading government party has weakened the political weight of, in particular, several finance ministers, who have 'come from outside', lacking either party membership or a parliamentary mandate. Neither Ferenc Rabár (finance minister from May to December 1990), nor Mihály Kupa (finance minister from December 1990 to February 1993), nor Lajos Bokros (finance minister from February 1995 to February 1996) was a member of parliament at the time of his appointment, and thus none was a party group member. László Békesi (finance minister from July 1994 to February 1995) was a member of parliament, but he did not maintain a close relationship with the MSZP parliamentary group during his period as minister, preferring to leave that to his political state secretary. In the absence of strong support from the parliamentary party, Békesi was, in consequence of a personal and economic-policy conflict with the prime minister, eventually forced to resign (Kóczián and Weyer, n.d.: 98–102).

These examples also show that the real political limitation upon the prime minister and the government is imposed above all by the prime minister's own party—and the parties of the government coalition—and not by the opposition. The opposition cannot bring about the fall of a majority government or dismiss an individual minister: only the government parties are capable of this. Since the prime minister and the government cannot count upon the support of the opposition, their fate hangs upon the votes of their own party groups within parliament. The position of the prime minister, the political unity and stability of the government and the efficiency of the government's activities are secured by a strong base for the government in the parliament—that is, by the political loyalty of the government parties' parliamentary groups. Thus, in a parliamentary system, if a majority government is formed, the relationship between the government and the parliamentary groups of the government parties and, in the case of coalition government, the relationships among the coalition parties are, in a certain sense, more important than the relationship between the government and the opposition (Körösényi, 1992: 60).

Voting discipline within the Hungarian parliament runs at between 85 and 100 per cent, and is thus as high as in the British or German parliament. Because of this high level of discipline, the prime minister and the government have, in general, possessed the sources of political strength that have been outlined. Thus, the kind of parliamentary domination over the government that occurred in the French Third and Fourth Republics has never emerged in Hungary. On the other hand, the leadership crises that have developed in almost every parliamentary party during the 1990s show that this cannot be counted on to occur automatically. For example, the consequence of the leadership crisis in the Smallholders' Party in 1991 and 1992 was that the re-elected leadership of the extra-parliamentary party organization left the government coalition, while the majority of the members of the parliamentary party remained loyal to the government. The parliamentary majority of the government was maintained only through the split of the majority of the Smallholder members of parliament from the party. In the spring of 1993, the opposite type of party split occurred within the MDF: the party leadership and the bulk of the party's parliamentary group continued to support the moderate-pragmatist policies of the conservative government, while the national radicals left both the party and the centre-right coalition. In early 1996, meanwhile, the liberal-centrist group led by Iván Szabó left the party and its parliamentary group and formed the MDNP.

The fact of coalition, which we generally consider to be a political limitation upon the prime minister, can also become a source of strength.

The introduction of a coalition partner into the government can reduce the dependence of the prime minister upon his or her own party and parliamentary deputies. If his or her party is not united, the prime minister will be at the mercy of the various groups within the party. The party élite of the MSZP at the time of the formation of the government in 1994 was, in terms of its political and personal composition, divided into three or four groups. The internal divisions within the party and the relationship between the party leader and the various groups provide one explanation for the decision to enter a coalition with the SZDSZ. The participation of the SZDSZ in the government strengthened the position of the MSZP president (that is, the prime minister) within his own party and increased his room for manoeuvre: first, he could more easily achieve balance between the rival groups within his own party that might otherwise have endangered his own position; second, conflicts with the SZDSZ could have the effect of increasing the internal cohesion of the MSZP (Körösényi, 1995, 1995a).

Coalition Government

Coalition is always a factor weakening the political unity of the government. Alongside, and independently from, the provisions enshrined in law, a key role is played in the development of the scope for ministerial discretion and of the relationship between the prime minister and the individual ministers by the *parliamentary party system* and the party composition of the government. The parliamentary party system is central in determining, first, whether a single-party or coalition government is formed and, second, whether that government is a minority or a majority government.

When we analyse the influence of the parliamentary party system and the coalitional character of the government upon the operation of the government and upon the division of powers—both within the government and between the government and other institutions—we enter a field in which law has no role to play: here, the laws that operate are the laws of the political game. The constitution and the law at this point do not regulate or limit the behaviour of political actors. Regarding the influence of the party system and the party composition of the government, the most important feature is that, while in *single-party government* political power is concentrated to a large extent in the hands of the prime minister, with *coalition government* power is divided more between, on the one hand, the prime minister and, on the other hand, the leaders of, and the ministers from, the coalition partners. Furthermore, if high parliamentary fragmentation leads to a multi-party coalition in which the participating parties have more or less equal strengths in the parliament—as in, for example, Belgium and the Netherlands—even the identity of the prime minister is likely to be the result of agreement between the parties forming the coalition.[3] In such circumstances, the prime minister plays not so much a political leadership role as a balancing role, seeking agreement and compromise between the coalition partners. If, however, there is, in terms of the distribution of parliamentary seats, a dominant party within the coalition—as in Germany and Austria, and as in Hungary following each of the three parliamentary elections to date—the power concentrated in the hands of the prime minister will be greater than that of the prime minister in the multi-party case, though still less than that of the prime minister of the single-party government (Rose, 1991: 16–19).

Government formation has been relatively straightforward in Hungary following each of the elections since 1990. There has been no need before the formation of any of the governments for the president of the republic to engage in lengthy exploratory talks in order to establish which party in the (moderately) multi-party parliament, or which respected politician, might be able to form a majority coalition. By contrast, this frequently occurs in, for example, Italy and the Netherlands. In Hungary, the division of parliamentary seats has always determined the leading party of the government coalition—in the first elections, the MDF secured 42.5 per cent of the seats; in the second elections, the MSZP won 54 per cent; and in the third elections, Fidesz won 38 per cent (see Appendix B). Earlier, in the chapter on the party system (Chapter Three), we saw that following each of the three elections to date, the party leader entrusted with the task of forming a government (Antall, then Horn, then Orbán) formed a coalition with the party or parties closest to his own in the political spectrum. We saw also that in all three cases a coalition broader than that needed for a parliamentary majority came into being: in the centre-right Antall government, the KDNP was a 'surplus' member; in the centre-left Horn government, the SZDSZ was in the same position; and in the centre-right Orbán government it was the MDF that was not needed to give the coalition its parliamentary majority.

All four of the governments formed to date have been coalition governments (an overview is given in Appendices A and C), even if the relationships between the coalition parties, and between the prime minister and his coalition partners, have been very different in each case. While the political unity and operation of the Antall government rested upon the authority of the prime minister, in the Horn government this function was filled by the coalition agreement, along with the detailed government programme and the procedural and institutional provisions regulating the operation of the coalition (the deputy prime minister from the junior coalition partner, the Coalition Reconciliation Council, and so on). The difference is thus that, while for Prime Minister Antall the coalition created only a *political* limitation, for Prime Minister Horn the agreement signed with the SZDSZ led to *procedural* and *institutional* limitations too. Bccausc of its institutionalized veto right, the SZDSZ had a stronger position within the Horn government than did the smaller parties in the Antall government (the KDNP and the FKGP). (It is, however, an unanswered question whether the stronger position of the SZDSZ was the result or the cause of these institutionalized provisions.) A further difference between the two governments was that, while the parliamentary majority of the Antall government was provided by the MDF's coalition partners, the absolute majority of the Socialists after 1994 meant that the withdrawal of the SZDSZ from the coalition would not have endangered directly the position of Horn as prime minister. Nevertheless, it would appear that the SZDSZ acted as a stronger limitation upon Horn than did the FKGP and the KDNP upon Antall.

Irrespective of these differences, however, every Hungarian prime minister to date has had to deal with the problems of retaining the support of his own party and maintaining the unity of the coalition. These will be discussed separately below.

The Distribution of Posts in the Coalition Government

The coalitional character of the government influences the division of governmental posts both quantitatively and qualitatively. It influences also the selection of government members.

DISTRIBUTION BETWEEN PARTIES • The first decision in the distribution of portfolios concerns the number of ministries that will be filled by each party in the coalition. This is of great importance, since each ministerial post is accompanied, on the one hand, by a multitude of patronage positions and, on the other hand, by a range of power sources and goods for distribution—all of which it is among the goals of the parties to obtain. The proportions of posts going to each party in European coalition governments reflect the proportions of parliamentary seats held by each party or the bargaining strengths of the various parties (Laver and Schofield, 1991; Budge and Keman, 1990). The first of these patterns has been followed in Hungary: after each of the three elections, the number of ministries going to each party has closely reflected the distribution of parliamentary seats.

PREFERENCES REGARDING MINISTRIES • It is not unimportant, however, which ministries are obtained by which party in the coalition bargaining. One reason for this is that the different portfolios differ significantly in their respective weights—there is an informal or formal hierarchy among the ministries. In Hungary today the highest-ranking ministries are the Interior Ministry and the Finance Ministry. Another reason is that particular ministries are considered important by different parties. For example, the Smallholders sought and obtained the Agriculture Ministry in 1990 and the Ministry of Agriculture and Rural Development in 1998, and the Christian Democrats sought the Ministry of Welfare in both years. In the light of this, it is somewhat surprising that the Free Democrats sought the ministries concerned with public administration and with law and order in 1994. (An overview of the distribution of ministerial portfolios among coalition members is given in Appendix C.)

THE SELECTION OF GOVERNMENT MEMBERS • At the time of coalition talks, bargaining concerns not only the government programme and the distribution of portfolios between the parties, but, in general, also the question of which individuals will fill the governmental posts. MDF president József Antall was in an exceptionally strong position in choosing the members of his government *when forming that government* in 1990. The personal authority of Antall, who one and a half years earlier had been offered the presidency of both the Smallholders' Party and the KDNP, ensured that he towered above the other politicians of the parties forming the coalition. He thus enjoyed almost total autonomy in the selection of government members: he was not at all limited by the smaller coalition partners, and his own party limited him only slightly. The formation of the 1994 government was very different. The expectations of the two coalition parties regarding personnel differed markedly from each other. While the Socialists wanted the party having control over a particular ministry to have a free hand in appointments to ministerial and state-secretary posts, the Free Democrats preferred a mutual veto. It was the latter approach that was finally accepted and enshrined in the coalition agreement. The SZDSZ vetoed the appointment of three Socialist nominees for ministerial or state-secretary positions. In 1998, the parties of the government had a free hand in making appointments to their own ministries.

INDIVIDUAL MINISTRIES: SINGLE-PARTY OR DIVIDED CONTROL • A further question concerning the division of powers between the parties forming the coalition is that of whether individual ministries should be exclusive domains for particular parties, or whether the positions within a ministry—in Hungary, the positions of minister and political state secretary—should be split between the coalition parties. The second solution creates a political control, or 'counterweight', within each ministry, such that the division of powers within the government is carried to the level of the individual ministries too.

Of the thirteen ministries of the Antall government in 1990, only two were 'pure' reserves of particular parties (in both cases, of the MDF). A further nine ministries were mixed in their party composition, while in the remaining two, non-party ministers (Rabár in the Finance Ministry and Kádár in the Ministry of International Economic Relations) were accompanied by MDF political state secretaries. In 1994, the Socialists argued against the SZDSZ for the establishment of some mixed ministries—that is, for ministries in which the minister and the political state secretary came from different parties. The final outcome was that in half of the cases—that is, in six ministries—single-party control was established, while four ministries were mixed and the remaining two had a Socialist minister and a non-party political state secretary. In 1998, only 'pure' ministries were formed.

The importance of personnel policy at the time of the formation of the government and the filling of patronage positions underlines the fact that political and personal trust and loyalty are the most important principles of selection in political appointments.

3. The Prime Minister's Sources of Power, and the Political Unity of the Government

In the preceding section we considered the influence of various political factors external to the government—above all concerning the party system—upon the operation and political unity of the government. We assessed the way in which, and the extent to which, the prime minister rises above the government and becomes the political leader of the government, as well as the question of what political obstacles limit the prime minister in achieving this. In what follows we discuss the question of what sources of power the prime minister can derive from his or her position as head of government in respect of the control of government members and the creation of political unity within the government. There is a link between the political unity of the government and the power of the prime minister within the government. The unity of the government, along with the concentration of governmental power in the hands of the prime minister, gives the prime minister a stronger position, while legal decentralization or political fragmentation within the government weakens his or her position. The question of the centralization or decentralization of power within the government depends, however, upon three mutually independent factors: the *legal* situation; the character of the *party system*; and the *personality* and leadership style of the prime minister. The differing roles played by Prime Ministers Antall and Horn can also be explained using these factors: they strengthened the position of the former within the government coalition, while weakening the position of the latter.

Governmental power in Hungary is heavily concentrated in the hands of the prime minister. This is not a matter simply of the constructive vote of no confidence and the inability of the parliament to dismiss ministers: it is related also to a range of further powers, such as the patronage power of the prime minister and his or her ability to determine the structure and size of the government. In what follows we consider the sources of power available to the prime minister.

The Prime Minister's Patronage Power

Among these sources of power, the most important is that of patronage. Within this, appointment to political positions is of primary significance. The Hungarian prime minister has a legal right of discretion in the selection of his or her ministers and political state secretaries. In the choice of ministers, key roles are played by political and personal loyalty and considerations of party tactics and politics. The prime minister must attend continuously to the maintenance of the *political unity* of the government. The most important (and final) instrument of this is the second element of patronage power—the right of dismissal. This right has often been exercised by Hungarian prime ministers. Changes in the personnel of government can be necessitated by frequent changes in government policy and by the need to create or maintain the political and administrative unity of the government. During the three and a half years of the government of József Antall, thirty-two personnel changes took place, of which two-fifths were moves from one post to another within the government. Of these changes, sixteen were at the ministerial level and sixteen at the level of political state secretary. During the first three years of the Horn government, there were sixteen personnel changes, but only a quarter of these were transfers within the government: in three-quarters of the cases, the individual concerned left the government.

One of the most important questions concerning the position of the prime minister within the government—and concerning his or her relationship with the parliamentary groups of the government parties—is that of the extent of the autonomy possessed by the prime minister in the choice of ministers. During the *authority-based* Antall government between 1990 and 1993, the prime minister himself chose the ministers, including those from the smaller coalition partners. By contrast, the autonomy of Prime Minister Horn was limited both by the veto right of the Free Democrats that was enshrined in the coalition agreement, and by the right of the Free Democrats to nominate the ministers for three portfolios—those of interior affairs, transport, and education and culture. This is perhaps also connected with the fact that, while József Antall frequently employed the instrument of the government reshuffle (that is, moving ministers from post to post within the government), Gyula Horn used it relatively rarely. The great majority of the personnel changes in the Horn government occurred as a result of the resignation of the minister concerned. This can be explained by constant personal tensions, by the hectic changes in the policies being advanced by the prime minister, and by the lack of political unity within the government and the government parties.

The Determination of the Structure and Size of the Government and the Distribution of Responsibilities

Legally speaking, the prime minister has a right of discretion not only in respect of the appointment of government members, but also in regard to the determination of the structure and size of the government. The appointment of ministers without portfolio, political state secretaries and titular state secretaries gives the opportunity for the expansion and transformation of the circle of patronage positions. This gives the prime minister an instrument that increases his or her room for manoeuvre in the interests of the maintenance or alteration of the political balance between the coalition parties.

In the case of coalition government, the prime minister can, through the appointment of his or her own confidants as political state secretaries, exercise control over the ministers of the coalition parties. Prime Minister Antall often used this instrument, on eight occasions reshuffling political state secretaries (and on a further five occasions reshuffling ministers) to different positions within the government. Under the Horn government, as was seen in the discussion of the distribution of portfolios, this technique was used by the government parties for the exercise of mutual control.

The prime minister also has the ability to change the *structure of the government*. At the time of the formation of the first post-communist government in 1990, Prime Minister Antall scrapped the National Planning Office and the Price Office, merged the industry and trade ministries, and, out of part of the apparatus of the latter, created the Ministry of International Economic Relations. When the Horn government was formed in 1994, the Ministry of International Economic Relations was, in fulfilment of an electoral pledge, incorporated into the Ministry of Industry and Trade.

In political terms, however, limitations do exist upon the power of the prime minister in this sphere. The SZDSZ, for example, on several occasions vetoed the plans of Prime Minister Horn for the modification of the structure of the government and the changes in the personal composition of the government that that would have entailed.

The Prime Minister's Personal Staff and Advisors

The prime minister, like the individual ministers, has his own private staff—the so-called *cabinet office*—which is organized as a unit within the Office of the Prime Minister. But while in most ministries the personal staff of the ministers rarely numbers as many as a dozen members, the cabinet office of the prime minister is, in both size and function, comparable to the French ministerial *cabinets*. The prime-ministerial cabinet office, employing almost one hundred people, is the prime minister's personal political and organizational staff, the activities of which are difficult to delimit. Alongside certain routine tasks—such as dealing with the correspondence of the prime minister—it carries out its activities according to the personal demands of the prime minister. This is more a type of political management than any form of traditional administrative activity. The cabinet office's work extends from the day-to-day business of the prime minister, through the maintenance of ties with the ministries, parties, parliamentary party groups and other political actors, to the shadowing of the activities of the ministries to monitor compliance with government decisions and the wishes of the prime minister. The leader of the Office of the Prime Minister is a person possessing the confidence of the prime minister.

Legal-Political Conditions and the Role of the Prime Minister

We discussed earlier the conditions in terms of the legal setting and the party system for the pre-eminence of the prime minister over the government. Such pre-eminence is best created by a centralized governmental system and single-party, majority government. Of the European parliamentary democracies, the British is the closest to the ideal-type of this. Against this, both the internal decentralization of governmental power (ministerial government) and the coalitional character of government (stemming from a fragmented party system) weaken the position of the premier. For these reasons, among all of the parliamentary systems in Europe, that of Italy has had the weakest prime ministers.

The power of the Hungarian prime minister of the 1990s has been increased by legal factors, but limited by the coalitional character of government. Following Richard Rose's typology, these circumstances lead to the *juggler* type of prime minister (Table 2).

Table 2. Typology of the role and power of the prime minister according to legal jurisdiction and the party system

	Legal centralization	Legal decentralization
Single-party government	*leader* United Kingdom	*bargainer* Canada
Coalition government	*juggler* The Netherlands, Denmark, Hungary	*symbol* Switzerland, Italy

Source: Based upon Richard Rose (1990: 19).

If we take into account two further dimensions beyond those concerned with law and the party system—namely, first, *personality* and *character as a politician* and, second, motivation for action (policy or career orientation)—the positions of the prime ministers in the typology may change somewhat. Taking these into account, Horn remains very close to the *juggler* ideal-type, but Antall moves from the *juggler* to the *leader* type. Antall, unlike Horn, was able, through his personal authority and leadership style, to run his government as a quasi-single-party government.

Both this move within the typology and the difference in the political characters of the two prime ministers that has been shown above are strengthened by the inclusion in the analysis of the factor pertaining to *political motivation* and the role of orientation towards policy (programme) or position (career). While Horn can be regarded above all as a career- or position-oriented politician, Antall's political character was much more strongly oriented to a programme and values. The career-oriented politician is best described as a *juggler*. He or she is more flexible in changing his or her policy position and subordinates that position to obtaining and retaining office. The pragmatic Horn had almost no independent political position or programmatic goal that he held to for its own sake and that he sought to realize during his period in office. Unlike Antall, he had no goals of social transformation, no 'vision', and was always capable of changing his viewpoint and his policy. His frequent improvisations—which often came as a surprise even to his party and ministerial colleagues and to his narrow circle of confidants—support this characterization.

Among the prime-ministerial, cabinet and departmental principles (*Kanzler-*, *Kabinetts-* and *Ressortprinzip*), the first is legally superior. In the political sense, however, the relationship between the three depends largely upon the influence of the party system, the coalitional character of the government and the mode of operation of the coalition. Both the Antall and the Horn governments were coalitional, but this coalitional character played roles of differing weights in the operation of the two governments; the restrictions delimiting and regulating the operation of the two governments and the range of action of the government worked in somewhat different ways. While the fact of coalition caused little change in the mode of governance of the prime-ministerial Antall government (despite the fact that one of the coalition parties left the government, and a part of the leading government party also left the coalition and formed a new party), this factor played a larger role with the Horn government—at least during the first half of the parliamentary cycle. We cannot state simply that the weight of the *Kabinettsprinzip* and the *Ressortprinzip* rose up under Horn at the expense of prime-ministerial government. A range of party-political conciliation mechanisms were institutionalized within the government (the Coalition Reconciliation Council, the deputy prime minister for the smaller coalition partner, the veto right for the smaller coalition partner over the statutes of the government) that were outside the rules of the constitution and of law, and that cut across or replaced those rules. As regards the cabinet-style operation of the government, in the field of decision-making, a party (minority) veto appeared alongside the majoritarian principle. The nature of the political responsibility of individual ministers changed: the responsibility of the Free Democrat ministers towards the prime minister was reduced, since the prime minister could dismiss those ministers only with the agreement of the SZDSZ leadership. Through all of this, the division of power at the level of party politics moved inside the government and, furthermore, became formally institutionalized. The government was politically more united between 1990 and 1994, and it became both politically and (because of the Coalition Reconciliation Council, the governmental statutes and so on) institutionally more divided after 1994.

But though the Antall government was politically a more united actor, its freedom of political action was severely limited by factors *external* to the government: it did not possess a two-thirds majority in parliament; and, in the sphere of legislation, parliament as an institution acted as a significant counterweight to its power. The Horn government was both politically and institutionally divided and, in consequence of the institutionalized internal 'counterweight' role of the junior coalition partner, was a less united actor. But the external political and institutional factors limiting its freedom of action were weaker. The party-political background to the government was more united. Though the prime minister was limited by strong opposition forces within his own party, party cohesion was still stronger than that of the MDF before 1994: it was not weakened by political desertions as were the parliamentary parties behind Antall. In addition, the parliamentary position of the Horn government was—in consequence of the government's two-thirds majority in parliament, the strengthening of party discipline through the broadening of the instruments of discipline in the parliamentary standing orders, and the rationalization of parliamentary decision-making in the amendment to the standing orders of 1994—more favourable in both party-political and institutional terms.

4. The Position of the Prime Minister and the Government: An International Comparison

In Hungarian politics and Hungarian political science, the strength of the position of the prime minister is often analysed in comparison with the German chancellor—an example of a head of government possessing a particularly strong position. These analyses refer to the two constitutional provisions in the Bonn Republic that strengthen the position of the head of government and that have been adopted in the Hungarian constitutional system: the constructive vote of no confidence against the head of government, and the lack of a vote of no confidence against individual ministers.

These provisions do certainly strengthen the position of the chancellor and of the prime minister. But contrary to a belief prevalent in Hungarian political thinking, the German chancellor is far from possessing a power in the government or in the wider political system similar to that of, for example, the British prime minister. All the same, the frequent references to the chancellorial power of the Hungarian prime minister are not wrong—that power is 'chancellorial' precisely in so far as that term indicates intermediate power for the head of government.

Table 3. The extent of the power of the government and of the head of government

	UK	Germany	Hungary	Italy
Legal/constitutional powers	+ + +	+ +	+ +	+
Government-parliament relationship	+ + +	+ (+)	+	+
Influence of the party system	+ + +	+ +	+ +	+
Political cohesion of the government	+ + +	+ +	+ +	+
Role of the legislative system	+ +	+ +	+	+
Mandate of the head of government	+ + +	+ +	+ +	+
Administrative co-ordination	+ + +	+ + +	+ +	+

Note: + + + = great/strong; + + = intermediate; + = slight/weak

The concept of *chancellor democracy* was first used in German political science in the 1950s to signify, somewhat pejoratively, what many saw as the excessive power of the head of government during the chancellorship of Konrad Adenauer. Later, during the 1980s and 1990s, this was superseded by the concept of 'co-ordination democracy' ('*Koordinationsdemokratie*') (Helms, 1996: 103), which stresses the limits imposed by law and the party system on the very same head-of-government power, and gives priority to the role of the head of government in the co-ordination of various constitutional and political factors and counterweights. Using the concepts of Table 2 above, this approach emphasizes, in place of the dominant *leader* role of the chancellor, the fact that, because of the need to obtain the necessary party support and of the coalitional character of the government, the chancellor rather takes on the role of *juggler*, and, furthermore, that, in consequence of legal decentralization, he becomes more of a *bargainer*. The chancellor system is thus, in German and international political science, far from synonymous with the powerful head of government. The German chancellor instead possesses an intermediate power: his or her constitutional position and political power are, in almost every respect, weaker than those of the British prime minister, but they are, in almost every respect, stronger than those of the Italian premier.

In what follows we refine the rather too general thesis of 'intermediate strength' by considering, in international comparison, seven factors influencing the power of the government and head of government (Table 3). We summarize the key characteristics of Hungarian government through comparison with the three types of governmental power and government operation in Europe that have been mentioned: those of the United Kingdom, Germany and Italy.[4]

Legal and *constitutional* factors promote the British prime minister within the government and *vis-à-vis* the parliament more than they do either the German chancellor or the Hungarian prime minister:

– the British prime minister is the leader not only of the party and of the government, but of the party's parliamentary group as well;

– he or she has the power (found nowhere else) to dissolve the parliament at any time and call new elections;

– he or she can, without parliamentary approval, change the structure of the government and create or disband ministries (in Hungary, the ministerial organization of the government is regulated by law);

– he or she can decide the agenda of the government as he or she wishes (in Hungary this is the power of the government);

– his or her power of patronage is also greater: he or she not only can appoint the members of the government, but also exercises control over the top civil servants in the ministries; in Germany and Hungary, this is the right of the individual ministers.

The Italian premier, like the heads of government of Germany and Hungary, lacks these powers. But he or she is weaker than his or her German and Hungarian counterparts: unlike them, his or her authority over the ministers is limited, since he or she cannot reshuffle the government at will and is hardly able to intervene in the affairs of the individual ministries.

The British government is again the strongest in the *relationship between government and parliament*: the British 'debating parliament' is a much weaker institution than the 'working parliaments' of Germany, Hungary and Italy, and the government rules more powerfully over the legislative process. The power of the German government is further limited by the strong *Bundesrat* (where the government parties may well be in a minority), while the upper houses of the British and Italian parliaments do not act as effective counterweights. In the case of the unicameral Hungarian parliament, the two-thirds laws have the effect of strengthening the legislature as a counterweight to the government. The room for manoeuvre of the three continental governments is restricted by constitutions that are protected by an amendment process requiring a qualified majority, and by the operation of constitutional courts. In the United Kingdom there is no written constitution and no constitutional court, and legislation in all spheres is carried by simple majority. In Germany, the powers of the federal government and chancellor are further narrowed by the federal structure of the state.

The effects of the *party system* point to the same three-way division: the German and Hungarian governments and heads of government lie between their strong British and weak Italian counterparts. In consequence of the two-party system, British governments are single-party in form, and the prime minister maintains a tight grip over the party group in parliament (through the distribution of government positions and through the 'whip' system). Governments in Germany and Hungary have been formed from two or three parties, with the leader of the largest party becoming prime minister. In part because of the coalitional character of the government and in part because of the character of the legislatures as 'working parliaments', the tasks of maintaining control over the government-party groups in parliament and of securing the unity of the government are more difficult. Nevertheless, the German chancellor and the Hungarian prime minister are the clear *leaders* of their respective governments. The Italian prime minister, by contrast, is at the mercy of the leaders, ministers and parliamentary groups of the often large number of coalition parties. Frequently, he is little more than a puppet. He is often not the leader of the largest party, but rather a 'compromise' candidate agreed upon among the competing leaders of the parties forming the coalition, and he cannot reshuffle his government as he wishes. Both legal/constitutional factors and factors pertaining to the party system play a part in the fact that the *control of the government and head of government over parliament* (over parliamentary groups and over the parliament as a whole) is strong in the United Kingdom, intermediate in Germany and Hungary, and weak in Italy. The Italian government has the fewest constitutional and political instruments for the realization of its policies in legislation: the Italian parliament has perhaps the strongest committee system in Europe, and it is here that the least united and least disciplined parliamentary parties are to be found.

The position of the Italian government is further weakened by the extensive powers of the parliament in the process of legislation, which are comparable to those introduced in Hungary at the time of the democratic transition. In the United Kingdom and Germany, meanwhile, the executive has broader powers to issue decrees.

As a result of the influence of the respective party systems, there is a fundamental difference in terms of the *personal and political coherence of the government* between the politically united, prime-ministerial British government and the fragmented, ministerial government found in Italy. In this respect too, the German and Hungarian governments lie between the almost ideal-type extremes of the United Kingdom and Italy.

The cohesion of the government is linked also to the authority of the head of government and the character of his or her mandate. The position of the British prime minister is strengthened by his or her *mandate as head of government*. In consequence of the two-party system and the direct electoral competition between the party leaders, he or she possesses an authority to lead the government of the country almost directly from the electorate. The mandate of the German and Hungarian heads of government from the electorate is weaker than this, but there remains a visible link between the preferences of the voters and the choice of prime minister. There is hardly any such link in the case of the Italian premier: he is nominated to his post by the leaders of the *partitocrazia*.

Governmental cohesion in Italy is weak not only in the political domain, but also in the sphere of *administration*. Fragmentation is increased by the multitude of sectoral and functional ministries: the government generally has more than thirty ministers. Co-ordination of governmental decision-making is minimal and decision-making is segmented: the key power lies within the individual ministries. The government as a collective body is powerless. The capacity of the prime minister in respect of governmental co-ordination, despite the huge prime minister's office, is weak, and it has grown only in the wake of the organizational reforms of the 1980s and the 'régime change' that has affected the entire governmental and political system during the 1990s. The administrative unity of British and German government is much stronger. This is guaranteed in the former case by the decision-making structure, and in the latter case by the powerful chancellor's office with a staff of some 450 individuals.

The German chancellor's office mirrors the whole governmental (ministerial) structure. The whole office is concerned with the tasks of the chancellor, in contrast with the prime-ministerial offices in Italy and Hungary. The Hungarian Office of the Prime Minister (MEH) is equal in size to the German chancellor's office. But, as has been seen, only a small part of it operates under the prime minister; the rest is tied to competences that are located within the MEH and carried out by a minister without portfolio and a political or titular state secretary. Thus, the MEH, in terms of its functions, cannot be compared to the office of the German chancellor (Helms, 1996; Hine, 1993).

Notes

1. Besides Germany, Spain too uses such rules.

2. In modern party-based parliamentary systems, *governments of experts* in general occur only in the face of exceptional external or internal danger or in the event of some kind of catastrophe or political vacuum. An example of this in Hungary is provided by the Németh government of 1989–90. This was not, however, the situation following the elections of 1990. The expectation of a government of experts was a reflection, in part, of the animosity towards parties that can be discerned in Hungarian political culture, and in part of the political ambitions of the 'independent' experts who exercised influence during the 1980s through the economic reform committees, and of the technocrats who held office in the Németh government.

3. Such negotiations concerning the identity of the prime minister were demanded by the SZDSZ from the MSZP at the time of the elections in 1994. Because the MSZP obtained an absolute majority in parliament, however, the influence of the SZDSZ and of the president of the republic was reduced to a minimum, and the identity of the prime minister was decided by the balance of forces within the Socialist Party (Kóczián and Weyer, n.d.: 44, 54).

4. In the cases of the United Kingdom and Germany, we take into account the main features of the governmental systems as they existed between 1950 and 1990; in the Italian case we consider the features of the system in operation until the mid- to late 1980s and not the subsequent changes that have taken place.

Chapter Eleven

Governmental Decision-Making and Control over the Administration

Hungary is not a federal but a unitary state. Nevertheless, its public administration is divided into two parts: the *centralized* state administration that is subordinate to the central organs of state and, in general, ultimately to the government; and the *functional self-governments and local councils* that possess considerable powers and autonomy aside from their executive-type administrative activities. The extent of decentralization in the Hungarian administration—the breadth of the jurisdiction and power of the self-governments and local councils—is considerable—above all in regard to decision-making jurisdictions but also in respect of financial independence. Local councils are particularly strong at the local level, though local-government bodies do also exist at the regional (county) level. Since our current topic is the political system on the national level, we will not deal in detail with the regional and local levels here. We restrict the discussion of political control over the administration in the current chapter to the *centralized* state administration. Similarly, we will not discuss in this chapter the functional self-governments, or the so-called national institutions (the National Bank of Hungary, public-service television, the Hungarian Academy of Sciences and so on), which act as a political-institutional limit on the government as political leader.[1]

1. The Organization of, and Political Control over, the Hungarian Public Administration

The leading body of the entire Hungarian public administration is the government, and the whole state administration is subordinate to it. Governmental control—direction and supervision—over all activities of the state administration is a basic principle of the constitution, and it is the basis of the political responsibility of the government: the government or one of its members can intervene directly in any matter lying within the responsibilities of the state administration; further, the government can place any branch of the administration under its direct supervision, and can create special organs for this purpose.

With regard to political control, the central organs of the state administration are divided into two large groups: ministries and public agencies. The difference between them is partly of political and hierarchical character, something that may be explained in administrative and historical terms. The public agencies generally have responsibilities of an *executive* form. However, the ministries, while having such responsibilities, are simultaneously institutions for *decision-making and the development of political programmes.* The latter thus form part of the so-called political administration, which will be discussed at greater length later.

At the head of each *ministry* stands a minister—a member of the government, and thus a *politician.* Reflecting continental traditions, the minister is the direct leader of the central administrative organ subordinate to him or her. In 1990, the Antall government divided the administrative organs lying under direct political control into thirteen ministries (Appendix C, Table 1). The Horn government in 1994, by merging the Ministry of Industry and Trade and the Ministry of International Economic Relations, reduced their number to twelve (Appendix C, Table 3). The number of people employed in each ministry lies on average between three hundred and six hundred, while the total number of people working in the ministries as of August 1994 exceeded seven thousand (Table 1).

From the point of view of government policy, the ministries are more important than the public agencies: while the ministries are headed by politicians (government members), the public agencies are headed by civil servants. The location of these latter bodies within the administrative hierarchy and the character of the political control exercised over them deviates from the position regarding ministries and takes several forms: they may be supervised by a particular ministry and minister—as in the cases of the Hungarian Office of Energetics and the National Office of Physical Education and Sport—or by the government (by a minister without portfolio, or by the political state secretary of the Office of the Prime Minister)—as in the cases of the Office for Hungarian Minorities Abroad and the Office of National Security.

Table 1. The ministries of the Horn government, 1994.

	Number of Employees	Expenditure (HUF × million)
Office of the Prime Minister	506	1135
Ministry of the Interior	540	1354
Ministry of Foreign Affairs	1620	7623*
Ministry of Defence	325	634
Ministry of Justice	320	379
Ministry of Finance	541	1594
Ministry of Industry and Trade	950	1910
Ministry of Agriculture	511	1594
Ministry of Transport, Communications and Water Management	338	500
Ministry of Culture and Education	610	768
Ministry of Welfare	269	785
Ministry of Labour	220	772
Ministry of Environmental Protection and Regional Development	415	635
Total	7165	19,683

* Excluding foreign representatives, 969.
Source: *HVG*, 6th August 1994: 9.

The number of public agencies is greater than the number of ministries, and it changes frequently. Furthermore, the character of political supervision over them and their place within the governmental-administrative hierarchy are also changeable. One reason for this is that, while the title of ministry is generally the product of a long period of administrative development and signifies the stabilization of the given grouping of issues, the situation with respect to the public agencies is very mixed. Some of them are institutions with long traditions that are integrated into the governmental structure, such as the Central Statistical Office, which operates under direct governmental supervision. Others are organizations serving the *ad hoc* needs and rapidly changing demands of the government of the day, such as the Office of Compensation (Lőrincz, 1993: 43).

The Administrative-Executive Organs of the Public Administration

The executive and managerial organs of the public administration take two principal forms: the local councils and the so-called deconcentrated organs. The *local councils*, besides their own jurisdictions, also have state-administrative responsibilities. The so-called *deconcentrated organs* are the regional organs of the state administration: they operate beneath the central administrative organs (ministries or public agencies) and thus lie within the administrative competence of the government.

The Hungarian public administration operates from the regional-administrative point of view on three levels. The *intermediate and intermediary level* between the central administration and the deconcentrated organs and local councils is traditionally filled by the *counties*. The powers of the county-level assemblies are very modest. In consequence of the evident 'anti-county' political atmosphere that existed when the 1990 local government law was drafted, the responsibilities of regional government were performed during the 1990–94 governmental cycle by the so-called representatives of the republic (*prefects*) and their county offices. The government that came to office in 1994 ended the institution of the representatives of the republic, and in their place established county-level administrative offices that were placed under the control of the Ministry of the Interior.

2. The Classical Separation of Administration and Politics

No great clear-out of personnel occurred within the Hungarian civil service in 1990, despite the fact that not merely a change of government, but rather a change of political régime occurred. The changes among top-level civil servants in 1990 were on the same scale as—and perhaps even less extensive than—those that followed the formation of the Socialist-liberal government in 1994. Of those appointed to the top civil-service posts—the administrative state secretaries and deputy state secretaries, who numbered fifty-two in 1990 and sixty-four in 1994—69.2 per cent in 1990 and 62.5 per cent in 1994 came from within the bureaucracy of the ministries. The proportion of those 'parachuted in' from outside was thus 30.8 per cent in 1990 and 37.5 per cent in 1994 (Table 2). According to another study, from among those appointed between 1990 and 1993, 72 per cent had risen steadily through the ranks through their careers, while 28 per cent leapt suddenly into their top-level posts (Lengyel and Martin, 1996: 27–28).

Table 2. The appointment of civil servants and of 'parachutists' from outside to the posts of state secretary and deputy state secretary following the changes of government in 1990 and 1994

	1990 number	1990 %	1994 number	1994 %
Ministerial civil servants	36	69.2	40	62.5
'Parachutists' from outside	16	30.8	24	37.5
Total	52	100.0	64	100.0

Source: Calculations by the author based upon figures in *HVG* (14th July 1990: 72; 19th November 1994: 112).

Of the fifty-two top civil servants appointed in 1990, eight were party members—four of the MDF and four of the MSZP. Of those appointed in 1994, five were party members—four of the MSZP and one of the SZDSZ—though a further two refused to say whether they were party members. Of those appointed to top civil-service posts within the economic ministries between 1990 and 1993, 58 per cent had worked in the same branch before their appointment and thus were not parachuted into the posts from outside (Lengyel, 1995: 319). Alongside all of this—in Hungary's relatively open administrative personnel system—a high rate of fluctuation has emerged. This fluctuation was higher during the early 1990s among top civil servants than among company managers, though it was no higher than that found in the banking sector (Lengyel, 1995: 317).

In consequence of the régime change of 1989–90, the direct party supervision of the administration and the existence of workplace party organizations both ended. With this, Hungary returned to the twentieth-century European tradition according to which the government—the political head of the executive—and the administration—the entire institutional and personnel apparatus of state administration—are separated from each other. Promotion of civil servants within the state administration is based upon a system of merit: upon expertise (academic qualifications, administration examination), performance (evaluation by superiors) and seniority (length of service).

3. Governmental Control of the Administration: The Legal, Administrative and Personnel Instruments of Political Control

The extent to which, and efficiency with which, the political leadership is able to control the administration to suit its political goals—or, conversely, the extent to which the administration is autonomous and institutionalizes rule by the bureaucracy—depends decisively upon the degree to which, and instruments by which, it rules over the top, ministerial tier of the administration—the *political administration*. There are three different modes or instruments for political control by the government over the state administration. That political control is achieved, first, through *legal rules* (laws or, more often, decrees issued by the government or by government members), second, directly through the political leadership activities of the government (that is, by *individual directives* and circular letters) and third, through *personnel policy* and the power of patronage.

Government through Legal Rules

The form of political control over the administration that touches the administration most generally is control by *legal rules*—by laws passed in parliament, or by decrees issued within the powers of the government and the ministers. In European democracies, the overwhelming majority of legal rules—generally 90 to 95 per cent—are laid down by means of governmental or ministerial decree, and only the remaining 5 to 10 per cent are laws passed by parliament (Sári, 1994: 140). Almost everywhere the extent and significance of rule-making by decree has grown to the detriment of legislative rule-making.

In Hungary, as a counter-reaction to the communist period during which governance was almost exclusively by decree, and as a product of the anti-executive (anti-government) approach that dominates political thought, the constitutional order and the practice of legislation are such as to give parliament greater weight than is often the case elsewhere. All the same, governmental and ministerial decrees account for around four-fifths of all legal rules: 82 per cent between 1990 and 1993. The proportion of rules introduced by means of law is higher in Hungary (at 18 per cent between 1990 and 1993) than is generally the case (Sári, 1994: 154). The Hungarian constitution (Act XXXI of 1989) and the Law on Legislative Process (Act XI of 1987) guarantee the decree rights of the government on the basis of both the 'original' governmental responsibilities listed in the constitution and the powers deferred to it by parliament. The former, however, plays an ever smaller role in the government's decree-making (Lőrincz, 1993: 37).

Government through Powers of Leadership and Direction

The government's activities regarding the control of the state administration are hierarchical. The government can intervene directly in any issues, but in general the various areas of state administration are led and controlled—in accordance with the *Ressortprinzip*—by the ministers, with the help of the ministries (Lőrincz, 1993a: 21). The *minister* leads as an individual. The minister as political leader possesses, first, the right of normative regulation over the whole administrative territory below him or her and the instruments associated with that (the power to issue decrees), and, second, direct or indirect *leadership and direction* powers. That is, alongside the powers of regulation by norms, he or she can issue individual, concrete directives. Within the framework of regulation by norms, the minister can issue both rules that have general application, and decisions, instructions and guiding principles that are binding upon the bodies beneath him or her. Within the context of the concrete, individual directions, he or she can give tasks and individual instructions to the administrative organs directly beneath him or her, or can change decisions reached in those organs (Takács, 1993: 26–28). The minister is able to restructure the organs beneath him or her and to rearrange both responsibilities and personnel. He or she has freedom in how part of the budget of the ministry is used, and is thus able, through the reapportionment of resources, to support certain programmes and restrict others.

Government through Personnel Management: Patronage in the Administration

In addition, the political leadership possesses *patronage* powers with respect to the upper tiers of the administration. Since the members of the political leadership—the ministers—are also the leaders of the central institutions of the administration—the ministries—we turn our attention in what follows primarily to the relationship of the political leadership with the ministerial bureaucracy. It is here that the legal rules—bills and decrees—are prepared and the directives and guiding principles are issued through which the executive apparatus of the administration is controlled.

The relationship of trust and loyalty between the minister and the administrative apparatus beneath him or her constitutes an important element of governability. Since control over the hugely swollen administrative apparatus by a single person is not possible, the problem of governability has generally been solved in European democracies through the creation of a *layer of political officials*, recruited in general from the administration, which is placed between the politician heading the ministry and the permanent administrative apparatus. The members of this layer are, in most cases, chosen by the minister from among those whom he or she trusts both personally and politically. Appointments to these posts constitute the primary sphere of patronage. Changes of personnel in these posts are a product of the political process, not of bureaucratic rules: they are tied above all to the political cycle (changes of government or of ministers) or to major policy changes—that is, to the routine operation of the political process (Körösényi, 1996a).

In Hungary, as in most other European democracies, the system of political bureaucrats is not explicitly formalized. But it has nevertheless developed in practice, above all within the sphere where the ministers have the rights of employers—the rights of appointment and dismissal—over the bureaucrats. These rights give a legal framework to what is, in practice, the institutionalization of political patronage. These political posts may be divided into three groups within the ministerial organization, and six groups altogether.

1. The first is composed of the generally two or three levels of *senior civil servants* who occupy the highest positions within the organizational hierarchy of the ministry beneath the minister. The top three ranks

within the ministries—those of administrative state secretary, deputy state secretary and division leader—have become elements of the patronage system. Across the whole government, this involves more than five hundred posts—the number of administrative and deputy state secretaries in 1994 was sixty-four, while the number of division leaders was around five hundred (*HVG*, 19th November 1994: 115). In practice, usually the first level and sometimes the second level of these top civil-service positions are filled by political appointees. The third level is reached by political patronage only rarely.

2. The second sphere of potential patronage positions is formed by a number of *organizational units under the direct control of the minister* that rise above the hierarchy of the ministry. Personnel, press, public relations and planning divisions often take this form. This sphere has become part of ministerial patronage in some ministries but not in others, and thus no general picture can be offered.

3. The third sphere consists of the personal secretaries and immediate work colleagues of the minister. The most complete and institutionalized form of this sphere is the French system of the ministerial *cabinet*. In Hungary, only very restricted *cabinets* consisting of a few individuals are to be found. Their members are, in general, recruited not from the bureaucracy but from among the previous colleagues of the minister—such as the members of his or her campaign staff—or from among the party's experts. Though the members of the *cabinet* are tied personally to the minister, they nevertheless, in general, have the status of civil servants (*HVG*, 8th October 1994: 115). This again shows that no sharp borderline has developed separating the civil service from the political sphere.

4. The fourth sphere is that of the *personal advisors* or advisory body of the minister. This is not, in general, part of the official machinery of the ministry or of the civil service, and its members often come from outside that machinery. Such advisors are to be found almost everywhere in Europe—prime-ministerial advisors were, for example, particularly influential during the second half of the Thatcher era. A politically significant system of advisors operating alongside the ministers as an important and permanent institution of government exists, however, only in the American administration. In Hungary, as in Europe generally, broad circles of ministerial advisors or advisory bodies have not been established. Some ministers—such as the two SZDSZ ministers for education and culture, Gábor Fodor and Bálint Magyar—have employed such personal advisors.

But only Prime Ministers József Antall and Gyula Horn have experimented with circles of advisors on a larger scale.

5. The fifth group is composed of the functional or regional administrative organizations that lie outside the structure of the ministries but under their direct control. In the cases of some ministries, several dozen such organizations exist. The appointment of their leaders generally falls within the competence of the minister.

6. The final group consists of the members and chairmen of committees and other bodies set up by ministers. The preparation of decisions by the ministries, the making of recommendations and the taking of decisions are not restricted to the civil service machinery and the political leadership of the ministry. Ministers often establish temporary or permanent committees or councils with advisory or co-ordination functions. These bodies offer opinions on plans for reforms or for legislation, and they distribute financial or symbolic resources and support.

There are, in general, several dozen such committees and councils in each ministry. The number of members in each differs widely, generally lying between seven and sixty (Lőrincz, 1993a: 25). Among the members of most committees can be found one or two civil servants who are responsible for the issues under discussion, civil servants from other ministries and public agencies that are affected, representatives of interest groups, professional organizations, parties and civil associations, the leaders of some larger institutions affected by the issues, and one or two experts from the world of academia. These committees make it possible to achieve interest reconciliation before decisions are taken, and give occasion for lobbying, the flow of information, and communication between individual actors within the given sphere. They also have a legitimizing function for the minister and the ministry. The appointment of several hundred committee members, and of the committee chairmen, further extends the patronage powers of each minister.

4. The Process of Governmental Decision-Making and the Organization of the Government

An important question regarding any government is whether it is politically united and has an independent policy programme, or whether government policy is largely subservient to the different aims of the parties forming the government, to the personal ambitions of the ministers, to the pressure of lobbyists and to the goals of the administrative apparatus. Regarding the internal structure of government, this question amounts to whether ministers are the executors of government policy in the ministries or the representatives of the interests of the ministries in the government. In other words: Is there a united government policy or only the aggregation of the activities of the ministries? Is there a unity of policy action across the government?

The question of the unity or fragmentation of government policy raises the problem of *co-ordination*. During the 1980s, the ability of the ministries to realize their own interests in Hungary prevented the development of a unified economic policy. Political economists and economic sociologists have identified as the causes of this the system of so-called branch ministries and the strength of large enterprises and economic lobbies in satisfying their interests. These problems are not, however, unique to the communist systems: they characterize democratic governments too. International comparisons generally identify the American presidential system as the clearest example of strong cohesion and unity, and the Swiss collegiate executive as the example of greatest disunity. Considering the parliamentary governments that resemble more closely the Hungarian system, the British and Italian governments give examples of, respectively, relative unity and disunity, while the German government lies somewhere between them. These differences are explained by a combination of factors pertaining to the constitution, law, administration and the party system. In what follows, we survey the organizations, instruments and institutions of governmental policy co-ordination operating in Hungary.

Political and Administrative Institutions of Co-ordination

The *political* instruments and institutions of governmental co-ordination were considered in the previous chapter. One consists of the powers of political leadership, administration and patronage of the *prime minister*. Another is the classical co-ordinating institution of the cabinet system—the government meeting itself—at which the outcome of disputes between ministers is decided and a united government standpoint is determined. A third possible political instrument in the case of coalition government is the *coalition policy reconciliation forum*, which may exist formally or informally, outside the government, and which may operate not only during talks on coalition formation, but throughout the term of the government. During the Antall government, this function was filled in Hungary, alongside the fortnightly meetings of the political state secretaries, by the prime minister's informal discussions and by the government meetings themselves. During the Horn premiership it was performed by a formalized institution operating outside the organization of the government—the so-called Coalition Reconciliation Council.[2]

Alongside political co-ordination, government involves *administrative* co-ordination—the harmonization of the operation and direction of the huge administrative machines that are separated from each other into departments. In Hungarian government, administrative instruments and institutions of co-ordination exist on three levels.

The first is the level of the public administration and the reconciliation by the public administration of the various programmes and draft bills put forward by the ministries. When, for example, a ministry produces a draft bill, that draft is, as early as the planning stage, sent out for consultation to interested ministries and public agencies, and often to organizations outside the state administration, such as interest representatives, the employers' and employees' sides within the Interest Reconciliation Council and the parliamentary groups of the government parties. On the basis of the remarks of these groups, the ministry generally modifies the draft law, taking into account the opinions of the other affected ministries. Finally, the ministry sends the draft, through the Office of the Prime Minister (MEH), to a meeting of the administrative state secretaries.

The second level of co-ordination has emerged within the government. It involves, first, the development of a hierarchy among ministers and ministries and, second, the creation of narrower bodies that prepare the ground for decision-making such as *cabinets*, committees and advisory councils. The hierarchy among ministries is based upon political and sociological rather than legal foundations.

Traditionally there has always been a certain informal 'inequality' among the ministries. Particular ministries and their ministers traditionally possess greater prestige than do the others. In the current governmental system, following the prime minister it is the finance minister and interior minister who top this hierarchy. The basis of the preeminence of the *finance minister* is his or her control over the budget, which gives what amounts to a veto right over the excess demands of the individual ministers. The Ministry of Finance is always at the heart of the rivalry between ministries competing for funds. During the 1990s, the Ministry of Finance has been the most important ministry in the government, and the finance minister has thus been the most prominent individual within government behind the prime minister. Finance ministers during the 1990s have striven to obtain control over all aspects of governmental economic policy. On the one hand, this has further increased their conflicts with the other economic ministries. On the other hand, in the interests of the protection of political balance within the government and the prevention of excessive strengthening of the finance minister that might threaten the position of the prime minister, it has encouraged prime ministers to create counterweights to the power of the finance minister. One instrument used by prime ministers to counter the rise of finance ministers has been their frequent replacement: between mid–1990 and mid–1997 there were a total of six finance ministers. In 1998, the Ministry of Finance was weakened by the incoming Orbán government: its powers were curtailed, with some being transferred to the Ministry of Economic Affairs and the Office of the Prime Minister.

Alongside the finance minister, the interior minister also heads the governmental hierarchy. In the Antall and Boross governments, the interior minister had the right to deputize for the prime minister. During the Horn government, the Free Democrat interior minister (Gábor Kuncze) was the prime minister's so-called coalition deputy—it was above all he who exercised the right of reconciliation and of veto established in the coalition agreement. It followed from this, for example, that the head of the ministerial *cabinet* at the Ministry of the Interior, like the administrative state secretary of the MEH, received every draft law in advance at the stage of administrative preparation.

The pre-eminence of the prime minister, the finance minister and the interior minister within the government is indicated and strengthened further by the fact that they are the leaders of the three so-called *cabinets* that operate within the government as smaller decision-making bodies. While formally these *cabinets* only prepare the ground for government decisions, in practice they have become decision-making organs: within their competences they possess essentially decisive power; their decisions are generally not debated in depth at government meetings, and instead their recommendations are simply accepted.

The third level of co-ordination respecting the activities of the government is filled by the Office of the Prime Minister (MEH). Because of its important political and administrative role, we will deal with this in greater depth. The Office of the Prime Minister is as large as a ministry—during the 1990s, its staff has numbered between four and five hundred people. It has three functions. First, it organizes the work of the prime minister. Second, it has responsibilities of administration and co-ordination respecting the operation of the government—that is, it is expected to ensure the unity of the governmental apparatus. Third, in organizational terms, the ministers and political state secretaries without portfolio and the prime minister's advisory apparatus both fall within its domain. Reflecting these three functions, the MEH was divided into three distinct and independent organizational sections under the Antall and Horn governments. The Orbán government that entered office in the summer of 1998 plans the reorganization and strengthening of the MEH along the lines of the chancellor's office in Bonn. Further, the leader of the MEH has gained the rank of minister. At the time of writing, however, the new structure of the MEH remains uncertain. Therefore, in what follows, we describe the arrangements that have existed to date.

1. THE CABINET OFFICE • The Cabinet Office is the *personal staff* of the prime minister, responsible for political planning and organization. It is headed by the prime minister's cabinet chief. It is organized into divisions that monitor different areas of government policy and that report directly to the prime minister. The cabinet chief and his or her deputies, who have the rank of titular state secretaries, are participants in government meetings, just as are the government spokesman and the head of the prime minister's press office. The prime minister's secretariat engages in the day-to-day organization of the prime minister's personal matters and programme. The responsibilities of the divisions—of which there were eight in 1993—do not correspond exactly to those of the ministries, and there are fewer divisions than there are ministries.

2. THE ADMINISTRATIVE APPARATUS • The administrative apparatus of the Office of the Prime Minister is led by an administrative state secretary. On the one hand, he or she is, like the administrative state secretaries in the ministries, traditionally the leader of the office. On the other hand, however, as a result of the leadership function of the prime minister, he or she exercises a form of general control over the

entire governmental apparatus (Müller, 1991: 1080). The role of political work in the activities of the administrative apparatus is not as direct as in the case of the Cabinet Office. Its responsibilities include the administration of the preparatory, co-ordinative and executive tasks of the prime minister as government leader, as well as the co-ordination of the activities of the ministries, the preparation of government meetings and the guaranteeing of the execution of government decisions. The administrative state secretary organizes, sets the agenda of, and chairs the meetings of administrative state secretaries that precede government meetings. He or she also recommends an agenda for, and organizes the government meetings themselves. Generally it is at the meetings of administrative state secretaries that it is decided what issues will be placed on the agenda of the government meetings. During the process of legislation, the link between government and parliament is maintained in part by the presence of the members of the government in parliament; but in part it is achieved also through the Office of the Prime Minister and the Office of the National Assembly, and through the fact that civil servants from the MEH and the ministries are present during the parliamentary decision-making process.

3. UNITS HEADED BY MINISTERS WITHOUT PORTFOLIO AND POLITICAL STATE SECRETARIES • Certain political responsibilities that, by virtue of their political importance, are not assigned to a public agency led by a civil servant but rather placed under direct political control, but that nevertheless are not integrated into the ministerial structure, are led or supervised in Hungary by ministers without portfolio or political state secretaries. These fall within the domain of the Office of the Prime Minister. The matters dealt with in this way are, first, those that have not yet found a stable place within the ministerial structure (such as youth policy) and, second, those that, because of their political or strategic importance, are placed in the apparatus lying directly below the prime minister (such as the secret service and press and information policy). From the administrative point of view—as in the administration of wages and staff—the apparatus of these units falls under the administrative state secretary of the MEH (Szilvásy, 1994: 462). Meanwhile, the politicians who lead or supervise the units—the ministers and state secretaries without portfolio—are subordinate to the prime minister.

5. The Mixing of the Roles of Politician and Civil Servant and the Politicization of the Administration

The politicization of the civil service currently taking place to a greater or lesser extent in all democratic states involves two processes. First, pressure is exerted in this direction by the politicization of the role and function of the top-level civil service within the ministries: in place of execution, these officials now prepare and take decisions. Second, the extension of the requirement for political loyalty to the top civil servants in the ministries and the broadening of the patronage power of the political leadership over civil servants also enhances politicization and blurs the division between political and administrative leadership.

In Hungary, too, the function of civil servants is becoming politicized and is penetrating into the classical territories of politics and government. We have already referred to the participation of civil servants in the governmental activities of decision preparation and decision-making (for example, in the formation of legal rules). Between 1990 and 1997, the administrative state secretary leading the MEH, who co-ordinates the activities of the whole government, was a civil servant. He or she prepares government meetings, organizes reconciliation between ministries and, since 1994, represents the government in the parliamentary House Committee. That is, he or she performs clearly political and governmental functions. The law on state leaders passed in the summer of 1997, however, makes it a matter for prime-ministerial discretion whether the leader of the MEH will be given the rank of administrative state secretary as before, or that of minister (*HVG*, 5th July 1997: 11).

The political role and influence of civil servants is not, however, confined to the ministries' work in the preparation of decisions. In Hungary, as in many European democracies, high-ranking civil servants represent and deputize for ministers or political state secretaries—that is, politicians—in political arenas such as government meetings, parliament and parliamentary committees. In the Hungarian parliament, particularly in committee discussions concerning bills, it has become the practice that the ministry proposing the bill be represented not by a politician (the minister or political state secretary) but by a civil servant (the administrative state secretary, deputy state secretary or division leader).

But civil servants participate also directly in the work of the government. The influence of the administrative state secretaries in Hungary has been enhanced in particular by the institution of the Tuesday meetings of administrative state secretaries, which take place in the week preceding the Thursday government meetings. This is the final 'professional filter' before a proposal reaches the government and is thus exceptionally powerful (Kéri, 1994: 84; Verebélyi, 1996; 1996a): anything not supported by the administrative meeting does not go before the government.

The civil servants leading the ministries are present not only in parliamentary committee discussions: before the parliamentary discussion of some bills, they appear also at the meetings of the government parties' parliamentary groups—at the party-political level of policy reconciliation (Bánsági, 1996: 149). During the process of governmental decision preparation and decision-making, civil servants perform a policy reconciliation function in a broader sense too: draft bills are sent for comment and reaction not only to the organs of the state that are affected, but also to the more important social organizations and professional and interest representatives. Civil servants often deputize for government politicians, even in the political limelight. Often it is the civil servants, and not the politicians, who represent, explain and justify the necessity and propriety of the government's legislative proposals before the public. They thus take on a role, and responsibility, in direct political campaigning.

Nevertheless, we must emphasize the limits on politicization in the case of the Hungarian administration: the laws and norms on incompatibility; the low prestige of party politicians and the anti-party atmosphere; the weakness of the penetrative power of the parties; and the dominance of the internal career path in the administration. Compared, for example, with the 1945–47 period or with régime changes in other countries, the politicization of the Hungarian public administration in the 1990s can be regarded as relatively modest.

Notes

1. For more on the functional self-governments, see footnote 14 in Chapter Five ('Political Elites').

2. During the first years of the MSZP–SZDSZ coalition, the Coalition Reconciliation Council met regularly—at times, almost weekly. It sat less frequently during the second half of the government's term.

Chapter Twelve

The Parliament

We have already discussed the role of parliament in the process of government formation. In the present chapter, we consider the operation of the parliament as a legislative, decision-making institution, as well as the parliament's representative responsibilities and the functions of the parliament in respect of governmental oversight and political publicity.

1. The Separation of the Branches of Power and the Two Parliamentary Ideal-Types

European parliamentarism is built upon two traditions that differ from each other in many respects. In one, the parliament is above all the institution for the representation of the people and the bearer of popular sovereignty; in the other, it is rather an institution that assists governance (Döring, 1994: 336). The *dualist model* that embodies the principle of the separation of powers—that is, the institutional and functional separation of legislature and executive—survived for a long time on the European continent. In British parliamentarism, however, the governmental function moved into the foreground from the eighteenth and nineteenth centuries; the primary function of the parliament came to be not legislation, but rather government formation, the creation and maintenance of the political majority necessary for government formation, and the fulfilment of the government's legislative programme. By the mid-twentieth century, parliamentarism had come throughout Europe to signify the system of parliamentary government—that is, the entrance of parliament into the sphere of governance (Döring, 1994: 337–338). The government (executive) and the majority group (the group of the government party) in parliament became intertwined. This invalidated the old concept of division of powers and created a *new type of division of powers*: division between government and opposition (Döring, 1994: 336–338). Despite this change in the function of parliament, the two traditions of parliamentarism—those of the primacy of government and the primacy of representation—continue today to influence political behaviour and understandings of the role of parliamentary representatives.

In part because of these traditions, and in part in consequence of other factors, the role of parliaments within the political system has often been analysed in political science during the second half of the twentieth century in relation to two ideal-types. These two ideal-types are the *debating* parliament of the Westminster model and the *working* parliament of Germany. The government/opposition dichotomy is the principal rule in both models of parliamentarism, but the division of roles and functions between the government parties and the opposition are arranged differently.

In the *debating parliament*, the government, through its solid parliamentary majority, is able in a political sense to control the legislature. The separation of legislature and executive becomes, in political terms, fiction, since the government is formed from the leadership of the majority party in parliament. It controls the legislature in order to ensure the discipline of its parliamentary supporters. The political counterweight to the government is thus in reality no longer the whole parliament, but rather the parliamentary opposition. Thus, on the one hand, the parliament, through the governmental majority, ensures the ratification of the laws (worked out in the ministries) that are necessary for government, while on the other hand, through the activities of the opposition, it becomes a field for criticism of government policy and the place where an alternative government programme can be presented. The essence of parliamentarism here is *political debate*, and the contestation and criticism of government policy by the opposition. The most important institution of the debating parliament is the *plenary session*, where for the most part, including during the discussion of bills, general political debate takes place. This is where the battle is fought between arguments for and against government policy.

In working parliaments it is not simply or primarily political debate, or the contestation and criticism of government policy, or the ratification of bills proposed by the government that takes place, but rather the 'work of legislation'. The solid majority of the government in the parliament does not imply that the parliament becomes an institution of merely formal ratification and political legitimation: the parliament continues to have an important role in influencing the process of legislation. Working parliaments are genuine 'law factories' where, particularly in the committees, bills are discussed in detail and agreement is reached. That agreement often includes not only parliamentary actors, but also pressure groups and interest organizations operating outside the legislature. The committee system covers the whole governmental structure, and the committees possess broad powers. Their weight within the system is considerable: they are capable of exerting substantial influence over the legislative process by modifying the proposals before them. Working parliaments are further differentiated from debating parliaments by the extensive rights—in both legislation and executive oversight—of individual members, of the parliamentary minority and of the parliamentary opposition to the government. Despite the fusion of the executive and the legislature that characterizes parliamentary systems, the old principle of the branches of power as mutual counterweights continues to survive in working parliaments, though in altered form, through the broad powers of the committees and the opposition.

2. *The Hungarian Parliament*

The Hungarian National Assembly (*Országgyűlés*)—whether we look at its operational procedures or at its legislative activities and their results—operates as a genuine 'law factory': by international standards, it passes many laws and decisions. Not only does it discuss and pass many laws and decisions, it also considers a huge number of amendment proposals put forward by individual deputies and by the committees. In the course of the 378 sitting days of the first parliament, the deputies voted 21,500 times. Even so, more than one hundred bills that had already been placed on the agenda were left outstanding at the end of the parliament (*HVG*, 24th September 1994: 105). Between 3rd May 1990 and 31st August 1993, the parliament's twelve standing committees held 2,218 sittings (*Tényék és adatok...*, 1994: 104) and this activity did not decline during the second parliament. Regarding the debating- and working-parliament ideal-types, the Hungarian parliament, as we will see, stands between the two, though in certain respects it is closer to the latter.

In what follows, we sketch out the procedures by which the parliament operates.

The Representative Function and the Legitimacy of the Parliament

The Hungarian parliament is a *representative chamber*—it is built upon the traditional principle of parliamentary representation, and, through universal suffrage, it guarantees democratic political representation. The parliament is unicameral. But, as was seen in the chapter on the electoral system (Chapter Seven), it is formed on the basis of two differing representative principles: of the 386 seats, 176 are filled through single-member districts on the basis of the principle of *territorial (individual) representation*, while 210 are filled through party lists and *party-political representation*. In reality, however, the character of representation has become party-political even in the single-member districts—the great majority of voters in these districts cast their votes for the candidates of the parties. Nevertheless, the legitimacy of parliament (satisfaction with the parliament and with the character and efficiency of representation) is rather low, reflecting the antipathy towards parties and politics that is a part of Hungarian political culture.

Criticisms of the unicameral structure of the parliament are in part an expression of this dissatisfaction. This unicameral structure deviates from pre-1945 Hungarian parliamentary traditions and from the situation in most European countries. Because of the ending of the peerage and the prelature in 1945, the weakening or destruction of the historical institutions (such as the churches), and the absence of federalism or regionalism, the constitutional reforms of 1989–90 did not reinstate the institution of the second chamber. This was despite the fact that certain professionals (constitutional lawyers and political scientists), interest groups and institutions (including the trade unions and the Hungarian Academy of Sciences) pressed for a second chamber built, above all, on corporate lines. The pressure groups with the greatest bargaining power did, however, gain representation in the form of the Interest Reconciliation Council. Even if this is not a second parliamentary chamber possessing rights of legislation, it does have limited (but nevertheless formalized) rights to participate in the legislative process within the spheres of labour and income policy (see Chapter Eight, on interest organizations).

Parliament as a Legislature: Governmental Domination or Parliamentary Rule?

According to the classical conception of democratic popular sovereignty, the legislature takes priority in its relationship with the executive. The parliament convoked on the basis of the principle of popular sovereignty establishes general norms (laws), which the administration can only apply to concrete cases—that is, which it can execute. The liberal conception of the separation of powers emphasizes the autonomy of the legislature and the executive and the balance between the branches of power. But passing laws belongs to the competence of the parliament.

The political science of the last half-century, however, talks at great length of the 'decline of parliaments'. Growth has taken place not only in the political control of governments over the parliamentary legislature, but also in the independent law-making—that is, decree-making—activity of those governments (Mény, 1991: 162–166; Sári, 1994: 140). In most European countries today a total of 5 to 10 per cent of legal rules originate in the legislature. Parliaments, being incapable of restricting law-making by decree, have sought through the establishment of various constitutional safeguards to keep it within an appropriate framework under the supervision of parliament.

The change in judgements on the role of parliaments, which took place in Europe in the space of around a century, occurred in Hungarian political thought in under a decade. The hopes for parliamentarism that emerged in the second half of the 1980s were apparently replaced during the first years of the 1990s by disillusionment. The critics of the parliament have lamented the parliamentary dictatorship of the government and have seen the parliament as a mere voting machine. Public trust in the parliament as an institution has—as was seen in Chapter One, on political culture—sunk to low levels. All the same, the role of the parliament in law-making in Hungary is large by international standards: it is two to three times the 5 to 10 per cent proportion found in Western Europe, standing between 1990 and 1993 at 18 per cent (Kukorelli, 1995: 117; Sári, 1994: 140–141).

Organization and the Division of Labour

The unicameral Hungarian parliament is divided organizationally on the basis of three different principles: it is divided politically into party groups and functionally into committees, while in its operation it is structured by the hierarchy of the decision-making procedure. In charge of the parliament is the speaker (*házelnök*), who comes from the governmental majority. He or she also presides over the House Committee, which is composed of the leaders of the parliamentary party groups. In comparison with the House Committee, which is formed on the basis of the political principle, meetings of the committee chairmen act only as consultative fora. This shows that, of the political and the functional-professional principles, it is the first that has priority—as is the norm in parliamentary systems. The speaker controls the agenda of the parliament, and thus co-ordinates the operation of both the plenary sessions that take and ratify decisions, and the committees that consider matters in greater detail. Within some committees, sub-committees also operate.

As regards the division of time in the Hungarian parliament, the party groups meet on Monday mornings, there are plenary meetings on Monday afternoons and on Tuesdays, the committees sit on Wednesdays and Thursdays, and on Fridays the deputies from single-member districts attend to the affairs of their constituencies.

3. The Passage of Legislation and Resolutions

During the first parliament, 55 per cent of decisions in the legislature pertained to *laws*—the making of which is, in constitutional terms, the main function of the parliament. A further 44 per cent of decisions were so-called parliamentary *resolutions* (*határozatok*) concerning the deputies and the internal agenda or procedures of the parliament, or were decisions of a political character that did not create legal rules (Soltész, 1994a: 229). In what follows we focus upon the procedure of, and activities related to, law-making—which is more important from both constitutional and political points of view—even if often, above all because of the structure of the available data, we refer to bills and proposed resolutions together. Certain conditions are set on the operation of parliament and, within this, on the procedure for law-making and the passing of

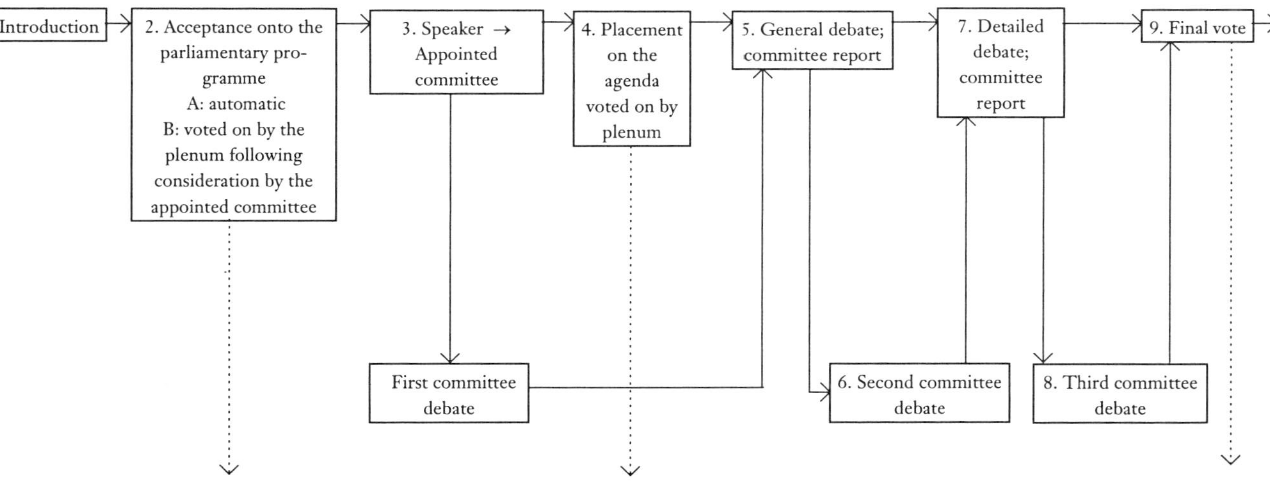

Figure 1. Procedure for the discussion of bills and proposed resolutions

A = Government proposal
B = Private member's motion

Note: The dotted vertical arrows show those points where a proposal can fail or become permanently locked in the legislative process.

resolutions by the constitution, the Law on Legislative Process and the standing orders of the house. The route taken through the parliamentary decision-making system by a bill or other proposal, or by an agenda item such as a report, is shown in Figure 1 (Gonda, 1994).

The processing of each bill, from the time it is introduced in the parliament until its acceptance, takes several months. In exceptional cases, the parliament can, on the recommendation of the government, push a bill through the entire parliamentary process in one or two weeks. At the other end of the scale, it can happen that a bill comes to a standstill at a particular point in the process for several years, only to lapse automatically at the end of the parliament.

The reason most bills and proposed resolutions do not become laws or resolutions is not that they do not receive the necessary majority when put to the final vote, but rather that they are filtered out at the stage of the fixing of the parliamentary programme, the setting of the weekly agenda or the preliminary discussions that take place in committee. The role of the parliament in selecting and modifying is shown well by the fact that, of the 628 bills and proposed resolutions that were unsuccessful during the first parliament, only forty-eight (8 per cent) fell at the stage of the final vote; the remaining 580 (92 per cent) never reached the final vote, but rather failed earlier on in the parliamentary process.

Of all the bills and proposed resolutions introduced during the first parliament, 69 per cent failed to reach the final vote. Twenty-eight per cent were not placed on the parliamentary programme, 17 per cent did not reach the agenda, and 24 per cent were withdrawn. Twenty-seven per cent of committee proposals and 18 per cent of governmental proposals fell before reaching a plenary vote. On the other side, 81 per cent of governmental proposals, 59 per cent of committee proposals and 29 per cent of private members' proposals were—with a greater or lesser degree of amendment—in the end accepted.

In the second parliament, between 1994 and 1998, the chances of acceptance of governmental and committee proposals increased further, while those of private members' proposals fell.

The picture of parliament that has been sketched here shows that it is not an institution that controls the executive or that acts as a counterweight to the executive, nor merely a rubber stamp for the policy of the government. The rules and practice of legislation show that the Hungarian parliament is an organ with its own internal rules of operation, and that it is an independent institutional actor in the process of political decision-making that exerts a considerable independent influence over legislation. The influence of parliament can be comprehended fully only by looking at the activities of the various institutional and political actors within it—the individual deputies, the committees, the parliamentary party groups and the opposition. This is a task to which we now turn.

4. *Institutional Actors: The Government, the Speaker, the Plenum and the Committees*

The norms of Hungarian constitutional law (of the constitution and of the Law on Legislative Process) give the government a prominent role and considerable responsibility in the process of legislation. In consequence of this, and even more so of the political composition of parliament, first, the government is able to determine the legislative agenda of parliament and, second, the government's bills and proposals for resolutions have a much higher chance of being passed than do those initiated from within parliament—by either individual deputies or parliamentary committees (Table 1).

Table 1. Division by source of the bills and proposed resolutions introduced in, and passed by, the parliament during the first parliament (2nd May 1990–2nd May 1994) and during the first three years of the second parliament (28th June 1994–19th December 1996).

	Government		Committee		Deputy		President		Total	
1990–94	number	%	number	%	number	%	number	%	number	%
Introduced	622	44	195	14	604	42	5	0	1,426	100
Passed	506	63	116	15	173	22	1	0	796	100
Success rate	-	81	-	59	-	29	-	20	-	56
1994–96										
Introduced	464	48	200	21	304	31	2	0	970	100
Passed	403	67	145	24	48	8	2	1	598	100
Success rate	-	87	-	73	-	16	-	100	-	62

Sources: For the first parliament, Soltész, 1994a: 228–232; for the second parliament, data published by the *Országgyűlés Képviselői Tájékoztató Központja* (Parliamentary Deputies' Information Centre).

Government Bills

Table 1 gives a comprehensive picture of the sources of bills and resolution proposals during the first two parliaments, and the relative chances these had of being passed by the legislature. As the table shows, around a third of the motions introduced in the Hungarian parliament, and around two-thirds of those passed are initiated by the government. The dominant role of the government is shown by the fact that the success rate of its proposals, at over 80 per cent, is significantly higher than that of the proposals of either the parliamentary committees or the deputies.

If, from among all the proposals introduced to the parliament, we consider only the bills, the dominant role of the government becomes still stronger. Though the constitutional rules give the right of initiation to a relatively broad range of actors—not only the government, but also the president, parliamentary deputies and committees—the majority of bills (around two-thirds) are proposed by the government. Furthermore, around nine in ten of the bills passed are initiated by the government.

Parliament thus debates, amends and passes bills that are prepared by the government and the administration—that is, by the *executive*. Government bills are written by the administration in the ministries under the direction of government members, and these are sent to parliament for debate.

The Setting of the Agenda

The central role of the government in the operation of the parliament is created in part, as we have seen, by constitutional and legal norms, in part (from the political point of view) by the government's parliamentary majority, and in part by the control over the decision-making and procedural system of parliament, as well as the operation of parliament, by a speaker who has the confidence of the government and by a governmental majority that can be mobilized for procedural votes. The speaker and the governmental majority have a decisive role in the setting of a legislative agenda that suits the intentions of the government. When discussing legislative procedure, we saw that the agenda is determined first by the process of placing items on the parliamentary programme, and second by the fixing of the weekly agenda itself. A decisive role is played in the determination of the agenda by the government, the speaker—who follows the intentions of the government—and the governmental majority in parliament. This is given significance by the fact that no bill or proposed resolution that fails to make it onto the parliamentary programme or agenda—that is not discussed at a plenary session of parliament—will ever become a law or resolution.

The government also has an advantageous position in plenary debates. The members of the government take part in parliamentary debates not as part of the parliamentary majority, but independently. According to the parliamentary standing orders, they can speak at any time during a parliamentary debate.

The government again plays a key role in the voting on proposed amendments to bills: every proposed amendment is sent to the appropriate minister in order that he or she be asked whether the government supports it or not. The government member, or his or her representative, is also present at committee meetings when agenda items introduced by him or her are being discussed.

By way of conclusion, we can state that the government, which in constitutional law is often referred to as the executive, in fact executes nothing. Rather, it governs. It controls the whole governmental system, from the legislature to the administration. Against the government, the parliament, as a functionally distinct and independent institution, has its own constitutional jurisdiction. In political terms, it has a role in influencing and supervising both legislation and execution—and thus, the government. The legislature in the parliamentary governmental system thus forms a part of *government* and has a governmental function. The extent of the autonomy of the parliament depends in large measure upon the organizational structure and procedural system of the parliament, and the relationships between parties within the parliament. In what follows, we turn our attention to how parliamentary institutions (committees, deputies) and political actors (the opposition) alter, influence, and on occasion thwart, the policies of the government.

The Plenum

The plenum, or plenary session, is the place where all parliamentary deputies deliberate together, where laws are passed, and where the government receives the confidence that allows it to exercise executive power. The plenary session is traditionally the most important forum of parliamentarism: it is here that public debate over bills, in which any deputy may speak, takes place, and it is here that proposals are voted on and either accepted or rejected. The plenary session guarantees the role of the parliament in political publicity: it is the most important location for opposition criticism of the government, where difficult questions can be put. It is also here that the opposition can articulate its alternatives to the proposals of the government. The plenary session of parliament passes or rejects all laws and amendments to laws—that is, the normative rules of the whole political community and the life of the state. In consequence of this symbolic, ratifying role, and of its role as the most important institution of political articulation and publicity, the plenum stands at the centre of public attention to politics and is of great significance from the point of view of the legitimacy of parliamentarism. From the point of view of the legislative process, however, it rarely has an independent role to play: we should speak of its role rather as being one of ratification. It is in general the legitimation of decisions reached elsewhere—at government meetings, within the party groups or in committee—that occurs here.

The parliament as an independent political actor *vis-à-vis* the government is structured in two ways. It is divided functionally by the system of permanent committees and politically by the parliamentary party groups.

Permanent Committees

Several types of committee exist in the Hungarian parliament. Permanent committees are involved above all in the process of legislation, in governmental oversight and in the management of matters relating to deputies and the internal affairs of the parliament. The activities of temporary (*ad hoc* or investigative) committees, meanwhile, last for only a short time; investigative committees play a role in governmental oversight in connection with single concrete cases. Within the permanent committees, sub-committees also operate. The composition of the permanent committees that are discussed below in general reflects the party composition of parliament, and thus the government parties have a majority on these committees. However, the House Committee and, for example, the investigative committees, are composed differently, with the parliamentary party groups each having equal representation on them. Meanwhile, the composition of sub-committees is often determined more or less independently from party considerations (Fogarasi, 1994).

The committee system that has developed in the Hungarian parliament is a strong one. The permanent committees have broad powers and a considerable weight in the legislative process (Soltész, 1994: 91–93). This increases the significance of the parliament *vis-à-vis* the government. Four-fifths of the deputies are committee members, and some are members of more than one committee. At the end of 1996, there were 466 posts on permanent and temporary committees filled by 319 deputies. Thus, 83 per cent of deputies were committee members (*Adatok…*, 1996).

The permanent committees have rights of independent initiation, proposal and opinion expression, and in certain cases they also have the right to make decisions. These committees are *specialized* and their structure follows that of the government departments. Initially, ten permanent committees were established in 1990. This number increased to twelve in 1992 when the committee structure was changed to reflect more accurately the structure of government (Soltész, 1994: 31). It subsequently grew further as the specialization of the committees was increased. Structuration matching that of the government enhances the ability of the committees to discuss and amend in detail the proposals of the government and to supervise the activity of government. The structure of permanent committees in the Hungarian parliament is thus closer to the committee systems of the strong German and Italian parliaments than to the less specialized committees of the weaker British and French parliaments.

Equally important is that, while in less specialized committee systems—such as that of the French National Assembly—the large committees operate as 'mini National Assemblies' similar to the plenary sessions in their degree of politicization, in Hungary (as, for example, in the German *Bundestag*) the smaller, more specialized committees operate almost as committees of experts. Membership of the same committee over a number of years leads to the development of specializations and feelings of solidarity in deputies in the matters they deal with—even if the extent to which this occurs should not be exaggerated. The *professional principle* has come to be used by party groups in the distribution of committee posts—something that is far from standard in parliaments generally. Thus, the members of economic committees are mostly economists, those of the agricultural committee are predominantly specialists in agriculture, those of the constitutional affairs and human rights committees are for the most part lawyers, and those on the culture and education committee generally have a background in the humanities. The deputies' committee memberships often correspond to their memberships of specialized working groups within their parliamentary parties. Thus, the permanent committees cannot be regarded, despite their composition reflecting the relative strengths of the parliamentary parties, as simply following the policies set by the parties. Rather, to a certain extent, they have been able to develop their own independent role.

The role of committees is further increased by the rule that bills, after being placed on the agenda, are discussed first by the committees and not by the plenum. Thus, the committees have a right of veto and a filtering role—even if not very strong—on proposed legislation: the committee must give its recommendation before plenary debate is possible. If none of the committees to which a proposal has been sent for preliminary opinion gives the proposal its blessing, that proposal is returned to the initiator, who may rework or withdraw it. In the case of private members' bills, since the amendment of the standing orders in 1994, committee support is required before they can even reach the parliamentary programme.

The most important function of the permanent committees in the legislative process is, however, not that of filtering out or proposing bills, but rather that of *amending* them. The committees express their views on bills and on amendments proposed by deputies and can also propose amendments of their own. The opinion of a committee regarding a proposed amendment—and particularly that of the committee appointed to consider the bill that the proposed amendment refers to—has considerable influence over whether the government and the majority will support the amendment in the subsequent plenary debate. Government proposals can often be amended in considerable detail by the committee. Of the fifty-one significant amendments proposed to the 1997 budget that were supported by the Budget and Finance Committee, forty-two received the support of the government (*HVG*, 30th November 1996: 10). In contrast, of the proposed amendments not supported by the committee, only one received governmental backing. During committee discussion, in which a representative of the government (in this case, the Finance Ministry) is among the participants, negotiations and bargaining take place between the deputies (whose suggestions reflect also the efforts of various party initiatives, interest groups and lobbies) and the government.

As regards amendment proposals made by deputies, the amendment to the standing orders of 1991 made it a general principle that those proposals that do not receive the support of at least one-third of the members of the appointed committee cannot reach the stage of plenary discussion. This means that the appointed committees can not only express an opinion on the amendment proposals of deputies, but also veto and filter them.

In summary, we can say, looking at the whole legislative process, that the strongest role of committees is not one of decision-making, but rather one of political *influence*. As we have seen, it is the government that has the most important role in initiating and directing the legislative process. In contrast with this, the committees play a selecting, amending role—in part by expressing opinions on bills, in part by discussing and selecting the amendment proposals of the deputies.

5. Political Actors: The Government Side and the Opposition

Deputies

The most important actors within the classical parliament were the deputies. Based upon the principle of the free mandate, each individual deputy in nineteenth-century parliamentarism was a representative of the whole nation and country. Today's parliaments are structured by the parties, and the vast majority of deputies belong to one of the party groups. This applies as much to the Hungarian parliament as it does anywhere else. The decisive role of the *party principle* in the political structuring of the parliament and the behaviour of deputies is established in Hungarian parliamentary law. Furthermore, a series of changes to the standing orders during the 1990s have further strengthened that role and significantly limited the principle of the free mandate. Alongside their party-group membership, however, the deputies are actors possessing a certain autonomy and having their own political world-views and preferences, as well as differing socio-cultural backgrounds and differing conceptions of their role. They obtain their parliamentary seats and reach the parliamentary stage in their political careers in different ways and with the help of different supporters. Many can thank their parties for their seats, while others can thank their supporters and voters in their individual districts. Many political analyses reveal differences between those deputies with single-member-district seats and those with list seats in their behaviour and their understandings of their role (Table 2).

Table 2. The deputies' understandings of representation, by the character of their parliamentary mandates (percentages, based on the question 'Whom do you represent above all in your parliamentary work?')

	Single-member district	List	Total
Electoral district	43	3	23
Town, region	4	15	10
Party	9	23	16
Social stratum	4	17	10
Interest group, ethnic group	0	5	3
The citizens of the country	38	28	32

Source: Based on Ilonszki, 1993: 122.

THE DEPUTIES' UNDERSTANDINGS OF THEIR ROLE • One element of the deputies' conception of their role concerns what they see as the content of representation itself, and what role they consider their mandates to give them (that of representative, delegate or politician). The second element—the client-oriented dimension, concerned with the orientation of representation—refers to whom, or which group or organization, the deputies represent in the legislature (place of residence, electoral district, region, interest group, party). That is, it refers to the kinds of expectations that the deputies seek to respond to. The third element is that of goal orientation, concerning how the deputies see their place in the decision-making process (Ilonszki, 1994: 7). The behaviour of the deputies and their understandings of their role are affected by a broad range of cultural, legal, institutional and political factors: the demands of the voters; traditions (the system of electoral districts, parliamentarism, the recall of deputies); the character of the electoral mandate (single-member district or party list); the method of selection of individuals as electoral candidates (by the party leadership or the local organization); the parliamentary standing orders (for example, the rules on switching between party groups, and on group formation, the distribution of parliamentary posts, and financial incentives); party group rules; group discipline; and whether a deputy belongs to the government or the opposition side.

The traditions of the system of individual electoral districts are strong in Hungary. The effect of this can be seen in public-opinion research conducted in late 1989, showing that voters wanted the deputies, first, to deal at least as much with local issues as with national issues, and, second, to follow the wishes of the voters in parliamentary decisions against their own consciences and the interests of the party (Kurtán *et al.*, 1990: 450; Ilonszki, 1993: 11). The latter was presumably influenced by the official conception of parliamentarism during the communist era, and by the political activism of the anti-communist opposition at the time of the régime change (seen, for example, in the recall of several deputies).

The retention of the principle of single-member electoral districts and the selection of the parties' district candidates by the local party organizations also show the strength of the tradition of 'local representation'. In the cases of some political movements and parties, this is mixed with the populist principle of direct democracy (seen, for example, in the demand to allow the recall of deputies).

In 'mass-level' political culture, many see the deputy as, in Burke's sense, a 'delegate'—a direct representative of the wishes of the voters. Within the political élite, by contrast, the concept of the free representative mandate is dominant: according to one investigation, the overwhelming majority (86.3 per cent) of deputies saw their parliamentary activity as being directed by their own judgements based upon the national interest, while only a minority (13.7 per cent) considered that their activity was determined not by conscience but by the instructions of the party or electoral district (Ilonszki, 1993: 15).

Conceptions of the *orientation of representation* are, however, determined more than anything else by the character of a deputy's mandate. Most deputies from single-member districts see themselves as the representatives above all of their electoral districts, and the second largest group among them see their role as that of representing the citizenry as a whole. By contrast, the majority of those elected on party lists see themselves as the representatives above all of neither the district, nor the citizenry in general, but rather of an intermediate group—the party, social stratum, interest group, town or region (Table 2). A role may be played in this, alongside identity and psychological factors, by differences between district and list deputies in the nature of their political dependence and responsibility, and of their activities as deputies. Political responsibility and dependency are linked to the different systems used by the parties for selecting candidates for the district and the list seats. While in most parties district candidates are chosen by local party organizations, list candidates are chosen by county and/or national party leaderships, or by party fora. Through these lists, the parties generally place into parliament the representatives and leaders of interest groups and organizations that are linked to the party, or that may simply improve the party's image. Presumably connected with this is the fact that those elected on the lists—particularly the national lists—are more likely to consider the support of interest groups to be important than are their colleagues chosen in single-member districts (Montgomery, 1994: 37). The differences in the activities of the district and list deputies are shown by the differences in their schedules: district deputies spend more time attending to local issues and the affairs of their constituents; the time of list deputies is directed more to the business of parliament, party, parliamentary party group and national interest representation (Table 3).

Table 3. The deputies' timetables, by the character of their parliamentary mandates (averages, in percent)

	District	List	Average
Participation in plenary sittings	24	27	25
Participation in committee meetings	16	15	16
Preparation for sittings	15	16	16
Parliamentary party group activities	9	11	10
Party activities	7	11	9
National interest-representation business	6	9	8
Local matters, maintenance of links with voters	21	11	17

Source: Ilonszki, 1993: 120.

THE DEPUTIES' PARLIAMENTARY ACTIVITY • The operation of the party groups, the committees and the whole parliament depends upon the deputies. They introduce the bulk of the motions that originate from within the parliament (Table 1), as well as the overwhelming majority of amendment proposals. The amending, influencing role of the parliament *vis-à-vis* the dominant government is built upon the amendment proposals of the deputies. The extent of this is shown by the fact that the number of amendment proposals introduced by the deputies was, for example, over six thousand between 1990 and 1992, and more than eight thousand in 1996 (*Országgyűlési kézikönyv*, 1992: 398, Table 10). Nevertheless, the political autonomy of the individual deputies is limited. The deputies' proposals must, above all, receive the support of their own party group; in practice, only then can they enter the parliamentary decision-making process.

The political structure of modern parliaments is thus created by the *parliamentary party groups*. The party groups arc formed from among those who run as the parties' candidates and win seats, the overwhelming majority of whom are also party members. Most deputies in the Hungarian parliament are members of one of the party groups—the number of 'independents' (those not belonging to a group) is small. In 1990, six deputies entered the parliament as independents. In 1994 there were no such deputies (Kurtán *et al.*, 1995: 444), while in 1998 there was one. The number of independents generally increases as the parliamentary cycle proceeds. This, however, is the result of the internal rules of the parliament and of movements within the parties (Table 4).

The Party Groups and their Functions

Independent deputies in the Hungarian parliament are thus exceptions, and the vast majority of deputies belong to party groups. In this, the parliament simply mirrors the party-based nature of modern parliamentary democracy. The party groups are legally recognized and—compared with the independents—privileged institutions. Each of the three parliaments to date has initially contained six party groups. During both of the first two parliaments, however, their number later grew as a result of party splits (Table 4).

Table 4. Changes in the party composition of parliament, 1990–1998

	First Parliament		Second Parliament		Third Parliament
	1990	7th April 1994	28th June 1994	8th Sept. 1997	July 1998
MDF	165	136	38	19	17
MIÉP	–	12	–	–	14
MDNP	–	–	–	15	–
SZDSZ	91	83	70	67	24
FKGP	44	9	26	25	48
Smallholders '36'	–	36	–	–	–
MSZP	33	33	209	208	134
Fidesz	21	26	20	32	148
KDNP	21	23	22	–	–
Agrarian Alliance	1	–	–	–	–
Joint candidates	4	–	–	–	–
Independents	6	28	1	20	1
Total	386	386	386	386	386

Notes: The MDNP parliamentary group was formed on 11th March 1996 following its split from the MDF. The KDNP group ceased to exist on 24th July 1997 as a result of a party split (which caused its membership to slip below the fifteen deputies needed at the time for a party group to exist). Eleven of its members moved to Fidesz, while eleven became independents (*Magyar Nemzet*, 9th September 1997: 1).

Sources: For 1990, *Szabadon választott...*: 44; for April 1994, Kukorelli, 1995a: 125; for June 1994, *Adatok...*, 1996: 1–6; for 1997, *Magyar Nemzet*, 9th September 1997: 1; for 1998, *Magyar Közlöny*, 4th June 1998.

The parliamentary governmental system is now all but unimaginable without party groups. The groups operate at every level of the parliament's procedural and decision-making structure, and they bind together the whole system of parliamentary leadership (the speaker and his or her deputies, the minutes secretaries and the House Committee), plenary sessions and committees. The party groups penetrate all parts of the parliament—something in which the Hungarian parliament resembles most European parliamentary systems. Following elections, the leading positions in the parliament, along with the committee chairmanships, vice-chairmanships and memberships, are distributed on the basis of agreement between the parliamentary groups. The proportions of seats held by the groups act as a guiding principle in this distribution, but nothing flows from them automatically: the political weights of the committees differ, and thus the parties are not indifferent about which committee chairs they obtain or on which committees they have more representation. The party groups delegate deputies to fill the positions they obtain. This means that the distribution of parliamentary posts reflects not only the proportions of seats held by each party group, but also the personal and political balance of forces within the groups. That is, the filling of the posts is, by parliamentary convention, a matter for the discretion of the party groups. Meanwhile, the House Committee, which, under the chairmanship of the speaker, co-ordinates the activity of the parliament, is composed of the leaders of these groups.

The party groups operate as unitary political actors within the parliament. This can be seen in many ways.

1. They generally display political unity during parliamentary debate. This is shown by levels of group discipline in voting that exceed 90 per cent (Hanyecz and Perger, 1994: 426–428).

2. Genuine policy decisions are made not in the course of plenary debate, but rather behind closed doors at party-group meetings. It is there that policy debate within the group occurs, while in the plenary debates the groups strive to appear united. Contributions to plenary sessions generally follow each other according to the pattern determined at the party-group meeting or in the relevant working group. The presence of the deputies in reality becomes significant only at the time of voting.

3. Positions within parliamentary bodies and committees, and leadership posts within the parliament (the speaker and his or her deputies, the House Committee, administrative functionaries such as the minutes secretaries) are filled by deputies delegated by the party groups.

4. The presence of party groups also structures parliamentary debate, as is shown by the system of leading speakers (whereby each party nominates for each bill a 'leading speaker', who is given greater time to explain the party's position with regard to the bill), the ordering of interventions according to the parliamentary strength of the parties, and the dividing of time between the groups. The ability of the deputies to participate in parliamentary debate—their right to speak in parliament—is thus constrained by their group attachment. The ability to speak is also limited by formal and informal time restrictions. This limited time is distributed among individual deputies by (the leaderships of) the party groups.

5. The role of the parliamentary groups and parties is increased by the fact that the structure of their permanent *working groups* more or less follows that of the ministries and of the permanent committees in the parliament. The working groups discuss and express opinions on the bills and proposed amendments that fall within their competence. It is on the basis of their reports and proposals that the party-group meeting decides the official standpoint and voting strategy of the group. In addition, the deputies whom the party delegates to the various parliamentary committees are selected from among the members of the relevant working groups.

The Relationship between the Government and the Government Parties

In the modern parliamentary governmental system, the separation of powers and the principle of checks and balances are embodied not through the confrontation of government and parliament, but through the confrontation of governmental majority and opposition. The division of powers between them is not *simultaneous*, but occurs only over time, through changes in the composition of government. Thus, within a given parliamentary and governmental cycle, there is no division of powers with the opposition: where the government parties operate as a '*voting machine*', the stability of the government is guaranteed. Since the government cannot, in general, count on the support of the opposition, it depends upon the votes of its own parliamentary party group or groups. The stability of government and the efficiency of legislative and governmental activity can thus be secured through a solid parliamentary basis—that is, through the political loyalty of the parliamentary groups of the government parties. The relationship between the government and the government-party groups and, in the case of coalition government, the relationships among the coalition parties, have thus become more important than the relationship between government and opposition (Körösényi, 1992). Following from this, the principal limitation upon the room for manoeuvre of the government within parliament is imposed not by the opposition but by the government's own parliamentary base. Thus, we now concern ourselves first with the role of the government-party parliamentary group or groups, and then with the role of the coalition parties and party groups participating in government.

In the Hungarian parliament, because of solid *party-group unity* and the high level of voting discipline, the government can take its parliamentary base essentially as given. Party-group unity does not, however, appear automatically. While the sense of belonging to a common political camp and party is an important force creating political solidarity, it is not enough to maintain political unity from week to week, month to month, over a period of years: that unity must be continuously created afresh and strengthened anew. The difficulty of this can best be shown by the party splits that have occurred during the 1990s (in the FKGP, the MDF and the KDNP). These splits show also that the instruments available to the government parties are more efficient than those of the opposition parties in preserving party unity. This is due, in part, to the psychological factor of governmental responsibility, which strengthens cohesion within the government party, in part to the material or positional factor of the remuneration derived from governmental positions, and in part to the fact, already discussed, of the resources available to the prime minister for securing group discipline. From our current point of view examining the legislature, however, a more important question concerns the ability of the party groups and group members to realize their goals, along with the extent to which they participate in, and influence, the governmental and legislative decision-making process. That is, we are concerned with the parliamentary party group's side in the creation of harmony in policy and activity between the government and the parliamentary group.

As regards the legislative sphere, the government-party parliamentary group has what amounts at least to considerable influence over government bills—both before they reach parliament and during the process of parliamentary discussion.

1. During the course of the preparation of a bill in the ministry, the draft bill is discussed by the relevant working groups of the government-party parliamentary groups, and those working groups express their opinions on it. The working groups and the deputies dealing with the issues involved maintain ties with the relevant civil servants within the ministry. The viewpoint of the party group and the voting recommendations that are accepted at the party-group meeting are, in general, based upon the proposals of the working group.

2. The leaders of the working groups are also members of the appropriate parliamentary committees—and, being from the government party, are generally the leaders of those committees. They thus continue to ex-

press their views on, and often propose further amendments to, the version of the bill accepted by the government later in the legislative process, during the period of committee discussion. The government-party parliamentary groups are thus participants in the long and multi-layered process of law preparation and legislation. They channel various professional, political and lobby perspectives into the decision-making process. Their bargaining position and their influence are significant, since they secure the political support, and votes, necessary for the ratification of the law.

3. The government-party parliamentary groups also express opinions on, and make amendments to, the government's semi-annual legislative programme, which the parliament later accepts as its legislative schedule for the following six months. The setting of the legislative programme is an important channel of influence for policy and interest groups and for lobbies within the government parties.

From all of this it can be seen that the unity of the political action of the government and the parliamentary majority and the operation of the government-party 'voting machine' within the parliament (party discipline) cannot be presumed to emerge automatically. Rather, they come about as a result, among other factors, of a bargaining system within the party and between the government, the administration and the party group in which the party group can exert considerable influence—and ultimately exercise a veto—over the legislative process.

The Government and its Coalition Partners

The second condition for governmental stability is the maintenance of the *unity of the coalition*: the break-up of the coalition may lead to the fall of the government. The operation of coalition government carries internal, institutional contradictions: it requires parties with different political programmes, and politicians of very different characters, to co-operate on a day-to-day basis. In neither the Antall, nor the Boross, nor the Horn government, however, did disputes and conflicts within the coalition over policy or positions lead to the fall of the government. The first years of the MSZP–SZDSZ coalition formed in 1994 displayed clearly the difficulties of co-operation—the possibility of the break-up of the coalition was frequently raised among both politicians and analysts. It was, however, the Antall government that had to face the most serious coalition crisis, caused by the departure of the Smallholders' Party from the coalition in 1992. This was the product of serious conflicts over government policy, such as policy on privatization and compensation for losses incurred during the communist era. The political spectrum spanned by the participants in the 'natural alliance' formed in 1990 proved to be too broad, though the more radicalized right-wing that moved into opposition—the FKGP, and the MDF politicians who formed MIÉP—was not able to bring down Antall's conservative government.

The Opposition

Since the dualism of legislature and executive, parliament and government was replaced by that between government (government parties) and opposition, the role of the opposition in European parliaments has grown remarkably (Döring, 1994: 340–346). The opposition's principal function is, however, to provide the oversight and criticism of the government (about which more will be said later), as well as an alternative government leadership and programme. It is a question how active and influential a participant the opposition is in the legislative process. Besides the committee system, this depends upon what independent rights the opposition possesses *vis-à-vis* the government majority.

By international standards, the Hungarian constitution and parliamentary standing orders secure for the opposition relatively extensive rights in decision-making and, as we will see, in governmental oversight (cf. Döring, 1994: 343). The opposition possesses broad rights to speak in parliament, as is customary in most parliamentary systems. Its share of leading parliamentary positions reflects its share of the seats in parliament. And the so-called two-thirds laws (those requiring a two-thirds majority) give it unusually generous rights of co-decision and veto in parliamentary decision-making.

The reform of the standing orders of autumn 1994, by modifying the role of the committees, perhaps reduced somewhat the weight of the opposition *vis-à-vis* the government and the government parties in the legislative process. By contrast, however, the rights of the opposition in respect of parliamentary oversight of the government were increased (Kukorelli, 1995). During the first parliament, the role of the committees involved, above all, their broad rights to express their opinions on proposals; during the second parliament, meanwhile, it involved their increased role in decision-making.

The ability of the opposition to speak in parliament depends in part upon the number of days on which parliament sits. At ninety to ninety-five sitting days, the Hungarian parliament occupies an intermediate position among the parliaments of Europe. The opposition's opportunities to speak are increased by the extensive committee system and by the right of the committee minority to report to the plenary session. This latter provision is common, but far from universal, among European parliaments (Döring, 1994: 343). The distribution of parliamentary positions and offices according to the shares of parliamentary seats applies not only to the committee members, but also to the committee presidents and their deputies, and to the House Committee and the deputy speakers. This is again not unusual, but, equally, not universal, in European parliaments.

The Hungarian parliamentary opposition possesses a very broad *veto* right *vis-à-vis* the government majority, which the government can neutralize only if it can obtain more than two-thirds of the votes cast. This veto right includes *changes to the parliamentary standing orders* (Constitution, Art. 24, Para. 4) and *constitutional amendments* (Constitution, Art. 24, Para. 3). Decisions concerning the *rules for the preparation of a new constitution* require four-fifths of the votes of all deputies (Constitution, Art. 24, Para. 5). This was stipulated in order to ensure that the principle of the opposition veto would operate, even when the government majority exceeded the two-thirds level, during the second parliament, formed in 1994, in which the government coalition held 72 per cent of the seats.

Exceptionally among parliamentary systems, however, the principle of the minority veto extends to ordinary legislation too. The constitution requires the votes of two-thirds of the deputies for the enactment of laws in more than thirty legislative fields.

The position of the minority is also protected by the one-third voting rule used during decision-making in the permanent committees, according to which proposals need the support of one-third of the committee examining them in order to reach the plenary agenda. During the first parliament, the representation of the opposition on each of the permanent committees stood, in reflection of the seat shares in the parliament, at between 38 and 40 per cent. By the end of the cycle, as a result of the erosion of the government's majority, this rose to between 42 and 46 per cent (Soltész, 1994: 330–334). During the second parliament, when the seat share of the opposition was below 30 per cent, the operation of the one-third 'minority protection' rules was safeguarded by over-representing the opposition on the 'strategic' committees, giving them more than one-third of the seats on these committees (Soltész, 1995c: 590–595).

For the special parliamentary committee formed in 1995 with the aim of preparing a new constitution, still stronger minority veto rights were established, and an opposition majority on the committee was guaranteed. (The committee was composed of four representatives from each party, plus the Socialist speaker. Thus, of the twenty-five places on the committee, the opposition held 64 per cent.) Each party—the two government parties and the four opposition parties alike—had one vote on the committee, and the agreement of five of the six parties was needed for a proposal to be accepted. The ultimate veto power of the MSZP, which had an absolute majority in the parliament, was guaranteed by the fact that the votes of two-thirds of the deputies were needed for a constitutional amendment to be passed. The parliamentary parties also agreed in 1995 that, during the period of constitution-making, or at least until the end of the 1994–98 parliament, the constitution could be amended only according to the rules agreed for constitution-making. That is, in the event of the failure of the constitution-making process, the government could not use its 72 per cent majority to amend the constitution unilaterally (Arató, 1996: 26). (These procedures, requiring almost complete consensus, did not produce results: no new constitution was born, the proposals always falling to the veto of either the government parties or the opposition. Finally, in the summer of 1997, the government coalition repudiated the moratorium on constitutional amendments, and, as in autumn 1994, used its two-thirds majority to modify the constitution in several places.)

All of these minority rights signify not a control function for the opposition over the executive, but an unusually advantageous and legally defined role for the opposition in the legislative process.

The Dualism of the Government Majority and the Opposition

The breakdown of private-members' bills and amendment proposals by party and by the government/opposition dichotomy (Tables 5 and 6) shows that, though the activity of the deputies is significant on both the opposition and the government sides of the House—many proposals are presented from both sides—the consequence of the political logic of the parliament is that the chances of a proposal's acceptance differ greatly depending on whether it is from a government-party deputy or an opposition-party deputy. The success rate of proposals originating from the government side is several times greater than that of proposals coming from the opposition. At the same time, the passage of proposals coming from the government-party benches is not automatic, while those coming from the opposition benches are not condemned to defeat in advance. All of this points to the independent role of the parliament in forming and influencing policy. This is shown also by the fact that amendment proposals to government bills are tabled from the government as well as the opposition side.

Comparing the activity of government-party and opposition deputies, it can be stated that, while opposition activity is greater in regard to bills and proposed resolutions—deputies from the government parties are more 'satisfied' with the proposals of the government—in respect of amendments, the situation is more balanced.

Table 5. The number and success rates of private members' bills and resolution proposals during the first and second parliaments, divided between government and opposition

	Introduced		Accepted		Success rate
1990–93	number	%	number	%	%
Government party	120	34	32	46	27
Opposition	184	53	26	38	14
Other	45	13	11	16	24
Total	349	100	69	100	20
1994–96					
Government party	61	20	27	56	44
Opposition	205	67	14	29	7
Other	38	13	7	15	18
Total	304	100	48	100	16

Sources: For 1990–93, *Tények és Adatok…*, 1994: 58–59; for 1994–96, *Országgyűlés Képviselői Tájékoztató Központ* [Parliamentary Deputies' Information Centre].

6. The Responsibility of Government to Parliament: Votes of Confidence and No Confidence

The democratic transition in Hungary resulted in the creation (albeit with limits) of a parliamentary governmental system: the dependence of the government on the confidence of parliament and the responsibility of the government to the parliament are enshrined in constitutional law. The motion of no confidence against the government is the most important sanction the parliament can deploy in executing its governmental oversight function. The institution of the *constructive vote of no confidence*—introduced in Hungary following the German model—limits the power of this instrument. This has weakened the government's responsibility to parliament, and has thus elicited much criticism.

Table 6. The number and success rates of amendment proposals, by party group of origin, 1996

	Government		Opposition					
	MSZP	SZDSZ	Fidesz	FKGP	KDNP	MDF	MDNP	Ind.
Total	2190	1120	228	563	154	334	113	35
Accepted	1765	852	71	279	46	106	28	5
Rejected	425	268	157	284	108	228	85	30
Acceptance rate	81%	76%	31%	50%	30%	32%	25%	14%

Notes: The proposals shown are those reaching the plenary vote. Proposals initiated by several deputies from more than one party group are included in the table under each of the relevant groups.
Source: *Országgyűlés Képviselői Tájékoztató Központja* [Parliamentary Deputies' Information Centre].

The parliamentary bases of the governments during the first two parliaments in Hungary were so strong that no government to date has required to make voting on any bill a matter of confidence. Also connected with this is the fact that the 'constructive' nature of the motion of no confidence has not been significant in practice—no government to date has seen its parliamentary base weaken to such an extent that it was saved from falling only by this constructive formulation. The parliamentary parties have developed other instruments of reward and discipline—if only gradually and unevenly—through which governments have been able to maintain their stability in parliament.

7. *Non-Sanctionary Instruments of Parliamentary Control over the Government*

In consequence of the weakening of the role of the motion of no confidence in European parliamentarism in recent decades, non-sanctionary instruments of parliamentary control over the government and the executive have come to the fore.

Political Publicity

The most important institution of parliamentary control over the government and the executive as a whole is that of the political publicity provided by the parliament's plenary sessions. In the modern theory of democracy, the parliament is a key centre for political publicity (Oberreuter, 1994: 329). The Hungarian parliament is more a 'working' than a 'debating' parliament: direct political debate—the so-called *political debate day*—appears on the agenda only rarely. A consequence of this is that political debate occurs during the so-called *pre-agenda speeches*. These have come to constitute one of the most important institutions in Hungarian politics for the criticism of the government by the opposition and, as a result of television coverage and the presence of the press, for political publicity. It is possible here to put questions and initiate interpellations, which must be announced in advance and answered within thirty days. For this reason, it is here that the daily twists and turns of political life are to be found. It is within this context that the debate between government and opposition, characteristic of the debating parliament, is played out.

The classical channels for the political oversight of the government are provided by the institutions of *interpellations* and *questions*. Indeed, because of the extent of media attention, they, together with the pre-agenda debate, provide perhaps the most important instrument by which the opposition may exercise influence over the items on the policy agenda. In the Hungarian parliament, as in most European parliaments, it is not possible to append a motion of no confidence against an individual minister or the whole government to an interpellation. Nevertheless, or perhaps precisely because of this, the interpellation is one of the most important instruments in the oversight of the government. The importance of the interpellation is not due primarily to the fact that, if the parliament does not accept the answer given by the minister to an interpellation, the issue is passed to one of the parliamentary committees for further investigation and subsequent return to the plenum. The rejection of a ministerial reply constitutes more than just a loss of political prestige for the government. It means also that the issue stays on the agenda; it does not pass into oblivion, but rather returns again to the public eye.

Between mid–1994 and the end of 1996, contributions outside the agenda—that is, before and after the agenda business—amounted to around 10 per cent of plenary discussion time and included around 15 per cent of questions and interpellations. Questions and interpellations, meanwhile, which take up around a quarter of the parliament's discussion time, are the two forms of parliamentary debate in which the principal role is played not by the government or the government parties, but by the opposition. While the legislative agenda is controlled by the governmental majority, it is the opposition that dominates the choice of topics when it comes to questioning. During the two and a half years beginning in summer 1994, almost two-thirds of contributions outside the agenda came from the opposition ranks, as did the great majority of questions, immediate questions and interpellations. It is also true, however, that the governmental majority in most cases (in the first parliament, 83 per cent of cases, and in the second parliament 94 per cent of cases[1]) accepts the answer given by a minister to an interpellation, with the result that the issue is dropped from the agenda.

Organs for the Oversight of the Administration

The traditional method for parliamentary supervision of the government and the administration is the supervision of the execution of the budget. One form of this is the *debate on the appropriation accounts*. Another is the supervision carried out by the *National Audit Office*, which operates independently of the government, as an organ of parliament. The establishment of parliamentary commissioners (*ombudsmen*) has created a new institution for parliamentary control over the administration, focusing on wrongs done to individual citizens in the course of the execution of the laws.

The Requirement to Report to Parliament

A wide-ranging and constitutionally enshrined method of parliamentary supervision over the government, the administration and other state organizations, is the ability of parliament to require those concerned to report to it. According to the constitution, the government is required regularly (though for ministers without a fixed time) to report to parliament. Various laws set out requirements for the government or individual members of the government to report on specific matters.

During the first parliament, the plenary session debated two such reports—concerning the activities of the government during the first two years of its term, and the employment situation. A further seventeen reports were discussed only in committee (Soltész, 1995a: 45). In 1996, of seventeen reports submitted to parliament, three were discussed and accepted by the plenum (*Országgyűlés Képviselői Tájékoztató Központja* [Parliamentary Deputies' Information Centre]). All of this points to the legislative rather than debating character of the parliament.

In various other matters, the government, or the individual ministers, have a duty to report, or to give information, not to the parliament as a whole, but to particular committees (Soltész, 1995a: 45). The extent of the committee system and its structure mirroring that of the government allow the parliament to play a serious oversight role. It is frequently the case, however, even in committees, that reports submitted in writing are never discussed. Further, as the parliamentary cycle progresses, the backlog of business in the committees and parliament as a whole gradually builds up, until—because the new parliament does not inherit it automatically—it is simply disposed of when parliament is dissolved.

A further instrument for parliamentary oversight over the government and the administration is provided by *committee hearings*. According to the constitution (Art. 21, Para. 3), everyone has the duty to give the parliamentary committees any information they request, and to give testimony to those committees. The right to summon government members and civil servants to committee hearings is enshrined also in the parliamentary standing orders. On the other hand, the committees have no power to sanction those who do not conform with their requests.

All those committees less burdened by the preparation of laws devote a considerable amount of their time to these hearings. In addition to oral hearings, the committees request and debate both reports and information.

Investigative Committees

In principle, the investigative committees constitute one of the most important instruments of parliamentary oversight over the government and the administration. The basis of this is the ability of the parliament, set out in the constitution, to establish committees to examine any question, and the constitutional requirement that any information or testimony requested by the committee be provided (Soltész, 1995a: 47; 1995b: 107). But, as has been seen, there exist no means to force compliance with committee requests, since the investigative committees of the Hungarian parliament—in contrast, for example, with those in Poland or Italy—do not have judicial status. Further, the political significance of the investigative committees is shown by the fact that, during the first parliament, the government majority repeatedly voted down the proposals of the opposition deputies for the establishment of investigative committees: from thirty-one proposals, only a single investigative committee was created (Juhász, 1996: 94–95). A serious role was given to the investigative committees only during the second parliament. The reform to the parliamentary standing orders of 1994 reduced to one-fifth of the deputies the number of votes required for the establishment of an investigative committee, in consequence of which six such committees had been set up by May 1997 (Juhász, 1997: 94). Since the composition of investigative committees concerned with the activities of the government is based upon parity between the government parties and the opposition, and since the chairmen of such committees come from the parliamentary opposition, the investigative committees have become instruments of the parliamentary opposition against the government. The significance of investigative committees for the opposition is shown by the fact that they give the opportunity to examine scandals associated with the activity of the government and they ensure that the issue can be kept within the public eye for months while the committee conducts its investigations.

The issues involved are often issues that draw considerable public attention, such as the so-called Oilgate scandal and the Tocsik affair.

The establishment of an investigative committee, even when supported by 20 per cent of the deputies, is, however, not automatic: by mid–1997 opposition proposals to set up committees dating from 1994, 1995 and 1996 had still not been placed upon the agenda. Thus, the government majority is able, through its control over the agenda and by sinking issues in committee discussion, to prevent the creation of investigative committees (Juhász, 1997: 109–111).

In summary, we can say that, though there is virtually no element of sanction in the institutions and procedures of parliamentary oversight over the executive, these institutions and procedures are nevertheless important instruments for the supervision of the government. Their efficacy is provided by the fact that they form a part of political publicity—both directly and through the media. Without the media, the criticisms levelled at the government by the opposition would never reach the voters, and the effectiveness of the parliament's activity would remain very low. The institutions and procedures of executive oversight operate—through the media—above all as instruments for the opposition against the government.

The Supervision of Personnel Policy

One further means of supervision of the activity of the government and of enforcement of the principle of governmental responsibility is provided by the *parliamentary committee hearings* that precede appointments to leading executive offices. The range of posts subject to such hearings is very wide. It extends to almost every leading state position and includes all ministers and other government members. The committees conducting the hearings have no veto rights, but the questions put to the candidate and the voting of the committee often ensure that their views reach the attention of public opinion. During the first parliament between 1990 and 1994, a total of 235 candidate hearings took place in the committees of the Hungarian parliament, while during the first half of the second parliament, from June to December 1994, there were eighty-seven.

The role of the parliament in appointments is, however, more than merely supervisory and advisory. In some spheres, parliament is decisive:

it appoints the leaders of some public institutions itself. For example, the constitution stipulates that the votes of a majority of all deputies (50 per cent plus one vote) are required for the election of the prime minister. For the election of the president of the republic, the votes of two-thirds of the deputies are required in the first round, though in the end (the third round of voting) a simple majority of votes cast is sufficient. While the votes of a simple majority of deputies is sufficient for the election of, for example, the president and three vice-presidents of the supervisory committee of the National Bank of Hungary, a two-thirds majority of all deputies is required for the election of the Constitutional Court judges, the president of the Supreme Court, the chief public prosecutor, the president and vice-presidents of the National Audit Office and the ombudsmen.

The requirement for a two-thirds majority, as is usual when qualified majorities are needed, often slows down the process of decision-making. Vacant positions—for example, on the Constitutional Court—are often left unfilled for months or even years.

8. Conclusion

We have seen in this chapter how inadequate for understanding the operation of the modern governmental system in Hungary is the concept of dualism found in classical constitutional thought, which identifies the relationship between the legislative and executive powers with the relationship between parliament and government. If we examine the traditional relationship between parliament and government, we can state that a *fusion* has come about between the two branches of power—mainly on the political level, but in part at the legal level too. This is so even if, as has already been mentioned, the dualist elements of the Hungarian constitution limit its extent. The location of legislative activity is the parliament, but the key player within this is the government. The independent role that the parliament is able to play is one of exercising influence. A new dualism has emerged between the government (the government parties) and the opposition, replacing the old dichotomy of legislature and executive and determining the internal political structure of the parliament. The most important roles of the opposition are to be found in supervision and, even more so, in the sphere of political publicity and the statement of a political alternative. Depending upon the balance of parliamentary forces, however, it can also, within the sphere of the two-thirds laws, exert a power of veto. In its everyday decision-making, however, the government is primarily dependent not upon the opposition but upon the government-party parliamentary groups—it is they that constitute the most important political limitation upon the government.

The Hungarian National Assembly is more a 'law factory' working parliament than a debating parliament: it expends most of its energy and discussion time upon the process of legislation (Soltész, 1995a: 27). The explanation for this can be found, first, in the demand for legal reforms created by the democratic régime change; second, in the rather romantic illusions concerning legislation that can be found in Hungarian political thinking; and third, following on from the second, in the relatively broad legislative powers given to the Hungarian parliament *vis-à-vis* the government (Soltész, 1995a: 27–28).

The Hungarian parliament is representative in nature (it has the function of popular representation). Despite this, its role in the formation of governments and in executive oversight has, in many respects, entered the centre of political life, while, as we have seen, its *legitimation function* is, from the point of view of the political system as a whole, less significant. The latter is connected with the peculiarities of Hungarian *political culture*. Because of the consensus-oriented and anti-party, anti-élite character of that culture, judgements concerning debate and conflict between the parties (and thus within the parliament) are negative. The prestige of the Hungarian parliament—and even more of the parties structuring the parliament—is low.[2] Since the parliament is the fundamental institution of the political class, and since it is of crucial importance in the self-legitimation of the leading political stratum, its prestige in the context of the anti-élite political culture is low, and its function in régime legitimation is minimal.

The 'working-parliament' character of the operation of the Hungarian parliament is consistent also with the *conception of parliamentarism* dominant in Hungarian political culture and political thought. Parliamentary debates—particularly the pre-agenda debates—are often regarded by public opinion and the opinion-forming media as needless word-play that only hinders the *work* of legislating.

Notes

1. Based upon figures provided by the parliament.

2. We saw in the chapter on political culture (Chapter Two) that the under-valuation of the parliament as an institution is particularly striking in light of the fact that levels of public satisfaction with other *non*-party-political institutions or individuals (such as the president of the republic and the Constitutional Court) are significantly higher than those of the parliament.

Chapter Thirteen

The Constitutional Court

Among the constitutional courts of Western Europe, the strongest are those found in countries that experienced dictatorship during the inter-war period—it was here that, during the reconstruction of democracy in the aftermath of the Second World War, the perception of the need for a guarantor of the constitutional state was greatest. By contrast, in countries such as the United Kingdom and the Netherlands, the institution of the constitutional court continues to be absent. The countries of Central and Eastern Europe, including Hungary, have tended, in the wake of the collapse of the communist system, to follow the first path and to adopt strong constitutional courts: such courts have been seen as indispensable institutions for the establishment of the constitutional state.

In what follows we restrict ourselves to outlining and analysing the political role of the Hungarian Constitutional Court and its place in the political system. In consequence of the dominance of liberal thought and the concept of the *Rechtsstaat* in the democratic transition, the Hungarian Constitutional Court has become a central institution, and it plays a key role in the system of counterweights to the parliamentary majority and the government.

1. The Jurisdiction and Political Role of the Constitutional Court

Following European practice, constitutional review is carried out in Hungary by a single constitutional court that is distinct from the rest of the judicial system. The power and political role of the Hungarian Constitutional Court is unusual by European standards. The activity of the Court is often *political* in character—it decides between alternatives, all of which are possible from the constitutional point of view and in respect of issues that affect much or all of the population (Gyorfi, 1996: 64, 69). In what follows we show the extent of the role played by the Constitutional Court in the political process.

The Powers of the Constitutional Court

The powers of the Hungarian Constitutional Court are broad not in all spheres, but instead principally in the political sphere. The rights of the Court are limited, for example, in respect of the redress of infringements by the authorities of individual rights—that is, in respect of the so-called *constitutional complaint*. This restriction lies in the fact that the citizens—unlike those of many other countries[1]—cannot always lodge a constitutional complaint with the Court if their constitutional rights are infringed by an administrative action; they can do so only if the infringement is caused by the use of an unconstitutional legal rule. In Germany, where the institution of the constitutional complaint is broader in scope, these complaints form at least 90 per cent of the issues sent to the Court (Kerekes, 1994: 450; Takács, 1996: 358). In Hungary, by contrast, as Table 1 shows, that proportion is barely 1 per cent.

In contrast with this, the Hungarian Constitutional Court has uniquely broad powers in those fields that give it a political role and function. We can differentiate, both in theory and in terms of international practice, three levels of politicization of the constitutional court's role (Pokol, 1991: 92–94).

1. A constitutional court has the least powers where it can engage only in *concrete* norm control—that is, where issues can reach the constitutional court only in connection with concrete legal cases. This is the situation in the United States.

2. *Abstract* norm control —where laws are considered by the court not in connection with particular legal cases but rather on the initiative of state organs empowered to do so—gives greater powers. This is so even when the abstract norm control is only *a posteriori*—that is, where constitutional review occurs concerning laws already passed, but where those laws can be nullified. The activity of constitutional courts has moved in this direction in many European countries.

Table 1. Issues reaching the Constitutional Court, and the decisions of the Court

Issues, by sphere of powers	1990	1991	1992	1993	1994	1995*	1996
A priori norm control	–	3	1	4	1	–	2
A posteriori norm control	584	734	408	350	295	171	402
of this: laws	305	606	303	248	207	124	262
cabinet decrees	124	69	35	21	5	18	34
ministerial decrees	51	33	18	33	22	10	23
other	104	26	52	48	61	19	83
Conflict of legal rule with international treaty	1	2	1	–	–	–	3
Constitutional complaints	12	6	21	17	7	7	19
Constitutional infringements by omission	174	49	6	17	5	3	16
Conflicts between the powers of state organs	–	–	1	–	1	–	3
Abstract constitutional interpretation	8	4	4	–	1	2	–
Other spheres of authority defined by law	13	29	81	41	85	16	83
Other issues rejected as not belonging to the jurisdiction of the Court	833	1475	1177	894	703	408	881
Total**	1625	2302	1700	1323	1098	607	1543
Of this:							
Cases taken up by Court	735	792	460	369	451	204	447
Cases on which judgement reached***	487	705	342	405	344	147	239
Cases in progress	248	335	453	417	524	557	460+
Decisions of the Court							
Claims upheld	26	45	50	47	46	47	48
Claims rejected	58	135	117	98	103	61	n. a.
Injunctions	37	97	30	107	78	39	n. a.
Total	121	277	197	252	227	147	n. a.

* January–April.

** Total of all preceding lines.

*** Cases on which judgements reached during the given year, irrespective of the year the cases were introduced.

+ Includes only cases introduced during the year.

Sources: *Constitutional Principles and Cases*, 1996: 638–640, 644, 646. For 1996, the Constitutional Court of the Republic of Hungary.

3. A constitutional court has the greatest power and most politicized role if it has the right of *a priori abstract norm control*—that is, if constitutional review can be requested in regard to bills not yet passed or laws not yet promulgated. This has until now been employed only in the case of the French Constitutional Council, though the Council does not have the power of *a posteriori* norm control.

The Hungarian Constitutional Court possesses all three of these powers. Furthermore, it has an additional power that enables it to exert a significant 'constitution-making' role. This is the power of *constitutional interpretation*. Not even a concrete law proposal is required in order to activate this procedure: it is possible to request a decision from the Court as to the constitutionality of abstract decision-making alternatives. Requests for constitutional interpretation are generally made in cases of political conflict. For example, the conflict over rival referendum proposals concerning the issue of whether agricultural land should be sold to foreigners was sent to the Constitutional Court in 1997. The power of abstract constitutional interpretation, combined with that of *a priori* norm control, have given the Hungarian Constitutional Court a strongly politicized role (Paczolay, 1993a: 35).

The Power to Initiate Constitutional Court Proceedings

The extent of constitutional court activity and of the involvement of the court in the political system depends not only upon the powers of the court, but also upon the means by which court proceedings may be initiated. The circle of those who can initiate such proceedings is broad in Hungary by international standards. It includes the president of the republic, the government, individual ministers, the president of the National Audit Office, the president of the Supreme Court, the attorney general and groups of at least fifty parliamentary deputies in matters of abstract norm control, as well as individual citizens in issues affecting them. As a result, almost any conflict that cannot be resolved elsewhere may end up in front of the Constitutional Court, and the number of issues sent to the Court is very high (Table 1). The extent of the Court's powers and the broad range of initiators of Court proceedings mean that the Court can easily become the final arbiter in political conflicts, making it a central participant in the political process.

The Selection of Constitutional Court Judges

The political character of a constitutional court depends also upon the method of selection of the court judges. In Hungary, as in most countries with constitutional courts, attempts are made to reduce the political character of the activity of the Court and to increase the Court's political impartiality and its judicial character through the conditions of appointment of Court judges. Stipulations are made regarding the legal qualifications and experience of judges, regarding their minimum age and their irremovability, and their mandate is much longer than is the political cycle.

According to Hungarian law, members of the Constitutional Court must be at least forty-five years old, hold a degree in law and be legal theoreticians, university teachers, or acknowledged legal experts (judges, attorneys, lawyers) with at least twenty years' experience. No one can be appointed to the Court who has, during the previous four years, been a government member, been an employee of a political party or held office in the state administration. Candidates for positions on the Court are nominated by a parliamentary committee composed of one representative from each party's parliamentary group, and for election the candidates require the votes of two-thirds of all deputies. Thus, in Hungary as generally, the leading role in the composition of the Constitutional Court is played by the parties.

Through the strict rules on the incompatibility of service on the Constitutional Court with other posts, the legislators sought to isolate the members of the Court from political and interest groups, and to secure their existential and political independence. The nine-year term of the judges—longer than two parliamentary cycles—has the same effect (Takács, 1996: 364–365). Political balance is further increased by the fact that the Court judges are not all elected simultaneously. Rather, their elections are spread over three parliamentary cycles. The elections of Court judges in 1989 and 1990 occurred through rapid political compromise. Since 1994, however, in the absence of inter-party agreement, they have dragged out for years and have at times been interspersed with open political conflict. The election procedure for Constitutional Court judges ties the Court directly to the world of politics: the judges are chosen through a parliamentary political selection process that involves party-political bargaining and compromise. The selection of all leading state office-holders—including judges—has become a party-political question, as much in Hungary as elsewhere.

The Career Paths of Constitutional Court Judges

The examination of the career paths, world-views, party membership and political supporters of the Court judges assists us greatly in understanding the decisions of those judges (Landfried, 1988: 11, 13). As regards their professional backgrounds, the members of the Hungarian Constitutional Court were engaged, prior to their appointments, for the most part not in legal practice (as judges, attorneys or lawyers) but in university and theoretical legal work. Of the fourteen Constitutional Court judges chosen between 1989 and 1997, eight came from university or theoretical work, two had been judges, one had been a practising lawyer and three had had mixed careers beginning in legal practice and then going on to theoretical law. It is particularly striking that only two had previously been judges. This may have played a part in the fact that, in contrast to the role of the judge in concrete cases between two sides where the law is considered central, the decisions of the Constitutional Court have at times deviated from the concrete issues and the text of the constitution and reflected a more activist approach.

The political criteria for selection that exist alongside the professional criteria stipulate that the judges cannot be members of political parties and cannot engage in political activities. In other words, the judges, once elected, must give up their party memberships and suspend their political activities. The law itself assumes—rightly—that the judges do not lack their own world-views and political orientations. A significant number of Hungary's Constitutional Court judges have previously engaged in political activities and been party members. This is of course tied to the fact that both the body nominating Court judges and the body electing them are composed of party politicians. This political character of the selection process influences who is elected. Every party seeks to nominate and to have elected individuals who are close to it politically, personally or in terms of general world-views. Those who are selected often have clear party-political connections or direct party membership. In the opinion of one Constitutional Court judge, the result of the nomination system is that 'the road to a seat on the Constitutional Court passes through the parties' (Kilényi, 1990: 393, quoted in Törő, 1991: 281).

The Judges' Views on their Own Role

A role continues to be played in the development of the political role of the Constitutional Court by the understanding the judges have themselves of their role and by the philosophy those judges bring to bear in their deliberations. One basic factor explaining the activism of the Hungarian Constitutional Court is the activist understanding the judges have of their own roles. The Constitutional Court advertises itself as the trustee of the revolution to a constitutional state. It has sought to establish an invisible constitution based upon the principle of the constitutional state that deviates from the letter of the written constitution. It has taken an activist stance principally in the sphere of basic rights, but also in the development of the institutions of the state (Kukorelli, 1995: 20, 98–99; Pokol, 1992, 1992a; Sajó, 1993: 38). In addition to what has already been said concerning the legitimacy deficit surrounding the written constitution, we must add that the Constitutional Court has not itself seen that constitution as final; it has seen it rather as the 'constitution of the transition'—that is, as transitional (Sajó, 1993: 42).

Constitutional review of the law and the application thereof is thus based, in Hungary, not simply upon the text of the constitution, but also upon such principles of constitutionalism as the '*concept of constitutionality*' and the '*invisible constitution*'—concepts that have entered the Hungarian constitutional system precisely through the judgements and interpretations of the Constitutional Court (Paczolay, 1993: 45). There is thus no *absolute* interpretation of the concept of constitutional law, with the result that in borderline cases—when a choice must be made between mutually exclusive conceptions (for example, in the question of capital punishment, the concept of the right to life)—the Constitutional Court has freedom in reaching a decision, and can employ its own conception in making its judgement. In this way one of the possible interpretations of the constitutional law becomes binding. Though the Constitutional Court only interprets the constitution, 'through its continuous interpretation, it itself lays down the standard of that interpretation' (opinion of Judge László Sólyom annexed to Constitutional Court decision 23/1990 [X. 31]).

The Hungarian Constitutional Court is a strongly *politicized* institution both in its embeddedness into the political decision-making process (its powers and accessibility) and the activist view many of the judges have of their own role (Table 2). The Court's decisions are widely discussed in public and among politicians. This contrasts with the situation in, for example, Austria, where the Constitutional Court is an authoritative institution isolated from politics and public opinion, whose decisions do not become the subject of political consideration and debate.

Table 2. The politicization of constitutional courts as a function of conceptions of the courts' role and their embeddedness into the political process

	Level of integration	
Role understanding	Embedded	Isolated
Activist	+ / + Hungary	+ / – ?
Textualist	– / + USA	– / – Austria

The political role of the Constitutional Court in practice can be seen through the judgements it issues and the opinions attached to them. The judges often explain and justify their judgements through arguments that are not legal but political in character. These arguments include the allowable political role of the Constitutional Court, the identification of legal security with the protection of the *status quo*, the exceptional nature of the political and economic transition, and the workability, productivity and social acceptance of the state (Sajó, 1993).

Limits upon Activism and the Political Counterweights to the Court

While emphasizing the activism of the Hungarian Constitutional Court, we must also note that significant limitations to that activism do exist. The most important limitation is that the Court can deal only with questions that are sent to it by the actors empowered to do so. The Court is thus only a *reactive* body—it cannot initiate constitutional review of laws and other decisions. In addition, the Court's political role operates only through constitutional law—the political discretion of the Court is limited. Furthermore, the Court has no instruments at its disposal for the execution of its decisions.

The Court's activism is further limited by a feature of the judges' own understanding of their role. The Constitutional Court has developed a certain self-restraint in respect of abstract constitutional interpretation and *a priori* norm control. When a minister has turned to the Court before the government has made a decision in order to enquire as to the constitutionality of various versions of the decision, or when one of the parties has asked the Court to judge the constitutionality of a bill before parliament has reached a decision on it, the Court has rejected these requests, citing the principle of the separation of powers (Paczolay, 1993a: 35–36).

One final limitation is created by the fact that, while the Constitutional Court has no means of executing its decisions, the legislature and the executive are far from lacking instruments against the decisions of the Constitutional Court. The government and parliament act as counterweights to the Constitutional Court, possessing such instruments against the Court as the right to modify the law on the Court or the constitution itself, and the ability to exercise political control over the selection of Court judges. Furthermore, it is common for Court decisions to be 'sabotaged' by the executive, when a situation that the Court has deemed unconstitutional is allowed to continue for a long period. Finally, the parties and the government sometimes try (but the latter only very rarely) to exert political pressure over the Court during its deliberations over particular issues.

2. *The Consequences of the Constitutional Court's Activism: The Judicialization of Politics*

The constitutional review of political decisions and the resolution of political conflicts by Constitutional Court arbitration show the politicization of the Court's work. (The right of the Court to arbitrate such political disputes does not mean that the Court has genuine political discretion, but, while its interpretations are based on law, they are often far from lacking political considerations.) This activity, together with its effects upon the political process discussed below, are referred to as the 'judicialization' of politics (Paczolay, 1993: 45; Landfried, 1984, 1988; Favoreu, 1995: 93). The more political and legislative conflicts are pushed in front of the Constitutional Court, the more decisions the judges take. The Court's decisions thus increasingly reduce the autonomy of political decisions and the freedom of politicians, while simultaneously reducing the 'openness' of the constitution (Landfried, 1988: 12). The judicialization of politics pushes the other functions of politics into the background. It reduces the scope for discretionary political decisions, limits the autonomy of politics in the determination and fulfilment of the common good, and marginalizes the role played in politics by interest reconciliation and compromise. The anticipation of Court judgements in legislation and in parliamentary debates is symptomatic of the judicialization of politics. So too is the usage of the Court and the law as political instruments by the political minority—the defeated side in political conflict. As a result of the Constitutional Court's broad jurisdiction and the activist view it takes of its own role, all of these processes appeared very early in Hungary and have progressed a long way.

3. Conclusion

The activity of constitutional courts is often referred to as the activity of 'negative legislatures': the constitutional review of laws leads to the nullification of certain legislative acts—that is, to *negative* legislation—and constitutional courts say, on the basis of constitutional interpretation, what the legislature may *not* do; but they are silent (at least officially) as to what the legislature should do in order to pass a law on the given issue without infringing the constitution.

Constitutional courts, however, often do precisely the latter when, in long written judgements, they analyse what would be the criteria by which the laws or particular paragraphs that they have nullified would be judged constitutional.

We have seen in the above that the Hungarian Constitutional Court is a central actor in Hungarian politics. The Court's broad powers and activism, and the judges' philosophy of judgement and their understanding of their role according to which they may go beyond the text of the constitution, all show that the constitution and constitutional review do not involve some form of 'objective', neutral system of norms that exists above politics, but are instead a part themselves of the political process. It is not simply the case that different legal interpretations and legal philosophies exist that have different consequences when applied to concrete cases. Rather, it is possible to give constitutional arguments both for and against every one of the possible political answers to a given question (as seen in Hungary, for example, in connection with the issues of compensation and the statute of limitations; Sajó, 1993: 42–45). In such cases, the function of the Constitutional Court is that of choosing between the—irreconcilable—constitutional arguments. Its decision is thus based upon legal argument but is nevertheless *political* in character. In this way, the Court often performs the function of political arbitration.

Since its creation, the Hungarian Constitutional Court has, in quantitative terms, played an active role in the constitutional review of the legal system. In qualitative terms, meanwhile, it has acted not only as reviewer of the constitution but, through its abstract constitutional interpretations and its filling of constitutional lacunae, also as *constitution-maker* and *legislator*. The Court's constitution-making role has been increased by the stalling of the process of political constitution-making.

The Hungarian Constitutional Court does not fit into the system of branches of power, but has rather become a powerful counterweight to all other actors in the system—the government, parliament, the president of the republic, the Supreme Court and the local councils. By international standards, it possesses considerable *political* power, and its counterweight role is particularly strong in relation to the government and the government's parliamentary majority. Nevertheless, because of its *gouvernementale* standpoint, the decisions of the Court have not led to ungovernability. The Court played an important role in the creation of the constitutional state, and it has become the most important political institution for the defence of the constitutional state in Hungary.

Note

1. The institution of the constitutional complaint exists in fuller form in Germany, Spain and many post-communist states (such as Slovenia, the Czech Republic, Slovakia, Croatia, and Russia) (Sólyom, 1996: 8).

Chapter Fourteen

The Head of State

The head of state in Hungary is the president of the republic. The presidency was created by constitutional amendment on 23rd October 1989, and it was filled for the first time on 3rd August 1990, with the election of Árpád Göncz. Göncz continues to hold the office today. Reflecting the parliamentary nature of Hungarian government, the presidency is a weak institution. Its powers are largely ceremonial, and election to the post is indirect. Nevertheless, as will be seen, the particular political circumstances of the early 1990s gave the presidency, at least for a time, a greater role than its constitutional powers would suggest.

In what follows, we begin by outlining the circumstances that led to the creation of the presidency in the form that is seen today. We then consider in greater detail the powers of the presidency. Those powers are created not only by constitutional stipulation, but also by the nature of the election of the president, the status of the incumbent prior to his or her election, and the incumbent's views as to how the role of president should best be performed. We thus consider each of these in turn. We then briefly conclude by comparing the role of the presidency in Hungary's political system to that of the Constitutional Court.

1. The Régime Change and the Presidency

The nature of the presidency was one of the most hotly debated issues of the régime change. In the space of ten months in 1989 and 1990, it was the subject of two political agreements, three constitutional amendments, two referendums and five decisions of the Constitutional Court. The option of a presidential system was not raised during this period, but the semi-presidential approach was supported by the final communist government of Miklós Németh, by the MSZMP and, after its formation, by the MSZP. By contrast, the opposition—particularly the liberal opposition—favoured a fully parliamentary system of government, accompanied by only a weak presidency.

These positions can be explained by the perceived interests of the various parties at the time. While the communist (later, former communist) forces hoped that a direct presidential election would be won by the popular, 'nationally aligned' reform communist Imre Pozsgay (Bozóki, 1995: 112), the opposition lacked any nationally recognized personality who could be expected to perform well in such a contest. It was the opposition's viewpoint that eventually won through.[1]

That victory was, however, only the momentary outcome of heated political conflict. It did little to promote political consensus on the subject, and debate has continued on the nature of the presidency ever since. As will be seen later, that debate was fuelled in the early 1990s by the election to the presidency of Árpád Göncz, a member of the opposition to the incoming conservative government. The current debate concerns in particular the method of election of the president: while all of the major parties now agree that the presidency should be an institution with weak powers, some continue to call for direct election in order to give the president greater popular legitimacy.

2. The Power of the Presidency

We turn now to consider in greater detail the power of the presidency within the Hungarian political system. As has been indicated already, that power cannot be understood simply by listing the powers given to the president in the constitution: personal and political factors are also of great importance. Having assessed the constitutional powers that the Hungarian president possesses, we thus consider, in addition, the method of election of the president, the position of the incumbent before election to the presidency and the views of the incumbent as to the presidency's role.

Constitutional Powers

We divide the constitutional powers (Sári, 1996a: 291–298) and functions of the president into five groups. We seek to show where, when and to what extent the president can exert independent political weight.

1. The first group is formed by *representative and symbolic functions.* The president of the republic is the leading dignitary of the country, who represents the *entire* nation and state. He or she represents the Hungarian state on national and state occasions, and on the international stage, but does not participate in government.

2. Another symbolic function is that of the *countersignature* of ministerial decisions and the laws passed by parliament. Included here is the ratification of appointments and promotions made by the government (for example, appointments and promotions of state secretaries, ambassadors, university teachers and military generals) and parliament (such as the appointments of the presidents of the National Bank of Hungary and of public-service radio and television), and the strengthening of the personnel decisions of other bodies (for example, the appointment of the president of the Hungarian Academy of Sciences).[2]

3. Next come the president's 'reserve' powers, which operate when other constitutional organs are unable to function or to reach decisions. These are tied to crisis situations that endanger the functioning of the state (such as states of emergency and of war).

4. A second group of 'reserve' functions are those tied to situations that recur periodically in the normal course of the operation of the democratic institutions—such as the end of the parliamentary cycle, formation of a new government and calling of a parliamentary sitting. The head of state has a role in all parliamentary systems in the formation of governments and in the elimination of situations of ungovernability arising, for example, from the absence of a governmental majority in parliament.

The legal role of the president in this respect is more limited in Hungary than in most parliamentary systems, because the president does not appoint the prime minister—he or she nominates a candidate, who may then be elected by parliament. The president's right to dissolve parliament is also limited. The institution of the constructive vote of no confidence restricts the room for manoeuvre not only of the parliamentary opposition but also of the president in influencing changes of government or the composition of government. This room for manoeuvre has been further narrowed by the fact that the parties with a chance of forming the government have always been relatively united and have had a clear candidate for prime minister, such that the president has had no independent discretion in choosing his nominee.

5. The Hungarian president also possesses certain *discretionary political powers* during the normal operation of the government and the institutions of the state. These powers do not require ministerial countersignature or parliamentary initiation. They involve primarily the right to initiate actions by other state organs and the right to express a political viewpoint. The powers belonging here are the following:

– the right to participate and speak in parliamentary plenary and committee sessions;

– the proposal of bills;

– the initiation of referendums;

– the right to veto laws passed by parliament by referring them to the Constitutional Court for review (the *constitutional veto*) or by sending them back to parliament for reconsideration (the *political veto*) (if the president's objection is not accepted by the Court or the parliament, he or she must sign the law);

– the right to make political statements.

Election and Legitimacy

In presidential and semi-presidential systems, because of the need for greater democratic legitimacy, the head of state is elected directly. In European parliamentary republics, however, the method of election of the president bears no relation to the post's constitutional powers: there are stronger presidents who are indirectly elected—such as the Italian—and weaker, symbolic presidents who are directly elected—such as the Austrian (Dezső and Bragyova, 1989).

The debate in Hungary in 1989 and 1990 over the method of election of the president was greater than that concerning the president's powers, and it has continued to surface repeatedly during the 1990s. Besides political interests, this reflects, in part, strong traditions of personalism in Hungarian politics, and in part the Rousseauist (populist) conception of popular sovereignty that appeared at the time of the régime change.

While the political conflict over the powers of the president had largely died down by the mid–1990s as a result of the decisions of the Constitutional Court and the arrival of parties supporting President Göncz in governmental office, leading to a legal and political stabilization of the weak presidential institution,[3] the demand for direct presidential elections reappeared again and again. This is one question on which the parties were unable to reach consensus during the efforts to draft a new constitution between 1994 and 1997.

The constitutional arrangement that came out of these debates in 1990 is that the president is elected by parliament. A two-thirds majority is needed in the first two rounds, but if these are unsuccessful, only a simple majority of votes cast is required in the third round. The president's term—unlike the four-year term of the government—lasts for five years, and the incumbent can be re-elected no more than once. Árpád Göncz was elected president in 1990 as the only candidate, and the joint candidate of all the new parties. In 1995 he was re-elected in the second round as the candidate of the socialist-liberal coalition against the opposition candidate Ferenc Mádl.

Career Path, Recruitment, Party Affiliation

Besides legal powers and mode of election, the political weight of the president is influenced by the individual filling the post.

In the *semi-presidential system* it is generally the leading politicians of the largest governing party who compete for the post of president, and the elected president chooses his or her prime minister from among the other leading figures of his or her party (or its electoral allies). In France, for example, it is not the position of head of government but that of head of state that constitutes the summit of a political career. In *parliamentary republics*, meanwhile, it is unambiguously the head of government who lies at the centre of constitutional and political power, and the constitutional powers of the president are tightly constrained. His or her power is particularly slight because, while the leader of the victorious party becomes prime minister, it is a highly esteemed, but second- or third-ranking member of the government party who is nominated to the presidency.

A third situation is created, however, when the president is a politician belonging to the opposition to the parliamentary majority and the government. This situation gives the president a political 'counterweight' function *vis-à-vis* the government that is largely independent from his or her constitutional powers: it reduces the head of state's power in the semi-presidential system and increases it in the parliamentary system.

It was the third situation that emerged in Hungary in the wake of the régime change. The election of Árpád Göncz, a member of the SZDSZ, the largest opposition party in parliament, to the presidency in 1990 was the product of the agreement reached in April 1990 between the MDF and the SZDSZ.[4] Göncz was a highly respected person, but he had no political weight and was unknown outside certain literary circles and the veterans of the 1956 revolution. Even within the SZDSZ he did not belong to the core of the party and was not a member of the party leadership. His selection was assisted by his lack of political weight, his role in the events of 1956 (important at a time when those events were being 'rehabilitated' as a revolution) and an old personal tie he had with József Antall, the incoming prime minister.

The effects of party affiliation upon the political weight of the president have been clear in Hungary during the 1990s. Despite his narrow constitutional powers and indirect election, President Göncz's oppositional party affiliation allowed him to act as a political counterweight to the government during the first parliament. By contrast, during the second parliament, when the president's party was itself a member of the government coalition, his role as a counterweight was replaced by a symbolic, representative role, and he became a president with little political weight (Table 1).

Table 1. The power of the president

Recruitment	Function	Power
Leader of the political majority	governance (semi-presidentialism)	great
Second- or third-ranking politician from the political majority	symbolic, representative	slight
Opposition politician	counterweight	moderate/great

The President's Interpretation of His or Her Role and of the Constitution

As has been seen, during his first years in office, Árpád Göncz established for himself a counterweight role *vis-à-vis* the government. Reflecting this, he employed an expansive interpretation of his own constitutional powers: he often interpreted them more broadly than had either the participants in the constitution-making process, or the government, or the Constitutional Court when it was called upon to arbitrate in his disputes with the government. The issues at stake included those of the representation of Hungary in foreign affairs, the powers of the commander-in-chief of the army, the president's independent role in domestic politics (his political speeches and whether he should take a stance in party-political debates) and the question of whether the president could veto appointments to leading government offices. The president entered a series of political conflicts over these matters during the first parliament with the defence minister, the prime minister and the parliamentary majority.

As a result of all of this and of the view he took of his own role, during the first parliament Göncz created out of his mainly symbolic and representative constitutional powers a presidency of intermediate strength. This was helped by the actions of the opposition parties and the most influential opinion leaders in the press, who, despite the constitutional amendment of 1990 and the later Constitutional Court decisions, strove for a reinterpretation of the constitution that would create a counterweight to the government out of the 'neutral' presidency.

In contrast with this, the political activism of the president and his role as a counterweight to the government and the parliamentary majority were reduced during the second parliament beginning in 1994, when Göncz's own party was in government and greater harmony broke out between him and the government. In 1995, Göncz was able to secure re-election for a second five-year term against the candidate of the opposition, on the basis of the votes of the government coalition.

Nevertheless, it was probably a political backlash against the president's counterweight role between 1990 and 1994 that prompted the six-party parliamentary committee that functioned between 1995 and 1997 with the task of preparing a new constitution, to propose the radical curtailment of the constitutional powers of the presidency (*HVG*, 30th November 1996: 117–118).

3. The Constitutional Court and the President

By way of conclusion, we may consider how the powers of the head of state compare with those of the Constitutional Court. Despite all that has been said concerning President Göncz's ability to extend his role beyond that implied by the constitution, it is not the president but rather the Constitutional Court that, during the 1990s, has become the most important of the counterweights to the government and the parliamentary majority. In consequence of the political constellation of the régime change and the demands of the then opposition, the powers of the president were made very slight (and were later further limited by the decisions of the Constitutional Court), and the legitimacy afforded by direct election was denied. By contrast, in the interests of reducing the political uncertainty and risks of the transition, all sides in the formation of the new system sought to vest the Constitutional Court with the greatest possible powers. Of these two institutions, it is the Constitutional Court, which has always been willing to extend its own powers and to engage in political activism, that has become the stronger counterweight to the majority government. While the president is heavily dependent upon the parliamentary majority that elected him—a simple majority is enough for that election, his term lasts for five years and he can be re-elected for one further term—the judges of the Constitutional Court are less dependent—they are elected by a two-thirds majority and for a nine-year term (though they too can be re-elected once). Furthermore, the Constitutional Court, as a 'professional' body composed of lawyers and engaged in legal interpretation, is in principle above politics. The legitimacy of its decisions derives not from political support for them, but from their legal argumentation and that 'above politics' status.

Notes

1. The more moderate part of the opposition—above all within the MDF, the KDNP and the FKGP—argued in favour of direct election and presidential powers stronger than the purely symbolic. For most of them, the election of Pozsgay as head of state would have been acceptable.

2. For example, President Göncz refused to give his assent to the Antall government's appointees to the presidencies and vice-presidencies of public-service radio and television in 1991 and 1992, causing a 'mini' constitutional crisis. The decisions reached by the

Constitutional Court in regard to this conflict narrowed the president's room for manoeuvre.

3. The same is suggested by the fact that around 1996 to 1997, the proposals of the parliamentary committee responsible for drafting a new constitution involved the further narrowing of the president's powers.

4. The SZDSZ obtained the post of president of the republic in exchange for accepting the shortening of the list of decisions requiring a two-thirds majority in parliament.

Conclusion

Hungarian Democracy

In the thematic chapters we have surveyed the most important institutions of Hungary's political and governmental system and the most important cultural and behavioural characteristics of Hungarian politics. In what follows we do not wish to give a strict thematic summary of this—that would only repeat the conclusions given at the end of each chapter. Rather we will seek to build upon those chapters in order to develop a more analytical understanding of the character of the relationship between the cultural-behavioural and institutional levels. As the basis of this we take Arend Lijphart's *majoritarian* and *consensus* models of democracy, which have been widely used within the field of comparative politics (Lijphart, 1984). Lijphart's work is taken as the starting point, in part because of its empirical basis, and in part because, as here, it seeks to link the cultural-behavioural and the constitutional-institutional levels of politics and to analyse the links between them. In what follows we thus summarize briefly these two models of democracy. We then seek to locate the Hungarian political and governmental system within this framework. Finally, we tie to all of this the questions of political culture and the strategies of political actors.

1. The Majoritarian and Consensus Models of Democracy

One of the main questions of the majoritarian and consensus models of democracy is that of the extent to which political power is concentrated in the hands of electoral victors or is divided among different political forces (above all, parties and their constituent groups) and institutions.

The *majoritarian* model of democracy is based upon the British Westminster system, in which, in consequence of the structure of the governmental system and the nature of political divisions and the party system, power is concentrated in the hands of the majority party. Concentration of power characterizes the executive, since this is controlled by a single-party, majority government. The legislature and the executive are interlinked, since the government is responsible to the legislature but is, at the same time, able to control the legislature through the combination of its parliamentary majority and party discipline. This control is complete if the legislature is unicameral, and thus no second chamber of potentially different composition exists that might act as a counterweight to the lower house in which the governing party is dominant. The opposition is able to influence the legislature and the government only if the governing party is divided on a particular question. If the governing party is united—and in Europe this is generally the case—the function of the opposition is restricted to criticism of the government. The concentration of power is further increased if the structure of the state is unitary and centralized, if the sovereignty of parliament is not limited by a written constitution, and if the institutions of direct democracy (such as the referendum) are absent. The possibility for the concentration of power is most likely to emerge where the political culture is homogeneous, where the party system is unidimensional, and where, as a result of a majoritarian electoral system, a two-party system operates. Under these circumstances, single-party, majority government is most likely.

The second ideal-type is the *consensus* model, in which the executive and the legislature are divided among several parties, and in which minority government may occur. The institutional structure and political conventions make it possible for the minority to participate in power. In the ideal-type case, the division of power within the executive is ensured by a grand coalition. At the level of the branches of power, the executive and the legislature are strictly separated from each other. The legislature is bicameral and can thus guarantee the representation of various minorities. Government and the structure of the state are federal and/or decentralized. Rights and jurisdictions are fixed by the constitution and are protected by a minority veto over constitutional amendment. The institutions of direct popular participation (such as the referendum) create a further division of power. The political landscape is characterized by a multi-party system, which is the product of a heterogeneous political culture, multi-dimensional political cleavages and a proportional electoral system (Table 1).

Table 1. The majoritarian and consensus models

	Majoritarian	Consensus
Constitution	unwritten constitution; parliamentary sovereignty	written constitution; minority veto
Executive (government)	united (single-party majority government)	divided (grand coalition)
Legislature–executive relations	fusion	separation
Structure of legislature	unicameral (or asymmetric bicameral)	bicameral (with minority representation)
State structure	unitary; centralized	federal; decentralized
Character of representation	exclusively representative democracy	elements of direct democracy
Electoral system	majoritarian	proportional
Party system	two-party system	multi-party system
Political culture	unidimensional	multi-dimensional

Real-world political systems can be situated along a scale delimited at either end by the two *ideal-types* of majoritarian and consensus democracy. Among the European democracies, the United Kingdom lies closest to the majoritarian model, while Switzerland and Belgium are closest to the consensus model. New Zealand, Ireland, Iceland and Luxembourg are also very close to the majoritarian model, while Italy, Japan, Finland, the Netherlands and the French Fourth Republic are close to the consensus end of the scale.

2. *The Character of Hungarian Democracy*

In what follows we answer the question of which of these two models the Hungarian system is closer to. This we do by surveying and summarizing the main characteristics of the Hungarian political system within the analytical framework of the majoritarian and consensus models.

THE CONSTITUTION • Hungary is a parliamentary republic in which the principle of the separation of the branches of power is constitutionally enshrined. Legislative power is limited by a *written constitution*, and the stability of the constitution is protected by a minority veto. These are the characteristics of consensus democracy. They are further strengthened by the Constitutional Court, with its broad jurisdiction and political activism. Another important factor is the form of the state that the constitution stipulates: Hungary is a *republic*, and not a parliamentary monarchy. The head of state is the *president of the republic*, who wins office not by inheritance, but—indirectly—by election. The head of state is thus an elected politician—in Hungary, a party politician—and is thus not 'above politics'. His or her political role therefore depends upon the party-political composition of the government. Thus, during the first parliament the president acted as a 'counterweight' to the governmental majority, while during the second parliament his political role was more passive.

THE CENTRAL EXECUTIVE POWER: THE QUESTION OF CONSTITUTIONAL AND POLITICAL UNITY • Though in Hungary there has been no grand coalition including every important party, as in the ideal-type of consensus democracy, coalition government has become the norm. After all three parliamentary elections, *coalition* governments have been formed, independently of whether the largest party forming the government has had a relative or an absolute majority in parliament. (Even in 1994, when the Socialist Party gained an absolute majority, a coalition government was formed.) Furthermore, it is important from our point of view that, following all the three parliamentary elections, a *broader* coalition has been formed than was necessary in order to secure a majority. It follows from this that the central government is politically divided. During the early 1990s, efforts were made—originating from the president and the then opposition—to split up the constitutional unity of the executive. Following temporary successes, however, these ended in failure. Important factors in this failure were the decisions of the Constitutional Court and the fact that, following the change of government in 1994, political harmony emerged between the government and the head of state. In sum, primarily because of the political dividedness of the government—the government's coalitional character and the breadth of the coalitions—Hungary's executive can be placed between the majoritarian and the consensus models.

THE RELATIONSHIP OF THE LEGISLATURE AND THE EXECUTIVE: HUNGARIAN DUALISM • In presidential systems, the relationship between the branches of power—because of their separation from each other—is characterized by balance. In parliamentary systems, imbalance can develop in either direction, depending upon the degree of political fragmentation and the nature of the party system. In the United Kingdom, with its two-party system, the government dominates parliament. In Italy or the French Fourth Republic, with multi-party systems and fragmented parliaments, it was parliament that was dominant, while governments were weak. Political development has given Hungary a parliamentary system, a multi-party political landscape and a (moderately) fragmented parliament. The basic structure that has emerged exhibits something of the 'strong parliament; weak, unstable government' model that is a feature of the consensus democracies. This basic structure, however, also displays a range of constitutional provisions that are peculiar to Hungary and that have mutually contradictory effects. In one group may be placed those constitutional arrangements that—reflecting concern over the dangers of a fragmented parliament and coalition government, and above all of the weakening of the executive—strengthen the power of the government, and within it the prime minister, against the parliament. Included in this group are the constructive vote of no confidence and the absence of parliamentary responsibility for individual ministers. Other constitutional provisions—such as that requiring a two-thirds majority for certain laws—strengthen the legislature over the executive. The two-thirds laws create the institution of a minority veto, significantly limiting the legislative power of the parliamentary majority. By institutionalizing a wide-ranging power for the legislature over the executive, this limits constitutionally the workability of parliamentary government. The parliament is further strengthened against the government by the unusual constitutional provision that the head of government cannot initiate the dissolution of parliament. Since some of the unusual provisions of the Hungarian constitution give special rights to the government or head of government while others give such rights to parliament, they strengthen the separation and mutual independence of the branches of power, as was analysed in detail in the chapter on the constitutional and governmental system (Chapter Nine). Because of this, in respect of the relationship between executive and legislature, Hungary is situated between the two models. But the *dualist* structure means that it lies closer to the consensual than to the majoritarian model of democracy.

THE STRUCTURE OF THE LEGISLATURE • The structure of the legislature, as in the majoritarian democracies, is *unicameral.* It is worth noting, however, that Hungary's unicameral parliament is closer to the model of a 'working parliament' than to the confrontational parliament of the Westminster model: the parliament, through the strong committee system, the two-thirds laws and so on, has a strong power of influence and amendment *vis-à-vis* the government.

THE STRUCTURE OF THE STATE • The governmental system and the structure of the state are *unitary*. It is thus similar to that of the majoritarian model of democracy and contrasts with the federal arrangement that is characteristic of consensus democracy. This model is, however, modified by the fact that an unusual level of administrative decentralization has been established in Hungary and that the local councils possess extensive autonomy in respect of decision-making. It is worth mentioning the corporatist Interest Reconciliation Council, which has the right to voice its opinions, or even to exercise a legislative veto, on certain labour issues. The 'functional self-governments' were also established (and operated until 1998) and were given powers in parallel with the government in regard to the pension- and health-insurance systems. Thus, in sum, the Hungarian state is unitary, but also markedly decentralized. In this respect too it can be regarded as lying between the majoritarian and consensus models.

REPRESENTATIVE AND DIRECT DEMOCRACY • The power of the representative institutions of democracy in the Hungarian constitutional and governmental system is not exclusive. The sovereignty of parliament is limited not only by the constitution and the Constitutional Court, but also by the institution of direct democracy. The principle of direct democracy is institutionalized by the *referendum*, which in Hungary can be initiated relatively easily by the citizens (until 1997, through the collection of 100,000 signatures; since then, through gathering 200,000 signatures), and which can be held over a very wide range of issues. This further increases the constitutional division of power. The political significance of this constitutional provision has, however, been reduced by the fact that, in consequence of the restrictive decisions of the Constitutional Court and the parliament, only a small number of referendums have been held. The significance of the institution of the referendum is thus more limited in political practice than in constitutional law.

THE ELECTORAL SYSTEM • Hungary has a *mixed* electoral system, combining the majoritarian and proportional systems. Thus, in this respect too Hungary is located between the majoritarian and consensus models of democracy. Of the 386 seats in parliament, 176 are filled in a (two-round) single-member-district system, around 120 are distributed proportionally in a county-level party-list system, while the remaining ninety or so are allocated by means of a compensatory system on the basis of national party-lists.

THE PARTY SYSTEM • As regards the party system, what has emerged is not the two-party system that is characteristic of majoritarian democracy, but the *multi-party* system that is a feature of consensus democracy: in all three parliamentary elections that have been held to date, the six largest parties were able to secure representation in the legislature.

POLITICAL CULTURE • As the multi-party structure of the political landscape indicates, Hungarian political culture is *multi-dimensional.* In the chapter on political cleavages (Chapter Four), we saw that three major, cross-cutting cleavages divide Hungarian society. The political élite is particularly divided by these dimensions. As regards society, part is similarly fragmented, while another part forms a politically undifferentiated 'mass'. The fragmented, multi-dimensional character of political culture in Hungary again lies closer to the consensual than to the majoritarian model of democracy.

Having surveyed the nine elements that make up the two models, we can state that, with the exception of one element, Hungarian democracy shows the characteristics either of the consensus model or of a mixed system lying between the two models (Table 2). In sum, Hungary lies decidedly closer to the consensual than to the majoritarian model of democracy.

Table 2. The Hungarian political system and the majoritarian and consensus models

	Majoritarian	Intermediate	Consensus
1. Constitution			+ +
2. Executive (government)		+ +	
3. Legislature–executive relations		+	+
4. Structure of legislature	+ +		
5. State structure		+ +	
6. Direct democracy		+	+
7. Electoral system		+ +	
8. Party system			+ +
9. Political culture			+ +

Note: The symbol + indicates where the various institutional elements of the Hungarian political system are placed within the model.

This conclusion is in harmony with the picture that was discussed in the earlier thematic chapters and formed in particular in the survey of the constitutional and governmental system, according to which institutionalized political power is divided in Hungary to a great extent. The division of political power has emerged not only between the various institutions—that is, at the level of the governmental system—but also—as could be seen in the discussion of the political élites and political parties—between the various political forces and political parties (cf. Körösényi, 1993a, 1993b). The division of control and influence over the branches of power and the governmental institutions between various political forces and actors is further increased when—as during the first parliament—different political forces are in control of the central government and the majority of the local councils, and when the head of state is a politician from the parliamentary opposition to the government.

3. Is Hungarian Democracy Consensual? The Role of Elite Strategies

Our conclusion regarding the placement of Hungarian politics and the Hungarian political system within Lijphart's framework was that, on most of the nine factors comprising the model, Hungary lies closer to *consensual* than to majoritarian democracy. This statement, however, strongly contradicts the conventional picture of the character of Hungarian politics, especially in the first half of the 1990s, as *conflictual* and *ideological*. While this picture is, of course, exaggerated, it is not entirely unfounded. What explains this contradiction? In our view the explanation is that the nine factors comprising Lijphart's model neglect a further dimension of great importance—namely, the role of political élites and *élite strategies*. This factor is generally strongly emphasized in the literature on consociational democracy and is stressed elsewhere by Lijphart too. One typology that is of use to us here divides the possible élite strategies into the competitive and the co-operative (Lijphart, 1968). The literature on consociational democracy and the model of consensus democracy described here rests upon the assumption that the élites employ co-operative strategies. That is, in the latter model, the political decision-making system works in a consensual manner if—along with a pluralistic political culture and party system, and broad institutional division of powers—political élite groups pursue a strategy of *co-operation* rather than of competition. The institutional division of power and the system of checks and balances do not in themselves create political consensus: they only make more difficult, or impossible, decision-making and governance carried out by non-consensual, majoritarian means. That is, they lead easily to political and constitutional stalemate.

It was the presumption of the majoritarian and consensus models of democracy that, where political culture is homogeneous, the political alternatives offered by the various parties and élites are not widely different from one another, and thus that the majoritarian model of democracy—involving alternation of parties in office, a two-party system—does not do serious harm to the opposition or minority that rejects the policies of the government of the day. In consequence of the homogeneity of political culture, competitive élite strategies and party competition lead to moderate government—they promote *centripetal democracy*. The other side of the presumption is that, in the case of a fragmented political culture, the majoritarian model of democracy—governance according to the ideas of the majority of the day—seriously harms the interests of the political minority and opposition. From a normative point of view, such a situation is unjust; from the point of view of the political system, it brings the danger of instability. The possibility of political polarization increases, and *centrifugal democracy* can easily emerge. Thus, in our model, in the case of a fragmented political culture, the institutionalized division of power and the integration and participation in government of a wide range of political forces—that is, the *consensus-oriented* form of democracy—are appropriate both from the normative standpoint and from the point of view of institutional stability. The precondition for this, however—and here we return to our key line of argument—is that élites adopt a *co-operative* strategy: they seek agreement, they draw their political opponents into the governmental process, and, in general, they adopt the behaviour of consensus-oriented politics. Hungarian analysts employing the concept of consensus democracy often reproach the party élites precisely for their lack of such behaviour.

We may seek the answer to our original question in the light of this. Through the fragmented political culture and multi-dimensional party system, as well as the institutional system based upon the division of power, the conditions upon which the consensus model of democracy is based have emerged in Hungary. But the co-operative élite strategies that are an implicit presumption of that model have become widespread neither during, nor following, the democratic transition. For this reason, Hungarian democracy in the 1990s is not consensus democracy (as we have seen, it is not majoritarian democracy either).

In our view, however, there exists a readily available explanation for this paradox, which is related to the democratic transition. Above all, the reason élite strategies are not co-operative and consensus-oriented is that, during the period of the formation of the multi-party system and mass democracy, the task of the political and party élites was not the reconciliation of organized subcultures and political groups that were isolated from each other and in conflict with each other, but rather, precisely the opposite of this: the creation of such groups. The development of the 'social embeddedness' of the parties, the foundation of party organizations and the expansion of party memberships—in other words, the creation of political bases for the parties—demand the formulation of the parties' self-identities, the strengthening of ideology, the emphasis of differences with rival parties and the development of adverse images of rival political actors. The presentation of differences rather than similarities and the emphasis of individual rather than common characteristics are what go together with the development of mass democracy and are what serve the goal of political mobilization. The competitive strategy of the political élites is thus a functional element in the generation of multi-party democracy. Political mobilization and the development of party support bases—the political tasks that go along with the creation of mass democracy—are thus, at the same time, important limitations upon the employment of co-operative strategies.

Alongside the functional character of competitive strategies and the link between those strategies and the development of a democratic multi-party system, we must emphasize that all of this is occurring in a country in which the political culture is such that, despite the acceptance of the institutional framework of parliamentary democracy, political thought is traditionally characterized by an antipathy towards parties, and political culture is characterized by depoliticization. In political thought and in public opinion, technocratic government by experts, inter-party consensus and coalition government are highly valued. The parties' competitive strategies—partisanship, the placement of party interests in the centre ground and so on—thus confirm and intensify the distrust and animosity towards parties and strengthen the *legitimacy deficit* facing the political system.

4. Elite Strategies: The Combination of Competitive and Demobilizational Strategies

One of the characteristics of the competitive strategy employed by Hungarian party élites was that political competition emerged first and foremost along a *programmatic-ideological* dimension and was not linked—or was linked only to a very limited extent—to any strategy of mass mobilization and mass-party development understood in an *organizational* sense. None of the parties have become *mass parties*. This is, of course, far from being unique to Hungary. In fact, it has been a general phenomenon in Europe during the last third of the twentieth century. The conditions for mobilization and the generation of a party support base are different now from those of the turn of the century: they no longer demand a close organizational and membership bond between the parties and their voters. The prime instrument of political mobilization is now mass communication, while the construction of mass parties and mass organizations has fallen to second (or third) place in terms of importance. Societal and organizational mobilization play little or no part in the competitive strategies and electoral mobilization of the parties. While this may be regarded as a general characteristic of contemporary European politics, we must emphasize that the absence of organizational mobilization fits into the longer-term twentieth-century Hungarian political tradition of *demobilization*. Besides the absence of mass parties, the strategy of demobilization is also indicated by the systematic frustration or neutralization of attempts at the initiation of referendums on the part of the political élite—often through constitutional and political arguments of dubious validity.

The politics of demobilization and depoliticization is also tied, among other features, to the low level of political participation and to the continuation of atomization and the 'subject-status' mentality in Hungarian political culture. The success of the politics of demobilization is shown by the low level of political participation and protest, as well as the relative weakness of *organizational* links between, on the one hand, the parties and political élites and, on the other hand, the voters and groups within society. This is also the reason for the weakness of pressure and demands on the political élite and political institutions from groups within society. All of this increases the political autonomy of the entire political élite and the political (state) institutional system. In contrast with certain other analyses, we thus conclude that the capacity of the governing political élite is limited not by the pressure exercised by various external groups, but above all by the internal institutional division of power of the political élite, the party system and the governmental system.

The autonomy of the political élite and the governmental system does not, however, mean a strong state and a strong government. The weakness of the Hungarian state that has been emphasized by many analysts is the product of the legitimacy deficit, the civic attitudes and political culture that are ambivalent towards the state, and the low level of efficiency of the government and public administration. Also related to this are the low level of preparedness to pay taxes and the low level of compliance with the law—on the part not only of the citizens, but of the governmental and administrative institutions too. In our view, these problems were promoted during the 1990s by the decentralization and fragmentation of the state institutional and governmental system (through the empowerment of local government, the functional self-governments, and a range of semi-state and public bodies). Alongside this, the instrumentalization of the laws and the whole legal order occurred with the participation not only of the legislators, but also of the executive and other political actors.

In Chapter One, on political culture, we saw that attitudes towards the state are ambivalent and that the level of satisfaction with the state is low. The authority of, and respect for, the state are not very high; tax avoidance and the evasion of the prescriptions of the state are not only standard forms of behaviour, but are also—according to popular opinion—'forgivable crimes'. Among other factors—such as the weakness of the role of mass participation in the régime change, the absence of the revolutionary moment, and the failure to introduce a new constitution, which could have strengthened the constitutional patriotism and consciousness of identity of the political community—we can state on the basis of the above that the *legitimacy* of the political system—if this concept can be approached at all in such a way—is weak. The demobilization and low level of protest do, however, increase the stability of the political system. Political stability in the Hungary of the 1990s is thus the result not of the strength of the legitimacy of the system, or of the performance of the government, but above all of widespread political *apathy*.

Notes

1. Attempts have already been made to interpret the Hungarian political system within this model (Körösényi, 1993a, 1993b; Szegvári, 1994).

2. The ideal-type of this separation is found in the American presidential system. Meanwhile, in Switzerland, though the government is chosen by the legislature, this is for a fixed, four-year term, during which it does not depend politically upon the confidence of the legislature. There is no motion of no confidence.

3. This is far from a merely formal observation. Of the European democracies that have been stable since 1945, one-half are republics (Ireland, Finland, Germany, Austria, France and Italy), while the other half are monarchies (the United Kingdom, Sweden, Norway, Denmark, the Netherlands, Belgium, Luxembourg). While in the monarchies the power of the head of state has, in the absence of democratic legitimacy, atrophied and become almost symbolic, the republics are divided in terms of the extent of the power of the president, depending on different constitutional arrangements and political situations (Lijphart, 1984: 85–89).

4. Despite this, the extent of the decentralization of financial resources, while far from negligible, is rather low by European standards (Körösényi, 1993a: 10, 18; 1993b).

5. Precisely because of this, not only do we regard the exclusivity of representative democracy (the absence of the referendum or other institutions of direct democracy) as

an element of majoritarian democracy, we also—unlike Lijphart—hold the reverse statement to be true: the presence of the institutions of direct democracy in the constitutional and governmental system also fits into the model of consensus democracy, which is characterized by the institutionalization of the division of power.

6. In Lijphart's two-dimensional model, Hungary belongs to the consensual-unitary category (Lijphart, 1984: 214, 216, 219).

7. Co-operative élite strategies, meanwhile, lead, in the case of homogeneous political culture, to the withdrawal of disputes and decision-making over political alternatives from public view, and thus to the depoliticization of democracy.

8. We assume that the gradual, peaceful and élite-based character of the régime change—and the absence of a radical 'revolutionary' break—may also be one source for the legitimacy deficit facing the régime. Not only the experience of a break in continuity, but also the fact of a legal break is lacking in the Hungarian transition: the decisions of the Constitutional Court that have strengthened continuity and the status quo (on, for example, compensation for property lost during communist times and the punishment of crimes committed under the communist régime) have, in the eyes of many, reduced the legitimacy of the new constitutional system.

Appendices

Appendix A. Elections and governments in Hungary, 1990–1998

Parliamentary elections*	Prime minister	Composition of government**	Period of office***
25th March and 8th April 1990	József Antall (MDF)	**MDF**-KDNP-FKGP	23rd May 1990–12th December 1993
	Péter Boross (MDF)	**MDF**-KDNP-FKGP	21st December 1993–15th July 1994
8th and 29th May 1994	Gyula Horn (MSZP)	**MSZP**-SZDSZ	15th July 1994–7th July 1998
10th and 24th May 1998	Viktor Orbán (Fidesz-MPP)	**Fidesz-MPP**-MDF-FKGP	7th July 1998–

* Two rounds.
** The largest parliamentary party is printed in bold.
*** Prime Minister Antall died on 12th December 1993.

Appendix B. Electoral results: percentages of party-list votes and the distribution of seats among parties

Table 1. The first elections: 25th March (second round: 8th April) 1990

Parties	% of votes	seats	% of seats
MDF	24.73	164	42.49
SZDSZ	21.39	92	23.83
FKGP	11.73	44	11.40
MSZP	10.89	33	8.55
Fidesz	8.95	21	5.44
KDNP	6.46	21	5.44
Others*	15.81	11	2.85
Total	100.00	386	100.00

* Others include independents and joint candidates.
Sources: Gábor, Levendel and Stumpf, 1994: 474; Szoboszlai, 1995: 25, 28.

Table 2. The second elections: 8th May (second round: 29th May) 1994

Parties	% of votes	seats	% of seats
MSZP	32.99	209	54.14
SZDSZ	19.74	69	17.88
MDF	11.74	38	9.84
FKGP	8.82	26	6.74
KDNP	7.03	20	5.70
Fidesz	7.02	20	5.18
Others*	12.66	2	0.52
Total	100.00	386	100.00

* Others include joint candidates.
Sources: Gábor, Levendel and Stumpf, 1994: 474; Szoboszlai, 1995: 25, 28.

Table 3. The third elections: 10th May (second round: 24th May) 1998

Parties	% of votes	seats	% of seats
Fidesz-MPP	29.48	148	38.34
MSZP	32.92	134	34.72
FKGP	13.15	48	12.44
SZDSZ	7.57	24	6.22
MDF	2.80	17	4.40
MIÉP	5.47	14	3.63
Others*	8.61	1	0.26
Total	100.00	386	100.00

* Others—independents.
Source: *Magyar Közlöny*, 1998, no. 47.

Appendix C. The composition of the Hungarian governments since 1990

Table 1. The composition of the Antall government, 23rd May 1990

	Minister	Party Membership	Member of Parliament
Prime Minister	J. Antall	MDF	MP
Minister of the Interior	B. Horváth	MDF	MP
Minister of Foreign Affairs	G. Jeszenszky	MDF	-
Minister of Defence	L. Für	MDF	MP
Minister of Justice	I. Balsai	MDF	MP
Minister of Finance	F. Rabár	-	-
Minister of Industry and Trade	Á. P. Bod	MDF	MP
Minister of International Economic Relations	B. Kádár	-	-
Minister of Agriculture	F. J. Nagy	FKGP	MP
Minister of Transport, Communications and Water	Cs. Siklós	MDF	MP
Minister of Labour	S. Győriványi	FKGP	MP
Minister of Culture and Education	B. Andrásfalvy	MDF	MP
Minister of Welfare	L. Surján	KDNP	MP
Minister of Environmental Protection and Regional Development	S. K. Keresztes	MDF	MP
Ministers without Portfolio			
– Land Property	J. Gerbovics	FKGP	MP
– Compensation	Gy. Kiss	FKGP	-
– European Union	F. Mádl	n.d.	-
– National Security	P. Boross*	-	-

* Appointed on 19th July 1990.
Source: Collected by P. Horváth.

Table 2. The composition of the Boross government, 21st December 1993

	Minister	Party Membership	Member of Parliament
Prime Minister	P. Boross	MDF	-
Minister of the Interior	I. Kónya	MDF	MP
Minister of Foreign Affairs	G. Jeszenszky	MDF	-
Minister of Defence	L. Für	MDF	MP
Minister of Justice	I. Balsai	MDF	MP
Minister of Finance	I. Szabó	MDF	MP
Minister of Industry and Trade	J. Latorcai	KDNP	-
Minister of International Economic Relations	B. Kádár	-	-
Minister of Agriculture	J. Szabó	FKGP	MP
Minister of Transport, Communications and Water	Gy. Schamschula	MDF	MP
Minister of Labour	Gy. Kiss	FKGP	-
Minister of Culture and Education	F. Mádl	MDF	-
Minister of Welfare	L. Surján	KDNP	MP
Minister of Environmental Protection and Regional Development	J. Gyurkó	MDF	MP
Ministers without Portfolio			
– Land Property	F. J. Nagy	FKGP	MP
– Privatization and Compensation	T. Szabó	MDF	MP
– Science, European Union	E. Pungor	-	-
– National Security	T. Füzessy	KDNP	MP

Source: Collected by P. Horváth.

Table 3. The composition of the Horn government, 15th July 1994

	Minister	Party Membership	Member of Parliament
Prime Minister	Gy. Horn	MSZP	MP
Minister of the Interior	G. Kuncze	SZDSZ	MP
Minister of Foreign Affairs	L. Kovács	MSZP	MP
Minister of Defence	Gy. Keleti	MSZP	MP
Minister of Justice	P. Vastagh	MSZP	MP
Minister of Finance	L. Békesi	MSZP	MP
Minister of Industry and Trade	L. Pál	MSZP	MP
Minister of Agriculture	L. Lakos	MSZP	MP
Minister of Transport, Communications and Water	K. Lotz	-	MP*
Minister of Labour	P. Kiss	MSZP	MP
Minister of Culture and Education	G. Fodor	-**	MP
Minister of Welfare	P. Kovács	MSZP	MP
Minister of Environmental Protection and Regional Development	F. Baja	MSZP	MP
Minister without Portfolio – Secret Service	B. Katona	MSZP	MP

* Member of the SZDSZ parliamentary group.
** Joined the SZDSZ in October 1994.
Source: Kurtán *et al.*, 1995, 368–387, and the daily press.

Table 4. The composition of the Orbán government, 8th July 1998

	Minister	Party Membership	Member of Parliament
Prime Minister	V. Orbán	Fidesz-MPP	MP
Head of the Office of the Prime Minister	I. Stumpf	-	-
Minister of the Interior	S. Pintér	-	-
Minister of Foreign Affairs	J. Martonyi	-	-
Minister of Defence	J. Szabó	FKGP	MP
Minister of Justice	I. Dávid	MDF	MP
Minister of Finance	Zs. Járai	-	-
Minister of Economic Affairs	A. Chikán	-	-
Minister of Agriculture and Regional Development	J. Torgyán	FKGP	MP
Minister of Transport, Communications and Water	K. Katona	Fidesz-MPP	-
Minister of Education	Z. Pokorni	Fidesz-MPP	MP
Minister of National Cultural Heritage	J. Hámori	-	-
Minister of Health	Á. Gógl	-	-
Minister of Family and Social Affairs	P. Harrach	KDSZ	MP
Minister of Environmental Protection	P. Pepó	-	-
Ministers without Portfolio			
– Phare Projects	I. Boros	FKGP	MP
– Secret Service	L. Kövér	Fidesz-MPP	MP

Source: Collected by the author from the daily press.

Bibliography

Aberach, J., R. Putnam and B. Rockman 1981: *Bureaucrats and Politicians in Western Democracies*. Harvard University Press.

Adorno, W. 1973: *Studien zum autoritären Charakter*. Frankfurt, Suhrkamp.

Adatok az Országgyűlés 1996. évi tevékenységéről [Data on the Activities of Parliament, 1996]. Budapest, Országgyűlés főtitkára, Mimeograph.

Ágh, A. 1994: *The First Steps. The Emergence of East Central European Parliaments*. Budapest, The Hungarian Centre for Democracy Studies.

—. 1998: *Emerging Democracies in East Central Europe and the Balkans*. Cheltenham, Edward Elgar.

—. 1998a: *The Politics of Central Europe*. London, SAGE Publications.

Ágh, A. and S. Kurtán, eds. 1995: *The First Parliament (1990–1994). Democratization and Europeanization in Hungary*. Budapest, Hungarian Centre for Democracy Studies.

Ágh, A. and G. Ilonszki, eds. 1996: *The Second Steps. Parliaments and Organized Interests*. Budapest, Hungarian Centre for Democracy Studies.

Almond, G.A. and S. Verba 1963: *The Civic Culture. Political Attitudes and Democracy in Five Nations*. Princeton, N.J., Princeton University Press.

— , eds. 1989: *The Civic Culture Revisited*. Newbury Park, London—New Delhi, SAGE Publications.

Alemann, von U. 1989: Parlamentarismus. In: Nohlen, D. ed.: *Politikwissenschaft*. Pipers Wörterbuch zur Politik. Munich, Piper, 650–656.

Alkotmányos elvek és esetek [Constitutional Principles and Cases], 1996. Budapest, Constitutional & Legislative Policy Institute.

Angelusz, Róbert and Róbert Tardos 1990: Politikai és kulturális választóvonalak a parlamenti pártok szavazótáborában [Political and Cultural Dividing Lines in the Electorates of the Parliamentary Parties]. *Társadalomkutatás*, No. 3–4.

—.1991: Pártpolitikai mélyrétegek. A parlamenti pártok szavazótáborának profiljához [Party Political Deep Layers: Towards a Profile of the Electorates of the Parliamentary Parties]. In: Kurtán, Sándor et al., eds.: *Magyarország politikai évkönyve 1991* [Political Yearbook of Hungary, 1991]. Budapest, Ökonómia Alapítvány, Economix Rt., 647–667.

—. 1994: Paletta fekete-fehérben [Palette in Black and White]. *Politikatudományi Szemle*, No. 3.

—. 1995: A választói magatartás egy mögöttes pillére. Az egykori MSZMP-tagság szerepe [An Underlying Pillar of Electoral Behaviour: The Role of the Former MSZMP Membership]. *Politikatudományi Szemle*, No. 4.

—. 1996: Választási részvétel Magyarországon, 1990–1994 [Electoral Participation in Hungary, 1990–1994]. *Politikatudományi Szemle*, No. 4.

Arató, András 1995: Parliamentary Constitution-Making in Hungary. *East European Constitutional Review*. Vol. 4, No. 4, 45–51.

—. 1996: Alkotmányozási végjáték [Constitution-Making Endgame]. *Beszélő*, No. 9.

—. 1996a: The Constitution-Making Endgame in Hungary. *East European Constitutional Review*. Vol. 5, No. 4, 31–39.

Bánsági, Zoltán 1996: A kormány munkája, döntéshozatali rendszere 1995-ben [The Work of Government and its Decision-Making System in 1995]. In: Kurtán, Sándor et al., eds.: *Magyarország politikai évkönyve 1996* [Political Yearbook of Hungary, 1996]. Budapest, Demokrácia Kutatások Magyar Központja Alapítvány, 146–156.

Berg-Schlosser, D. 1989: Politische Kultur. In: Nohlen, D. ed.: *Pipers Wörterbuch zur Politik*. Munich–Zurich, Piper.

Beyme, K. von 1993: *Das politische system der Bundesrepublik Deutschland nach der Vereinigung*, Munich—Zurich, Piper.

—. 1993a: *Politische Klasse im Parteienstaat*. Frankfurt, Suhrkamp.

—. 1994: *Systemwechsel in Osteuropa*. Frankfurt, Suhrkamp.

Bibó, István 1986–1990: *Válogatott tanulmányok* [Selected Works]. Volumes 1–4. Budapest, Magvető.

—. 1991: *Democracy, Revolution, Self-Determination*. Ed. Károly Nagy. Boulder, Coo.: Social Science Monographs.

Bihari Mihály, ed. 1992: *A többpártrendszer kialakulása Magyarországon* [The Emergence of the Multi-party System in Hungary]. Budapest, Kossuth.

—. 1996: *Magyar politika 1945–1995* [Hungarian Politics, 1945–1995]. Budapest, Korona.

Bíró, Lajos 1994: A választási eredmények regionalitása [The Regionalization of Election Results]. In: Gábor, Luca, Ádám Levendel and István Stumpf, eds.: *Parlamenti választások 1994* [Parliamentary Elections, 1994]. Budapest, Osiris-Századvég, 564–571.

Bogdanor, V., ed. 1987: *The Blackwell Encyclopaedia of Political Institutions*. Oxford, Basil Blackwell.

Bossányi, Katalin 1994: Megegyezéses díszdoboz, avagy: lesz-e szociális paktum? [Agreement in Gift Wrapping, or: Will there be a Social Pact?] *Mozgó Világ*, No. 11.

Bozóki, András 1990: Politikai irányzatok Magyarországon [Political Trends in Hungary]. In: Kurtán, Sándor et al., eds.: *Magyarország politikai évkönyve 1990* [Political Yearbook of Hungary, 1990]. Budapest, Aula–OMIKK, 184–192.

—. 1992: Post-Communist Transition: Political Tendencies in Hungary. In: Bozóki, A., A. Körösényi and G. Schöpflin, eds.: *Post-Communist Transition. Emerging Pluralism in Hungary*. London, Pinter Publishers–New York, St. Martin's Press, 13–29.

—. 1994: Confrontation and Consensus: On the Forms of Political Integration. In: Bozóki, András, ed.: *Democratic Legitimacy in Post-Communist Societies*. Budapest, T-Twins Publishing House, 66–82.

—. 1995: Hungary's Road to Systemic Change: The Opposition Roundtable. *East European Politics and Societies*, Vol. 7, No. 2. Spring, 276–308.

—. 1995a: *Konfrontáció és konszenzus* [Confrontation and Consensus]. Szombathely, Savaria University Press.

—. 1996: Modernizációs ideológia és materiális politika: szocialisták szocializmus után [Modernization Ideology and Materialist Policy: Socialists after Socialism]. *Századvég*, No. 3.

—. 1996a: Intellectuals in a New Democracy: The Democratic Charter in Hungary. *East European Politics and Societies*, Vol. 10, No. 2. Spring, 173–213.

—. 1997: The Ideology of Modernization and the Policy of Materialism: The Day after the Socialists. *Journal of Communist Studies and Transition Politics*, Vol. 13, No. 3. September, 56–102.

—. 1997a: Mozgalmi-értelmiségi politika a rendszerváltás után: a Demokratikus Charta [Movementist-Intellectual Politics after the Régime Change: The Democratic Charter]. *Politikatudományi Szemle*, No. 1, 98–136.

Bozóki András, ed. 1998: *Intellectuals and Politics in Central Europe*. CEU Press.

Bozóki, A., A. Körösényi and G. Schöpflin, eds. 1992: *Post-Communist Transition. Emerging Pluralism in Hungary*. London, Pinter Publishers—New York, St. Martin's Press.

Böhm, A. and Gy. Szoboszlai, eds. 1996: *Önkormányzati választások 1994: politikai szociológiai örkép* [Local Government Elections, 1994: Political-Sociological View]. Budapest, MTA PTI.

Brettschneider, F. et al. 1994: Materialen zu Gesellschaft, Wirtschaft und Politik in de Mitgliedstaaten der Europäischen Gemeinschaft. In: Gabriel, O.W. and F. Brettschneider, eds.: *Die EU-Staaten im Vergleich*. Opladen, Westdeutscher Verlag, 445–624.

Bruszt László 1995: *A centralizáció csapdája* [The Trap of Centralization]. Szombathely, Savaria University Press.

Bruszt László and János Simon 1991: A 'választások éve' a közvélemény-kutatások tükrében [The 'Year of Elections' in the Light of Public Opinion Research]. In: Kurtán, Sándor et al., eds.: *Magyarország politikai évkönyve 1991* [Political Yearbook of Hungary, 1991]. Budapest, Ökonómia Alapítvány, Economix Rt., 607–646.

—. 1992: A Nagy Átalakulás. Elméleti megközelítések és állampolgári vélemények a demokráciáról és a kapitalizmusról [The Great Transformation: Theoretical Approaches and Citizen Opinions Concerning Democracy and Capitalism]. *Politikatudományi Szemle*, No. l.

—. 1994: Az Antall-korszak után, a választások előtt avagy demokráciánk és pártjaink az állampolgárok szemével [After the Antall Era, Before the Elections, or, Our Democracy and Parties in the Eyes of the Citizens]. In Kurtán, Sándor et al., eds.: *Magyarország politikai évkönyve 1994* [Political Yearbook of Hungary, 1994]. Budapest, Demokrácia Kutatások Magyar Központja Alapítvány, 774–802.

—. 1994a: Pártválasztás kampány elotti szélcsendben [Party Choice in the Calm before the Campaign]. *Társadalmi Szemle*, No. 4.

Budge, I. and H. Keman, 1990: *Parties and Democracy. Coalition Formation and Government Functioning in Twenty States*. Oxford University Press.

CEU (Central European University) 1992, 1993, 1993a: *The Development of Party Systems and Electoral Alignments in East Central Europe*. Database. Budapest, Department of Political Science, Central European University.

Cox, T. and L. Vass, eds. 1994: Civil Society and Interest Representation in Hungarian Parliament. *The Journal of Communist Studies and Transition Politics*, Vol. 10, No. 3. 153–179.

Cox, T. and A. Furlong, eds. 1995: *Hungary. The Politics of Transition*. London, Frank Cass.

Csepeli, György, László Kéri and István Stumpf, eds. 1992: *Állam és polgár. Változás és folyamatosság a politikai szocializációban Magyarországon* [State and Citizen: Change and Continuity in Political Socialization in Hungary]. Budapest, MTA Politikai Tudományok Intézete – Magyarországi Politikai Képzési Központ.

—. 1993: *State and Citizen: Studies on Political Socialization in Post-Communist Eastern Europe*. Budapest, Institute for Political Science of the Hungarian Academy of Sciences.

Csizmadia, Ervin 1995: *A magyar demokratikus ellenzék (1968–1988)* [The Hungarian Democratic Opposition (1968–1988)]. Budapest, T-Twins Publishing House. Monograph.

—. 1995a: A nyolcvanas évek politikai bölcselete [The Political Philosophy of the 1980s]. *Kritika*, June.

Dahl, R. 1971: *Polyarchy. Participation and Opposition*. New Haven—London, Yale University Press.

Dezső, Márta and András Bragyova 1989: *A köztársasági elnök a parlamentáris rendszerekben* [The President of the Republic in Parliamentary Systems]. Budapest, MTA Államtudományi Kutatások Programirodája.

Dogan, M., ed. 1975: *The Mandarins of Western Europe. The Political Role of Top Civil Servants*. New York—London, John Wiley and Sons.

Döring, H. 1994: Parlament und Regierung. In: Gabriel, O.W. and F. Brettschneider, eds.: *Die EU-Staaten im Vergleich*. Opladen, Westdeutscher Verlag, 336–358.

Elster, J. 1997: *Institutional Design in Post-Communist Societies*. Cambridge, Cambridge University Press.

Enyedi, Zsolt 1993: Pillér és szubkultúra [Pillar and Subculture]. *Politikatudományi Szemle*, No. 4.

—. 1995: A katolikus-keresztény szubkultúra fejlodése. [The Development of the Catholic-Christian Subculture]. *Politikatudományi Szemle*, No. 4.

—. 1996: Organizing a Subcultural Party in Eastern Europe. The Case of the Hungarian Chrisitan Democrats. *Party Politics*, Vol 2. No 3., 377–396

—. 1997: *Az elkülönülés politikája. Szervezeti mobilizáció és szubkulturális politika a katolikus-keresztény pártok és mozgalmak körében* [The Politics of Separation: Organizational Mobilization and Subcultural Politics among the Catholic-Christian Parties and Movements]. MTA Politikai Tudományok Intézete, Ph.D. dissertation.

Fábián, György 1994: Választási rendszerek és a magyar megoldás megoldás [Electoral Systems and the Hungarian Solution]. *Társadalmi Szemle*, No. 4.

Fábián, György and Imre László Kovács 1995: Az arányosság újabb dimenziói. Az 1990-es és az 1994-es magyar parlamenti választások eredményeinek összehasonlító elemzése [New Dimensions of Proportionality: A Comparative Analysis of the Results of the Hungarian Parliamentary Elections in 1990 and 1994]. *Politikatudományi Szemle*, No. 2.

—. 1996: A választási rendszerek tipológiai problémái és a magyar választási rendszer [Typological Problems of Electoral Systems and the Hungarian Electoral System]. *Politikatudományi Szemle*, No. 2.

Fábián, Zoltán 1996: Szavazói táborok és szavazói hűség [Electoral Camps and Voter Loyalty]. *Századvég*, No. 1.

Farkas, E.J., Á. Vajda 1995: Candidates for Parliament. In: Tóka, Gábor ed. 1995: *The 1990 Election to the Hungarian National Assembly: Analyses, Documents and Data*. Berlin, Sigma, 67–83.

Farrell, David M. 1997: *Comparing Electoral Systems*. Hemel Hempstead, Herts.: Prentice Hall / Harvester Wheatsheaf.

Favoreu, L. 1995: Az alkotmánybíróságok [The Constitutional Courts]. In: Paczolay, Péter, ed.: *Alkotmánybíráskodás, alkotmányértelmezés* [Constitutional Review, Constitutional Interpretation]. Budapest, Dr. Varga Csaba, 53–116.

Fogarasi, Ágnes 1994: Az albizottságok rendszere és muködésük [The System of Subcommittees and their Operation]. In: Soltész, István, ed.: *A bizottsági munka* (part 1). Parlamenti dolgozatok I. [Committee Work (Part 1). Parliamentary Studies I]. Budapest, Parlamenti Módszertani Iroda, 40–50.

Fraenkel, E. 1991: *Deutschland und die Westlichen Demokratien*. Frankfurt, Suhrkamp.

Fricz, Tamás 1996: *A magyarországi pártrendszer 1987–1995* [The Hungarian Party System, 1987–1995]. Chapter II. Budapest, Cserépfalvi, 61–136.

Gábor, Luca, Ádám Levendel and István Stumpf, eds. 1994: *Parlamenti választások 1994* [Parliamentary Elections 1994]. Budapest, Osiris–Századvég.

Gabriel, O. W. and F. Brettschneider, eds.: *Die EU-Staaten im Vergleich*. Opladen, Westdeutscher Verlag.

—. 1994: Politische Einstellung und politische Kultur. In: Gabriel, O. W. and F. Brettschneider, eds.: *Die EU-Staaten im Vergleich*. Opladen, Westdeutscher Verlag, 96–136.

Gallagher, M., M. Laver and P. Mair, 1992: *Representative Government in Western Europe*. New York—London, McGraw-Hill, Inc.

Gazsó, Ferenc 1990: A káderbürokrácia és az értelmiség [The Cadre Bureaucracy and the Intelligentsia]. *Társadalmi Szemle*, No. 11.

—. 1993: Az elitváltás Magyarországon [Elite Change in Hungary]. *Társadalmi Szemle*, No. 5.

—. 1996: Volt egyszer egy állampárt [Once there was a State Party]. *Társadalmi Szemle*, No. 11.

Gazsó, Ferenc and Tibor Gazsó 1993: Választói magatartás és pártpreferenciák Magyarországon [Electoral Behaviour and Party Preferences in Hungary]. *Politikatudományi Szemle*, No. 4.

Gazsó, Ferenc and István Stumpf 1995: Pártbázisok és választói magatartástípusok [Party Electorates and Types of Electoral Behaviour]. In: Kurtán, Sándor et al., eds.: *Magyarország politikai évkönyve 1995* [Political Yearbook of Hungary, 1995]. Budapest, Demokrácia Kutatások Magyar Központja Alapítvány, 567–580.

—. 1995b: Pártok és szavazóbázisok [Parties and Electorates]. *Társadalmi Szemle*, No. 6, 3–17.

—. 1997: Pártok és szavazóbázisok [Parties and Electorates]. In: Kurtán, Sándor et al., eds.: *Magyarország politikai évkönyve 1997* [Political Yearbook of Hungary, 1997]. Budapest, Demokrácia Kutatások Magyar Központja Alapítvány, 515–531.

—. 1998: A pártok versenyképessége és szavazótábora [The Competitiveness and the Electorates of the Parties]. In: Kurtán, S. et al., eds.. *Magyarország politikai évkönyve, 1998* [Political Yearbook of Hungary, 1998]. Budapest, Demokrácia Kutatások Magyar Központja Alapítvány, 633–647.

Gerentsér Imre and Antal Tóth 1996: Az egyes tiltakozási fajták megítélése és a lakosság részvételi hajlandósága [Judgements on Types of Protest and the Willingness of the Population to Participate]. In: Kurtán, Sándor et al., eds.: *Magyarország politikai évkönyve 1996* [Political Yearbook of Hungary, 1996]. Budapest, Demokrácia Kutatások Magyar Központja Alapítvány, 638–644.

Gombár, Csaba 1989: Mentalitás, érték és politikai intézmény; Velleitásaink [Mentality, Value and Political Institution: Our Velleities]. In: Gombár, Csaba: *Borítékolt politika* [Politics in a Closed Envelope]. Budapest, Pénzügykutató Rt., 62–71, 166–191.

Gombár, Cs. et. al., eds. 1994: *Balance. The Hungarian Government 1990–1994*. Budapest, Korridor—Centre for Political Research.

—. 1995: *Question Marks: The Hungarian Government 1994–1995*. Budapest, Korridor—Centre for Political Research.

Gonda, Pál 1994: A törvényjavaslatok parlamenti tárgyalásának folyamata [The Process of Parliamentary Discussion of Bills]. In: Soltész, István, ed.: *A törvényalkotó Országgyűlés*. Parlamenti dolgozatok III [The Law-Making Parliament. Parliamentary Studies III]. Budapest, Parlamenti Módszertani Iroda, 62–72.

Grosser, D. 1994: Ordnungspolitische Orientierung und wirtschaftiche Entwicklung. In: Gabriel, O. W. and F. Brettschneider, eds.: *Die EU-Staaten im Vergleich*. Opladen, Westdeutscher Verlag, 384–421.

Győrfi, Tamás 1996: Az Alkotmánybíróság politikai szerepe [The Political Role of the Constitutional Court]. *Politikatudományi Szemle*, No. 4.

Halmai, Gábor 1991: Az alkotmányvédelem: az állami hatalom korlátozása [Constitutional Defence: The Limitation of State Power]. *Társadalmi Szemle*, No. 5.

—. 1993: Tiszta Amerika? Alkotmánybíráskodás nálunk és más nemzeteknél [Purely American? Constitutional Review Here and in Other Nations]. *Világosság*, No. 11.

—. 1995: The Constitutional Court. In: Király, K.B. and A. Bozóki, eds.: *Lawful Revolution in Hungary, 1989–1994*. Boulder, Colo.: Social Science Monographs–Highland Lakes, N.J.: Atlantic Research and Publications Inc.—New York: Columbia University Press, 243–258.

Hankiss, Elemér 1989: *Kelet-európai alternatívák* [East European Alternatives]. Budapest, Közgazdasági.

—. 1990: *The East European Alternative*, Oxford, Oxford University Press.

Hankiss, Elemér et al. 1982: *Kényszerpályán? A magyar társadalom értékrendszerének alakulása 1930 és 1980 között* [On an Involuntary Course? The Formation of the Value System of Hungarian Society between 1930 and 1980]. Vols. 1–2. Budapest, MTA Szociológiai Kutató Intézet.

Hann, Endre 1996: A politikai közvélemény a Medián kutatásainak tükrében [Political Public Opinion in the Light of Medián Research]. In: Kurtán, Sándor et al., eds.: *Magyarország politikai évkönyve 1996* [Political Yearbook of Hungary, 1996]. Budapest, Demokrácia Kutatások Magyar Központja Alapítvány, 602–622.

Hanyecz, Imre and János Perger 1994: A magyar parlament tevékenysége számokban [The Work of the Hungarian Parliament in Numbers]. In: Kurtán, Sándor et al., eds.: *Magyarország politikai évkönyve 1994* [Political Yearbook of Hungary, 1994]. Budapest, Demokrácia Kutatások Magyar Központja Alapítvány, 417–445.

Helms, L. 1996: Executive Leadership in Parliamentary Democracies: The British Prime Minister and the German Chancellor Compared. *German Politics*, Vol. 5, No. 1. (April).

Herzog, D. 1975: *Politische Karrieren*. Opladen, Westdeutscher Verlag.

—. 1982: *Politische Führungsgruppen*. Darmstadt, Wissenschaftliche Buchgesellschaft.

Héthy, Lajos 1994: Új vonások a vállalati munkaügyi kapcsolatokban [New Features of Business–Labour Linkages]. *Társadalmi Szemle*, No. 7.

—. 1996: Negotiated Social Peace: An Attempt to Reach a Social and Economic Agreement in Hungary. In: Ágh, A. and G. Ilonyszki, eds.: *The Second Steps. Parliaments and Organized Interests*. Budapest, Hungarian Centre for Democracy Studies. 147–157.

Hine, D. 1993: *Governing Italy*. Oxford, Clarendon Press.

Holló, András n.d.: *Az Alkotmánybíróság* [The Constitutional Court]. Útmutató Kiadó.

Horváth, M. Tamás 1993: Formák és határok. A helyi önkormányzatok politikai viszonyai [Forms and Borders: The Political Relations of Local Governments]. In: Horváth, M. Tamás: *Új változatosság. Politikai keretek és gazdálkodási stratégiák az önkormányzatokban*. Budapest, Helyi Demokrácia és Újítások Alapítvány, 9–92.

Ilonszki, Gabriella 1993: Ahogy a dolgok látszanak. A parlament a képviselok szemével [As Things Seem: Parliament through the Eyes of the Deputies]. In: Kurtán, Sándor et al., eds.: *Magyarország politikai évkönyve 1993* [Political Yearbook of Hungary, 1993]. Budapest, Demokrácia Kutatások Magyar Központja Alapítvány, 116–130.

Ilonszki Gabriella and R. Malcolm Punnett, 1993: Pártok és pártvezetők Magyarországon [Parties and Party Leaders in Hungary]. *Társadalmi Szemle*, No. 10.

—. 1994: Leading Democracy: The Emergence of Party Leaders and Their Roles in the Hungarian Parties. *The Journal of Communist Studies and Transition Politics*, Vol. 10, No. 3, September, 137–152.

Ilonszki, Gabriella and D. Judge, 1994: Képviselet és képviselői szerepek [Representation and the Roles of Representatives]. *Politikatudományi Szemle*, No. 2.

—. 1994 Representational Roles in the Hungarian Parliament. *The Journal of Communist Studies and Transition Politics*, Vol. 10, No. 3. September, 137–152.

Juhász, Gábor 1996: A vizsgálat bezárult... Parlamenti nyomozóbizottságok [The Investigation Closed... Parliamentary Investigative Committees]. *HVG*, 6th April.

—. 1997: Pünkösdi királyság? Parlamenti kisebbségi jogok [Pentecostal Monarchy? Parliamentary Minority Rights]. *HVG*, 24th May.

Katzestein, P.J.: *Mitteleuropa. Between Europe and Germany*. Providence-Oxford, Berghahn Books.

Kavanagh, D. 1972: *Political Culture*. London and Basingstoke, Macmillan.

Kecskés J. and Gy. Németh 1994: *Országgyűlési választások 1994* [Parliamentary Elections, 1994]. Kiskunfélegyháza, Press+Print.

Kende, Péter 1994: Politikai kultúra, civil társadalom, elit [Political Culture, Civil Society, Elite]. In: Gyurgyák, János, ed.: *Mi a politika?* [What Is Politics?] Budapest, Századvég, 233–261.

Kerekes, Zsuzsa 1992: Kilátás az elefántcsonttoronyból. Hatalommegosztás és alkotmánybíráskodás [View from the Ivory Tower: Separation of Powers and Constitutional Review]. In: Kurtán, Sándor et al., ed.: *Magyarország politikai évkönyve 1992* [Political Yearbook of Hungary, 1992]. Budapest, Demokrácia Kutatások Magyar Központja Alapítvány, Economix Rt., 141–149.

—. 1994: Szándékok és tények. Az Alkotmánybíróság elso négy éve a számok tükrében [Intentions and Facts: The First Four Years of the Constitutional Court in the Light of the Numbers]. In: Kurtán, Sándor et al., eds.: *Magyarország politikai évkönyve 1994* [Political Yearbook of Hungary, 1994]. Budapest, Demokrácia Kutatások Magyar Központja Alapítvány, 446–454.

Kéri, László 1994: A kormányzati döntéshozatal szervezet-szociológiai nézőpontból [Governmental Decision-Making from the Viewpoint of Organizational Sociology]. In: Gombár, Csaba et al., eds.: *Kormány a mérlegen 1990–1994* [Government on the Scales 1990–1994]. Budapest, Korridor, 78–93.

—. 1994a: Decision-making of the Government from the Point of View of Organizational Sociology. In: Gombár, Csaba et. al. 1994: *Balance: The Hungarian Government 1990–1994*. Budapest, Korridor—Centre for Political Research, 81–96.

Kilényi, Géza 1990: Gondolatok az Alkotmánybíróság háza táján [Thoughts on the Chamber of the Constitutional Court]. *Magyar Jog*, No. 5.

—. 1994: A parlament és a kormány viszonya a hatalommegosztás rendszerében [The Relationship between Parliament and Government in the System of Separation of Powers]. *Magyar Közigazgatás*, No. 5.

—. 1997: Interjú [Interwiew], *Népszabadság*, 30th May.

King, A. 1990: Modes of Executive–Legislative Relations: Great Britain, France, and West Germany. In: Norton, P., ed.: *Legislatures*. Oxford, Oxford University Press, 208–236.

Kiss, József 1991: Búcsú a pártoktól...? Többpártrendszer Magyarországon 1987–1990 [Farewell to the Parties...? The Multi-party System in Hungary, 1987–1990]. In: Kurtán, Sándor et al., eds.: *Magyarország politikai évkönyve 1991* [Political Yearbook of Hungary, 1991]. Budapest, Ökonómia Alapítvány, Economix Rt., 519–539.

—. 1993: *A Magyar Országgyűlés Almanachja* [The Almanach of the Hungarian Parliament] Budapest, Országgyűlés.

—. 1996: *Az 1994-ben megválasztott Országgyűlés Almanachja* [The Almanach of the Parliament Elected in 1994]. Budapest, Magyar Országgyűlés kiadása.

Kitschelt, H. 1992: The Formation of Party Systems in East-Central Europe. *Politics and Society*, No. 1.

Klingemann, H.-D. 1994: Die Entstehung wettbewerbsorientierter Parteiensysteme in Osteuropa. In: Zapf, W. and M. Dierkes, eds.: *Institutionvergleich und Institutionendynamik*. ZB-Jahrbuch 1994, Wissenschaftszentrum Berlin für Sozialforschung.

Konrád, György and Iván Szelényi 1992: Értelmiség és dominancia a posztkommunista társadalmakban [Intellectuals and Domination in Post-Communist Societies]. *Politikatudományi Szemle,* No. 1.

—. 1991. Intellectuals and Domination in Post-Communist Societies. In: *Social Theory in a Changing Society,* ed. Pierre Bourdieu and James Coleman. Boulder, Colo., Westview.

Kovách, Imre 1994: A gazdasági elit Magyarországon [The Economic Elite in Hungary]. In: Balogh, István (ed.): *Törésvonalak és értékválasztások.* Budapest, MTA Politikai Tudományok Intézete.

Kovács, István ed. 1988: *Nyugat-Európa alkotmányai* [The Constitutions of Western Europe]. Budapest, Közgazdasági.

Kovács, László Imre 1992: Voksok és mandátumok. Arányos-e a magyar választási rendszer? [Votes and Seats: Is the Hungarian Electoral System Proportional?] *Társadalmi Szemle,* No. 12.

Kóczián, Péter and Balázs Weyer n.d.: *Felelősök* [Those in Responsibility]. Budapest, Figyelő.

Körösényi, András 1988: A kritikai-ellenzéki értelmiség Közép-Európában. A totalitárius rendszerek bomlásától a pragmatikus-autoriter diktatúrák létrejöttéig [The Critical-Oppositional Intelligentsia in Central Europe from the Collapse of the Totalitarian Systems to the Emergence of the Pragmatic-Authoritarian Dictatorships]. *Századvég,* No. 6–7.

—. 1988a: The Emergence of Plurality Trends and Movements in Hungary's Society in the Mid–1980s. *Südosteuropa,* No. 11–12.

—. 1989: Újjáéledő politikai tagoltság [Rejuvenescent Political Divisions]. In: Kurtán, Sándor et al.: *Magyarország politikai évkönyve 1988* [Political Yearbook of Hungary 1998]. Budapest, R–Forma Kiadói Kft., 283–292.

—. 1990: Pártok és szavazók. Parlamenti választások 1990-ben [Parties and Voters: The 1990 Parliamentary Elections]. *Mozgó Világ,* No. 8.

—. 1990a: Hungary. *Electoral Studies* 9: 337–345.

—. 1991: Revival of the Past or New Beginning? The Nature of Post-Communist Politics. *Political Quarterly* 62 (1): 1–23; also in Bozóki, A., A. Körösényi and G. Schöpflin, eds. 1992: *Post-Communist Transition. Emerging Pluralism in Hungary.* London, Pinter Publishers—New York, St. Martin's Press, 111–131.

—. 1992: A hatalommegosztás és parlamentarizmus [The Separation of Powers and Parliamentarism]. In: Kurtán, Sándor et al., ed.: *Magyarország politikai évkönyve 1992* [Political Yearbook of Hungary, 1992]. Budapest, Demokrácia Kutatások Központja Alapítvány, Economix Rt., 58–62.

—. 1993: Politische Gliederung 1990. In: Bayer, J. and R. Deppe, eds.: *Der Schock der Freiheit. Ungarn auf dem Weg in die Demokratie.* Frankfurt: Suhrkamp Verlag, 118–127.

—. 1993a: Kié a hatalom? A hatalom pluralitása Magyarországon, 1990–1992 [To Whom Does Power Belong? The Pluralism of Power in Hungary, 1990–1992]. *Politikatudományi Szemle,* No. 4.

—. 1993b: The Divided Republic. The Distribution of Power in Hungary 1990–1992. Minza de Gunzburg Center for European Studies Program on Central and Eastern Europe Working Papers, No. 32. Cambridge, Mass.: Harvard University.

—. 1993c: Stable or Fragile Democracy? Political Cleavages and Party System in Hungary. *Government and Opposition* Vol. 28, No. 1: 87–105.

—. 1994. Relative Stabilität, strukturelle Dilemmata. Parteien, Eliten, Gesellschaft und Politik in Ungarn 1989–1992. In: Hatschikjan, A. M. and R.P. Weilemann, eds.: *Parteienlandschaften in Osteuropa*. Padeborn—Munich—Vienna—Zurich, Schöningh, 11–40.

—. 1995: Kényszerkoalíció vagy természetes szövetség? In: Gombár, Csaba et al., eds.: *Kérdőjelek: a magyar kormány 1994–1995*. Budapest, Korridor, 260–280.

—. 1995a: Forced Coalition or Natural Alliance? The Socialist-Liberal Democrat Coalition, 1994 [Forced Coalition or Natural Alliance]. In: Gombár, Csaba et al., eds. 256–277.

—. 1996: A magyar politikai gondolkodás főárama [The Mainstream of Hungarian Political Thinking]. *Századvég*, No. 3 (Winter).

—. 1996a: Demokrácia és patronázs. Politikusok és köztisztviselők viszonya [Democracy and Patronage. Relation of Politicians and Public Servants]. *Politikatudományi Szemle*, No. 4.

—. 1996b: Nómenklatúra és vallás–törésvonalak és pártrendszer Magyarországon [Nomenklatura and Religion: Cleavages and the Party System in Hungary]. *Századvég*, No. 1.

—. 1997 Das Parteiensystem Ungarns. In: Segert, D., R. Stöss and O. Niedermayer: *Parteiensysteme in Postkommunistischen Gesellschaften Osteuropas*. Opladen, Westdeutscher Verlag, S. 157–180.

—. 1998: Intellectuals and Democracy in Eastern Europe. In: A. Bozóki, ed.: *Intellectuals and Politics in Central Europe*. CEU Press, 227–244.

—. 1999 Cleavages and the Party System in Hungary. In: Enyedi and Tóka, eds.: *The 1994 Elections to the Hungarian National Assembly*. (Founding Elections in Eastern Europe). Berlin, Sigma.

Kőhegyi, Kálmán 1994: Egy lehetséges szociális paktum politikai veszélyei [The Political Dangers of a Possible Social Pact]. *Magyar Hírlap*, 13 June.

—. 1995: Több szerep keres egy szerzőt. A társadalmi-gazdasági megállapodás [Several Roles Seek an Author: The Social-Economic Agreement]. *Európa Fórum*, V, No. 3 (October).

Kukorelli, István 1995: A kormány és ellenzéke az új házszabályban [The Government and its Opposition in the New Parliamentary Standing Orders]. In: Gombár, Csaba et al., eds.: *Kérdőjelek: a magyar kormány 1994–1995*. Budapest, Korridor, 110–128.

—. 1995: The Government and its Opposition in the New Rules of Order of the House. In: Gombár, Csaba et al., eds.: 110–130.

—. 1995a: *Az alkotmányozás évtizede* [The Decade of Constitution-Making]. Budapest, Korona.

—. 1996: *Alkotmánytan* [Constitutional Studies]. Budapest, Osiris.

Kurtán, Sándor 1995: A legfontosabb közjogi intézmények vezetoi és az Országgyűlés tagjai [The Leaders of the Major Public Institutions and the Members of Parliament]. In: Kurtán, Sándor et al., eds.: *Magyarország politikai évkönyve 1995* [Political Yearbook of Hungary, 1995]. Budapest, Demokrácia Kutatások Központja Alapítvány, 368–383.

Kurtán, Sándor et al., eds. 1990: *Magyarország politikai évkönyve 1990* [Political Yearbook of Hungary, 1990]. Budapest, Aula–OMIKK.

—. 1995: *Magyarország politikai évkönyve 1995* [Political Yearbook of Hungary, 1995]. Budapest, Demokrácia Kutatások Magyar Központja Alapítvány.

Lackó, Miklós 1988: *Korszellem és tudomány* [The Spirit of the Age and Science]. Budapest, Gondolat.

Ladó, Mária 1996: Continuity and Changes in Tripartism in Hungary. In: Ágh, A. and G. Ilonszki, eds.: *The Second Steps. Parliaments and Organized Interests*. Budapest, Hungarian Centre for Democracy Studies, 158–172.

Ladó, Mária and Ferenc Tóth, eds. 1996: *Helyzetkép az érdekegyeztetésről (1990–1994)* [The Situation of Interest Reconciliation (1990–1994)]. Budapest, Secretariat of the Interest Reconciliation Council—PHARE Social Dialogue Project.

Landfried, C. 1984: *Bundesverfassungsgericht und Gesetzgeber*. Baden-Baden, Nomos.

Landfried, C., ed. 1988: *Constitutional Review and Legislation. An International Comparison*. Baden-Baden, Nomos.

Laver, M. and N. Schofield, 1991: *Multi-party Government. The Politics of Coalition in Europe*. Oxford University Press.

Lázár, Guy, ed. 1992: A politikai közvélemény a Medián kutatásainak tükrében [Political Public Opinion in the Light of Medián Research]. In: Kurtán, Sándor et al., ed.: *Magyarország politikai évkönyve 1992* [Political Yearbook of Hungary, 1992]. Budapest, Demokrácia Kutatások Magyar Központja Alapítvány, Economix Rt., 575–603.

Lázár, Katalin 1996: Parlamenti pártok közötti távolságok [Distances between the Parliamentary Parties]. Budapest, ELTE Jogi Továbbképző Intézet.

Lengyel, Emőke, Molnár Zoltán and Tóth Antal 1994: Magyar lakossági vélemények gazdaságról, politikáról és az európai együttmuködésről 1991–1993 [The Opinions of the Hungarian Population on the Economy, Politics and European Co-operation, 1991–1993]. In: Kurtán, Sándor et al., eds.: *Magyarország politikai évkönyve 1994* [Political Yearbook of Hungary, 1994]. Budapest, Demokrácia Kutatások Magyar Központja Alapítvány, 757–773.

—. 1996: Közép- és kelet-európai vélemények gazdaságról, politikáról és az európai együttmuködésről 1995-ben [Central and East European Opinions on the Economy, Politics and European Co-operation in 1995]. In: Kurtán, Sándor et al., eds.: *Magyarország politikai évkönyve 1996* [Political Yearbook of Hungary, 1996]. Budapest, Demokrácia Kutatások Magyar Központja Alapítvány, 623–637.

Lengyel, György 1995: A magyar gazdasági elit a kilencvenes évek első felében [The Hungarian Economic Elite in the First Half of the 1990s]. In: Kurtán, Sándor et al., eds.: *Magyarország politikai évkönyve 1995* [Political Yearbook of Hungary, 1995]. Budapest, Demokrácia Kutatások Magyar Központja Alapítvány, 314–323.

—. 1998: The Hungarian Economic Elite in the First Half of the 1990s. In: Higley, J., J. Pakulski, and W. Weselowski, eds.: *Postcommunist Elites and Democracy in Eastern Europe*. Houndmills—London—New York., MacMillan Press–St.Martin's Press, 203–212.

Lengyel László 1993: *Útfélen* [At the Halfway Point]. Budapest, 2000–Századvég.

Lijphart, A. 1968: Typology of Democratic Systems. *Comparative Political Studies*, Vol. 1 (April); reprinted. In: Lijphart, A. (ed.): *Politics in Europe. Comparisons and Interpretations*. Berkeley, University of California Press.

—. 1984: *Democracies. Patterns of Majoritarian and Consensus Government in Twenty-One Countries*. New Haven—London, Yale University Press.

—. 1992: Democratization and Constitutional Choices in Czechoslovakia, Hungary and Poland, 1989–1991. *Journal of Theoretical Politics*, Vol. 4, No. 2, 207–223

—. 1992a: *Parliamentary versus Presidential Government*. Oxford, Oxford University Press.

Lipset, S. M. and S. Rokkan 1967: Cleavage Structures, Party Systems and Voter Alignments. An Introduction. In: Lipset, S.M. and S. Rokkan, eds.: *Party Systems and Voter Alignments. Cross-national Perspectives*. London, Collier-Macmillan; New York, The Free Press, 1–64.

Loewenberg, G. 1993: Die neuen politische Eliten Mitteleuropas: Das Beispiel der Nationalversamm-lung. *Zeitschrift für Parlamentsfragen*, Heft 3/93, 438–457.

Lőrincz, Lajos, ed. 1993: *Közigazgatási alapvizsga* [Civil Service Examination]. BM Kiadó.

—. 1993a: *A közigazgatás alapintézményei. A közigazgatás központi szervei* [The Basic Institutions of the Public Administration. The Central Organs of the Public Administration]. Budapest, Államigazgatási Főiskola.

Machos, Cs. 1997: Elitenbildung und Elitenwandel in der Ungarischen Sozialistischen Partei (1989–1996). *Südosteuropa*. Heft 1–2, 65–89.

A Magyar Országgyűlés 1994–1996. évi tevékenységéről [On the Activity of the Hungarian Parliament, 1994–1996]. Budapest, Országgyűlés Képviselői Tájékoztató Központ.

Magyary, Zoltán 1942: *Magyar közigazgatás* [Hungarian Public Administration]. Budapest, Magyar Királyi Egyetemi Nyomda.

Marián, Béla, ed. 1996: A politikai közvélemény a Marketing Centrum kutatásainak tükrében [Political Public Opinion in the Light of Research by Marketing Centrum]. In: Kurtán, Sándor et al., eds.: *Magyarország politikai évkönyve 1996* [Political Yearbook of Hungary, 1996]. Budapest, Demokrácia Kutatások Magyar Központja Alapítvány, 571–601.

—. 1997: A politikai közvélemény a Szokai–Tocsik-ügy évében [Political Public Opinion in the Year of the Szokai–Tocsik Affair]. In: Kurtán, Sándor et al., eds.: *Magyarország politikai évkönyve 1997* [Political Yearbook of Hungary, 1997]. Budapest, Demokrácia Kutatások Magyar Központja Alapítvány, 532–567.

—. 1998: Választás előtt [Before the Election]. In: Kurtán, Sándor et al., eds.: *Magyarország politikai évkönyve, 1998* [Political Yearbook of Hungary, 1998]. Budapest, Demokrácia Kutatások Magyar Központja Alapítvány, 648–688.

van der Meer, A. et al. 1995: A parlamenti párt szerepe az új demokráciákban. Magyarország és Lengyelország esete. *Politikatudományi Szemle*, No. 4.

Mény, Y. 1991: *Government and Politics in Western Europe*. Oxford, Oxford University Press.

Mészáros, József and István Szakadát 1993: *Választási eljárások, választási rendszerek* [Electoral Procedures, Electoral Systems]. Budapest, BME Szociológiai Tanszék.

—. 1995: *Magyarország politikai atlasza* [Political Atlas of Hungary]. Budapest, Konrad-Adenauer–Stiftung.

A Miniszterelnöki Hivatal Évkönyve 1995 [The Yearbook of the Prime Minister's Office, 1995]. Budapest, Magyar Hivatalos Közlöny Kiadó.

A Miniszterelnöki Hivatal Évkönyve 1996 [The Yearbook of the Prime Minister's Office, 1996]. Budapest, Magyar Hivatalos Közlöny Kiadó.

Montgomery, K. 1994: *Interest Group Representation in the Hungarian Parliament.* Budapest Papers on Democratic Transition, Hungarian Centre for Democracy Studies Foundation, Department of Political Science, Budapest University of Economics.

—. 1996: *Interest Group Representation in the Hungarian Parliament,* In: Ágh, A. and G. Ilonszki, eds.: *The Second Steps. Parliaments and Organized Interests.* Budapest, Hungarian Centre for Democracy Studies, 430–450.

Müller, György 1991: A kormányzati struktúra változásai 1987–1991 [Changes in the Governmental Structure, 1987–1991]. *Magyar Közigazgatás,* No. 12.

Norton, P., ed. 1990: *Legislatures.* Oxford, Oxford University Press.

Oberreuter, H. 1994: Das Parlament als Gesetzgeber und Repräsentationsorgan. In: Gabriel, O.W. and F. Brettschneider, eds.: *Die EU-Staaten im Vergleich.* Opladen, Westdeutscher Verlag, 307–335.

Országgyűlési kézikönyv 1992 [Parliamentary Handbook 1992]. Budapest, Magyar Országgyűlés.

Őry, Csaba 1997: Ha elfogy a türelem... A Horn-kormány és az érdekképviselet [If Patience Runs Out... The Horn Government and Interest Representation]. *Magyar Nemzet,* 24th June 1997.

Paczolay, Péter 1993: The New Hungarian Constitutional State. In: Howard A.E.D., ed.: *Constitution-Making in Eastern Europe.* Washington, D.C., The Woodrow Wilson Center Press, 21–55.

—. 1993a: Könyörtelen bírói hatalom? A bírói alkotmányértelmezés politikai szerepe [Merciless Judicial Power? The Political Role of Constitutional Interpretation by the Judiciary]. *Jogállam,* No. 2.

Pesti, Sándor 1997: A bizottság-plénum viszonya a törvényalkotás során (1920–1994) [The Committee–Plenum Relationship in Law-Making (1920–1994)]. In: Soltész, István, ed.: *A plenáris ülés* (part 1). Parlamenti Dolgozatok VI [The Plenary Session (Part 1). Parliamentary Studies VI]. Budapest, Parlamenti Módszertani Iroda, 288–306.

Petrétei, József 1994: A 'jó' kormányforma [The 'Good' Form of Government]. *Társadalmi Szemle,* No. 3.

Pokol, Béla 1991: Alkotmánytani alternatívák [Constitutional Alternatives]. *Társadalomtudományi Közlemények,* No. 3–4.

—. 1992: *A professzionális intézményrendszer elmélete* [The Theory of the Professional Institutional System]. Budapest, Felsőoktatási Koordinációs Iroda.

—. 1992a: Aktivista alapjogász vagy parlament törvénybarát? A magyar Alkotmánybíróság jogkoncepciói [Activist Lawyer or Friend of Parliamentary Law? The Legal Conceptions of the Hungarian Constitutional Court]. *Társadalmi Szemle,* No. 5.

—. 1992b: Aktivizmus és az Alkotmánybíróság [Activism and the Constitutional Court]. In: Kurtán, Sándor et al., eds.: *Magyarország politikai évkönyve 1992* [Political Yearbook of Hungary, 1992]. Budapest, Demokrácia Kutatások Magyar Központja Alapítvány, Economix Rt., 150–155.

—. 1993: A politika nyelvezete [The Language of Politics]. In: Pokol, Béla: *Pénz és politika* [Money and Politics]. Budapest, Aula, 59–80.

—. 1993a: Professzionalizálódás, értelmiség, politika [Professionalization, Intellectuals, Politics]. In: Pokol, Béla: *Pénz és politika* [Money and Politics]. Budapest, Aula, 81–90.

—. 1994: *A magyar parlamentarizmus* [Hungarian Parliamentarism]. Budapest, Cserépfalvi.

Pridham, Geoffrey and Paul Lewis, eds. 1996: *Stabilising Fragile Democracies: New Party Systems in Southern and Eastern Euorope*. London—New York, Routledge.

Putnam, D. R. 1976: *The Comparative Study of Political Elites*. New Jersey, Prentice-Hall.

Rebenstorf, H. 1990: Politische Herkunft und politische Karriere. In: Klingemann, H-D., R. Stöss and B. Weßels, eds.: 1991: *Politische Klasse und politische Institutionen*. Westdeutscher Verlag.

Róna-Tas, Á. 1991: The Selected and the Elected: The Making of the New Parliamentary Elite in Hungary. *East European Politics and Societies*, Vol. 5, No. 3.

—. 1994: The First Shall Be Last? Entrepreneurship and Communist Cadres in the Transition from Socialism. *American Journal of Sociology*, Vol. 100, No. 1. July.

Rose, R. 1991: Prime Ministers in Parliamentary Democracies. *West European Politics*, Vol. 14, No. 2, 9–24.

Rudzio, W. 1991. *Das politische System der Bundesrepublik Deutschland*, Opladen, Leske & Budrich.

Rüb, F.W. 1993: Designing Political Systems in East European Transitions. A Comparative Study of Bulgaria, Czecho-Slovakia, and Hungary. *Papers on East European Constitution Building*, No. 3. Zentrum für Europäische Rechtspolitik. Universität Bremen, 1–68.

Sajó, András 1993: A 'láthatatlan alkotmány' apróbetűi: a magyar Alkotmánybíróság első ezerkétszáz napja [The Smallprint of the 'Invisible Constitution': The First 1,200 Days of the Constitutional Court]. *Állam- és Jogtudomány*, XXXV, No. 1–2.

—-. 1993a: Jövendő alkotmányos válságok elé elé [Before Future Constitutional Crises]. *Világosság*, No. 7.

—. 1996: A materiális természetjog árvái, avagy hogyan védi Alkotmánybíróságunk az elesetteket [Orphans of Material Constitutional Law, or, How Does Our Constitutional Court Protect the Dropouts]. *Magyar Jog*, No. 4.

Sári, János 1993: A rendeleti jogalkotás [Law-Making by Decree]. *Társadalmi Szemle*, No. 7.

—. 1994: A kormány és a rendeletalkotás [The Government and Decree-Making]. In: Gombár, Csaba et al., eds.: *Kormány a mérlegen 1990–1994* [Government in the Balance, 1990–1994]. Budapest, Korridor, 140–157.

—. 1994a: The Government and Legislation Decree. In: Gombár, Csaba et al., eds.: *Balance: The Hungarian Government 1990–1994*. Budapest, Korridor—Centre for Political Research, 144–161.

—. 1995: *A hatalommegosztás* [The Separation of Powers]. Budapest, Osiris.

—. 1996: A kormány [The Government]. In: Kukorelli, István, ed.: *Alkotmánytan* [Constitutional Studies]. Budapest, Osiris, 303–319.

—. 1996a: A köztársasági elnök [The President of the Republic]. In: Kukorelli, István, ed.: *Alkotmánytan* [Constitutional Studies]. Budapest, Osiris, 291–302.

—. 1996b: Constitutional Change of the Régime in Hungary. Principle and Methods. Old and New Institutions. In: Tóth, Károly, ed.: *System Transformation and Constitutional Developments in Central and Eastern Europe*. József Attila University, Faculty of Law—Károli Gáspár Reformed University, Szeged–Kecskemét, 51–76.

Sartori, G. 1969: From the Sociology of Politics to Political Sociology. In: Lipset, S.M., ed.: *Politics and the Social Sciences*. New York, Oxford University Press, 65–100.

Segert, D., R. Stöss and O. Niedermayer 1997: *Parteiensysteme in Postkommunistischen Gesellschaften Osteuropas*. Opladen, Westdeutscher Verlag.

Simon, János 1991: A 'nem-szavazók' választása [The Choice of Non-Voters]. In: Kurtán, Sándor et al., eds.: *Magyarország politikai évkönyve 1991* [Political Yearbook of Hungary, 1991]. Budapest, Ökonómia Alapítvány, Economix Rt., 120–127.

—. 1995: Mit jelent a demokrácia a magyarok számára? [What Does Democracy Mean to Hungarians?] *Politikatudományi Szemle*, No. 1.

—. 1995a: Freiheit oder Wohlstand? Zum Demokratienverstandnis der ungarischen Bürger. Südoseuropa, 44.Jhg. Heft 11–12. S. 711–727. SOCO Survey 1995.

Soltész, István, ed. 1994: *A bizottsági munka* (part 1). Parlamenti dolgozatok I [Committee Work (Part 1). Parliamentary Studies I]. Budapest, Parlamenti Módszertani Iroda.

—. 1994a: *A törvényalkotó Országgűlés*. Parlamenti dolgozatok III [The Law-Making Parliament. Parliamentary Studies III]. Budapest, Parlamenti Módszertani Iroda.

—. 1995a: A bizottságok szerepe a kormány ellenőrzésében ellenőrzésében [The Role of Committees in the Supervision of Government]. In: Soltész, István, ed.: *A bizottsági munka* (part 2). Parlamenti dolgozatok II. Budapest, Parlamenti Módszertani Iroda, 25–55.

—. 1995b: A vizsgálóbizottságok [Investigative Committees]. In: Soltész, István, ed.: *A bizottsági munka* (part 2). Parlamenti dolgozatok II [Committee Work (Part 2). Parliamentary Studies II]. Budapest, Parlamenti Módszertani Iroda, 107–131.

—. 1995c: *Országgyűlési kézikönyv* [Parliamentary Handbook]. Budapest, Unio.

Sólyom, László 1996: Az Alkotmánybíróság hatáskörének sajátossága [The Exceptionality of the Jurisdication of the Constitutional Court]. In: *Tanulmányok Benedek Ferenc tiszteletére* [Studies in Honour of Ferenc Benedek]. Pécs, Studia Iuridica Auctoritate Universitatis Pécs Publicata 123, 5–34.

Stumpf, István 1994: Választói magatartás a generációs és a vallási törésvonalak mentén [Electoral Behaviour alongside the Generational and Religious Cleavages]. In: Balogh, István, ed.: *Törésvonalak és értékválasztások. Politikatudományi vizsgálatok a mai Magyarországról* [Cleavages and Value Divisions: Political-Scientific Investigations Concerning the Hungary of Today]. Budapest, MTA Politikai Tudományok Intézete, 147–167.

—. 1996: Elszalasztott vagy elhalasztott politikai generációváltás? [Missed or Postponed Political Generation Change?] *Századvég*, No. 1.

Sugatagi, Gábor 1994: Politikuskiválasztódás, politikuskarrierek [Selection of Politicians, Careers of Politicians]. *Politikatudományi Szemle*, No. 4.

Szabadon választott. Parlamenti almanach 1990 [Freely Elected. Parliamentary Almanach 1990]. Budapest, Idegenforgalmi Propaganda és Kiadó Vállalat.

Szabó, Máté 1994: A társadalmi mozgalmak szerepe a demokratikus politikai rendszer intézményesedésének folyamatában Magyarországon [The Role of Social Movements in the Process of Institutionalization of the Democratic Political System in Hungary]. *Szociológiai Szemle*, No. 3.

—. 1995: A szabadság rendje. Társadalmi mozgalmak, politikai tiltakozás, politikai szervezetek a magyarországi rendszerváltás folyamatában [The System of Freedom: Social Movements, Political Protest and Political Organizations in the Process of Régime Change in Hungary]. *Politikatudományi Szemle*, No. 4.

—. 1995a: Politikai tiltakozás mint az új politikai kultúra eleme: Magyarország, Szlovénia, Szlovákia [Political Protest as an Element of the New Political Culture: Hungary, Slovenia, Slovakia]. *Szociológiai Szemle*, No. 3.

—. 1996: A tiltakozás kultúrái a posztkommunista társadalmakban: Magyarország, Szlovénia, Szlovákia [Cultures of Protest in Post-Communist Societies: Hungary, Slovenia, Slovakia]. *Társadalmi Szemle*, No. 1.

—. 1996a: Közép-Európa — a tiltakozás kultúrája a rendszerváltás előtt és után [Central Europe — The Culture of Protest before and after the Régime Change]. *Társadalmi Szemle*, No. 4.

—. 1996b: A kollektív tiltakozás trendjei [The Trends of Collective Protest]. In: Kurtán, Sándor et al., eds.: *Magyarország politikai évkönyve 1996* [Political Yearbook of Hungary, 1996]. Budapest, Demokrácia Kutatások Magyar Központja Alapítvány, 322–330.

Szabó, Miklós 1989: *Politikai kultúra Magyarországon, 1896–1986* [Political Culture in Hungary, 1986–1986]. Budapest, Medvetánc Könyvek.

Szakadát István 1992: Káderfo(r)gó [Cadre Trap, Cadre Rotation]. *Társadalmi Szemle*, No. 8–9; *Szakinfo* 49, September 1993.

Szalai, Erzsébet 1994: *Útelágazás* [Road Fork]. Budapest, Pesti Szalon Könyvkiadó; Szombathely, Savaria University Press.

Szelényi, I. 1993: Changing patterns of elite recruitment in post-communist transformation: first results from the Hungarian study. Ithaca, N.Y., Mario Einaudi Center for International Studies, Cornell University.

—. 1995: The rise of managerialism: the 'new class' after the fall of Communism. Budapest, Working Paper Series, Collegium Budapest, 30.

—. 1995a: A menedzserkapitalizmus [Managerial Capitalism]. *Lettre Internationale*, Autumn.

Szelényi I., G. Ezal and E. Townsley 1996: Posztkommunista menedzserizmus [Post-Communist Managerialism]. *Politikatudományi Szemle*, Nos. 2 and 3.

Szelényi, Iván and Szonja Szelényi 1991: Az elit cirkulációja? [Elite Circulation?] *Kritika*, No. 10.

Szilvásy, György 1994: A Miniszterelnöki Hivatal négy éve [The Four Years of the Prime Minister's Office]. In: Kurtán, Sándor et al., eds.: *Magyarország politikai évkönyve 1994* [Political Yearbook of Hungary, 1994]. Budapest, Demokrácia Kutatások Magyar Központja Alapítvány, 455–477.

—. 1995: A kormányváltás technikája [The Mechanics of Changing Government]. In: Kurtán, Sándor et al., eds.: *Magyarország politikai évkönyve 1995* [Political Yearbook of Hungary, 1995]. Budapest, Demokrácia Kutatások Magyar Központja Alapítvány, 465–483.

Szoboszlai, György 1994: A választási rendszer hatása a politikai tagoltságra [The Effects of the Electoral System upon Political Division]. In: Balogh, István, ed.: *Törésvonalak és értékválasztások. Politikatudományi vizsgálatok a mai Magyarországról* [Cleavages and Value Divisions: Political-Scientific Investigations Concerning the Hungary of Today]. Budapest, MTA Politikai Tudományok Intézete, 47–62.

—. 1995: Választási rendszer és parlamentarizmus. Az 1994. évi parlamenti választások [The Electoral System and Parliamentarism: The Parliamentary Elections of 1994]. In: Bőhm, Antal and György Szoboszlai, eds.: *Parlamenti választások 1994* [The Parliamentary Elections of 1994]. Budapest, MTA Politikai Tudományok Intézete, 13–55.

—. 1995a: An Electoral System and parliamentarism: The Parliamentary Elections of 1994. In: *Hungarian Parliamentary Election 1994*. Hungarian Centre for Electoral Research, Budapest, 5–18.

Szűcs, Jenő 1983: *Vázlat Európa három történeti régiójáról* [Sketch of the Three Historical Regions of Europe]. Budapest, Magvető.

—. 1990: Die drei historischen Regionen Europas. Frankfurt am Main, Verlag Neue Kritik.

Takács, Albert 1993: *A közigazgatás alapintézményei* [The Basic Institutions of the Public Administration]. Budapest, Államigazgatási Főiskola.

Takács, Imre 1996: Az Alkotmánybíróság [The Constitutional Court]. In: Kukorelli, István, ed.: *Alkotmánytan* [Constitutional Studies]. Budapest, Osiris, 341–372.

Tények és adatok az Országgyűlés tevékenységéről [Facts and Data on the Work of Parliament] 1994. Budapest, Országgyűlés Képviselői Tájékoztató Központ.

Tóka, Gábor 1992: A kelet-közép-európai pártrendszerek oldalnézetből [A Side View of East-Central European Party Systems]. In: Andorka, Rudolf, Tamás Kolosi and György Vukovich, eds.: *Társadalmi Riport 1992* [Social Report 1992]. Budapest, TÁRKI, 359–375.

—. 1992b: *Changing Dimensions of Party Competition. Hungary 1990–91.* Paper presented for the conference on 'Elections and Political Stability in East-Central Europe', Princeton, 1th–5th June 1992.

—. 1994: Pártok és választóik 1990-ben és 1994-ben [Parties and their Voters in 1990 and 1994]. In: Andorka Rudolf, Tamás Kolosi and György Vukovich, eds.: *Társadalmi Riport 1994* [Social Report 1994]. Budapest, TÁRKI, 460–489.

—. 1994a: Who is satisfied with democracy? In: Bozóki, András, ed.: *Democratic Legitimacy in Post-Communist Societies.* Budapest, T-Twins Publishing House, 242–266.

—. 1995: *Political Parties and the Bases of Party Support in East Central Europe.* Paper presented at the conference on 'Consolidating the Third Wave Democracies. Trends and Challenges'. Taipei, 27th–30th September 1995.

—. 1995a: Parties and their Voters. In: Király, K. B. and A. Bozóki, eds.: *Lawful Revolution in Hungary, 1989–1994.* Boulder, Colo. Social Science Monographs; Highland Lakes, N.J. Atlantic Research and Publications Inc.; New York, Columbia University Press, 131–158.

—. 1996: Parties and Electoral Choices in East-Central Europe. In: Pridham, G. and P. G. Lewis, eds.: *Stabilising Fragile Democracies. Comparing New Party Systems in Southern and Eastern Europe.* London—New York, Routledge, 100–125.

—. 1997: *Political Parties and Democratic Consolidation in East-Central Europe.* Glasgow, Centre for the Study of Public Policy, University of Strathclyde, 76.

Tóka, Gábor, ed. 1995: *The 1990 Election to the Hungarian National Assembly: Analyses, Documents and Data.* Berlin, Sigma.

Tomka, Miklós 1991: *Magyar katolicizmus 1991* [Hungarian Catholicism, 1991]. Budapest, Országos Lelkipásztori Intézet Katolikus Társadalomtudományi Akadémia.

—. 1994: Changes in Religious and Church Policy. In: Gombár, Csaba et. al., eds.: *Balance. The Hungarian Government 1990–1994.* Budapest, Korridor—Centre for Political Research, 267–287.

Tóth, István János 1992: Képviselők és frakciók a parlamentben [Deputies and Party Groups in Parliament]. In: Kurtán, Sándor et al., eds.: *Magyarország politikai évkönyve 1991* [Political Yearbook of Hungary, 1991]. Budapest, Ökonómiai Alapítvány, Economix Rt., 81–89.

—. 1993: Gazdasági érdekszervezetek és érdekérvényesítési eszközök [Economic Interest Organizations and the Instruments of Interest Attainment]. *Politikatudományi Szemle*, No. 2.
Tóth, Zoltán 1995: Az országgyűlési képviselőválasztások néhány fontos számadata [Some Important Numerical Data on the Parliamentary Elections]. In: Kurtán, Sándor et al., eds.: *Magyarország politikai évkönyve 1995* [Political Yearbook of Hungary, 1995]. Budapest, Demokrácia Kutatások Magyar Központja Alapítvány, 439–445.
Törő, Károly 1991: Az Alkotmánybíráskodás kérdőjelei [Questions Concerning Constitutional Review]. *Magyar Jog*, No. 5.
Tőkés, Rudolf 1990: *A posztkommunizmusból a demokráciába* [From Post-Communism to Democracy]. Budapest, Konrád Adenauer Alapítvány.
—. 1990a: Az új magyar politikai elit [The New Hungarian Political Elite]. *Valóság*, No. 12.
Tőkés, L. R. 1996: *Hungary's Negotiated Revolution: Economic Reform, Social Change, and Political Succession, 1957–90*. Cambridge, Cambridge University Press.
Trócsányi, László Jr. 1993: Közjogi változások és a rendszerváltás [Legal Changes and the Régime Change]. *Magyar Közigazgatás*, No. 7.
Varga, Károly 1994: Adózási szokásaink [Our Taxation Customs]. *Valóság*, No. 10.
Vecernik, J. 1996: Gazdasági nehézségek és politikai attitűdök [Economic Difficulties and Political Attitudes]. *Századvég*, No. 3 (Winter).
—. 1996a: Markets and People: the Czech Reform Experience in a Comparative Perspective. Avebury, Aldershot.
Verebélyi, Imre 1996: A kormányzás és a közigazgatás reformjának tervezete [Plan for Reform of Governance and Public Administration]. *Magyar Közigazgatás*, April.
—. 1996a: Interview. *HVG*, 12th October.
Wright, V. 1989: *The Government and Politics of France*. London, Unwin Hyman.
Závecz, Tibor 1994: A pártok megítélése a két választás között [Judgements on the Parties between the Two Elections]. In: Andorka Rudolf, Tamás Kolosi and György Vukovich, eds.: *Társadalmi Riport 1994* [Social Report, 1994]. Budapest, TÁRKI, 447–459.
—. 1995: Pártok, választások, közvélemény-kutatás [Parties, Elections, Public Opinion Research]. In: Kurtán, Sándor et al., eds.: *Magyarország politikai évkönyve 1995* [Political Yearbook of Hungary, 1995]. Budapest, Demokrácia Kutatások Magyar Központja Alapítvány, 524–531.

Documents

The Constitution of the Republic of Hungary. In: Ágh, A. and S. Kurtán, eds. *1995: The First Parliament (1990–1994). Democratization and Europeanization in Hungary*. Budapest, Hungarian Centre for Democracy Studies, 265–292.

The Hungarian Election Law. In: Tóka, Gábor, ed. 1995: *The 1990 Election to the Hungarian National Assembly: Analyses, Documents and Data*. Berlin, Sigma, 143–182.

Index

F

G

H

I

O

P